History in Depth

Collections of documents come in all shapes and sizes. Many
attempt to cover a very broad period; in consequence they
rely heavily on illustrative material which is thought to be
typical. In practice, this means a patchwork of often isolated
snippets, with material torn out of context. Single documents
or even fragments of documents have to bear the whole weight
of a period, a problem, a theme. Students derive from such
collections a mistaken impression of the nature of history, of
the character of historical research, and very often, a false
impression of the subject of study.

HISTORY IN DEPTH is based on the belief that historical
perception demands immediacy and depth. Working to the
principle that true breadth in history can be achieved only by
examining a concrete problem in depth, each volume in the
series is devoted to either a particular event or crisis of considerable significance, such as the Peasants' Revolt of 1381
or the British General Strike of 1926; or to a trend or movement running through a coherent period of time, such as
West African Nationalism from the middle of the nineteenth
century or the concept of Das Volk in the German lands; or
to a particular area of experience, such as the Victorian
underworld or Elizabethan Puritanism.

No artificial uniformity is imposed on the format of the
volumes; each is shaped by the dictates of its subject. But
there are certain basic elements common to all. The core of
each book is a major collection of original material, translated into English where necessary, with editorial decisions
on modernised punctuation and spelling governed by the
nature of the subject. Each editor provides an introduction
geared to the particular demands of his volume; each
volume carries a full working bibliography, interpretive
notes and an index.

This is a new approach to the teaching of history which
has been evolved in response to a demand from practising
teachers throughout the Commonwealth. The general editor
has selected the subjects and the volume editors with care,
so that each book stands in its own right and has something
of the quality of a monograph.

History in Depth

General Editor: G. A. Williams

Published

Henry S. Wilson: Origins of West African Nationalism
R. B. Dobson: The Peasants' Revolt of 1381
J. R. Pole: The Revolution in America, 1754–1788
D. S. Chambers: Patrons and Artists in the Italian Renaissance
H. C. Porter: Puritanism in Tudor England
Dorothy Thompson: The Early Chartists

In preparation

R. Martin: The General Strike
R. C. Mettam: State and Society under Louis XIV
P. Hollis and B. Harrison: Robert Lowery: Portrait of a Radical
Hans Koch: Das Volk
Raphael Samuel: The Victorian Underworld
Lionel Butler: The Fourth Crusade
W. H. Hargreaves-Mawdsley:
Spain under the Bourbons, 1700–1833

The Early Chartists

DOROTHY THOMPSON

Macmillan

First published 1971 by
THE MACMILLAN PRESS LTD
London and Basingstoke
Associated companies in New York Toronto
Dublin Melbourne Johannesburg and Madras

SBN 333 01164 3 (hard cover)

Printed in Great Britain by
ROBERT MACLEHOSE & CO LTD
The University Press, Glasgow

Contents

Part III: Chartist Activity

General Editor's Preface

Historical perception demands immediacy and depth. These qualities are lost in attempts at broad general survey; for the reader of history depth is the only true breadth. Each volume in this series, therefore, explores an important historical problem in depth. There is no artificial uniformity; each volume is shaped by the problem it tackles. The past bears its own witness; the core of each volume is a major collection of original material (translated into English where necessary) as alive, as direct and as full as possible. The reader should feel the texture of the past. The volume editor provides interpretative notes and introduction and a full working bibliography. The volume will stand in its own right as a 'relived experience' and will also serve as a point of entry into a wider area of historical discourse. In taking possession of a particular historical world, the reader will move more freely in a wider universe of historical experience.

*

In this volume, Mrs Dorothy Thompson explores the early years of Chartism, those crucial and formative years when a multiplicity of popular and populist campaigns fused into a movement national in scope and purpose and intensely class-conscious in spirit. In May 1838 the People's Charter was published and a national campaign formed around it; in July 1840, after the turmoil of the first Convention, the Petition, the spasmodic attempts at resistance, boycott, general strike and insurrection, the movement settled down for a long haul and, in the National Charter Association, regrouped itself in a national political organisation with an executive which had to submit itself to annual election — a process from which not even the charismatic Feargus O'Connor was exempt. In many ways, therefore, these years are decisive in the history of a movement which burned itself into the consciousness of a generation and into the memory of the generations which followed.

This is not to say that Chartism was in any fundamental sense a 'beginning'. Mrs Thompson points out that most of the delegates to the Convention had been active in the Reform crisis of 1831-2;

the labour historian Dolléans once argued that the labour move-ment first 'emerged' in both Britain and France in the years 1829-34. How can one so precisely date a birth-certificate, when at least five points of the Charter's six figured in a radical manifesto of 1780? Indeed, before a Co-operative Congress of 1831, the same Bronterre O'Brien who appears here joyfully acclaiming the radical unity of the Crown and Anchor meeting of February 1837 was bitterly denouncing working-class radicals for their dependence on 'middle-class' nostrums; only in their accents, he claimed, could they be counted 'working-class'.

Chartism had behind it fifty years of experiences whose sum constituted a tradition, from the first crystallisation of 'Jacobin' populism in the 1790s, through the underground of the Napoleonic Wars, Luddism, Peterloo, the 'decade of the silent insurrection' of the 1820s, to the 'hurling time' of the Reform crisis of 1829-34, when tension attained a 'European' intensity: fifty years when the old 'moral economy' crumbled, industrial structure and spiritual sensibility were transformed, when the thrust of Evangelicalism and Political Economy powered a triumphant 'middle-class' consciousness. Look at the documents Mrs Thompson has grouped in her Part II, 'Chartist Propaganda', savour their relentless rationality, their literacy, the bite and rhythm of their ultimately optimistic argument and sense how much they owe to a tradition of discourse and dialogue which stretches back to those high falutin Old Jacks of the 1790s. But look too at her exemplary selection in Part I, which illustrates and expounds motive, from the Tory paternalism of Richard Oastler through the tough plebeians of East London to that remarkable rebel 'autobiography', with its human revulsion from the paternal and revolt against humiliation, by the man who was 'a democrat in my Sunday School', and sense the sheer complexity and contra-diction, the transmission and transmutation which the 1780-1838 coupling suggests and which coloured the whole process of the 'nationalisation' of the working class.

The proximate source was evidently the slump of 1829 and the coincident political crisis (precisians might like to single out the Ramsay Spinners' Conference that winter, dominated by that John Doherty who was to launch his Owenite National Association for the Protection of Labour) and the resulting multiple campaigns whose threads Mrs Thompson weaves together — the Owenites in unions and co-operative cells, the 'infidels' in their journals, the mass movements with their Hunt and Cobbett totems, the war of the unstamped press, the elaboration of anti-capitalist economics, the battles for the 'honourable trades', the instinctive defence of what we have come to call (perforce) 'sub-cultures'. But the immediate stimulus was without doubt negative — the exclusion from citizenship in the Reform Act, the drawing of the £10 line across the face of the urban nation by what Frenchmen would call a *régime censitaire*, followed by the perceived humiliation of measure after measure, the New Poor Law, the restriction of the right of petition, the punishment of Dorchester labourers and Glasgow spinners, even the Anatomy Act and the pursuit of the propertyless beyond the grave, all climaxed by fear, of helplessness, of centralisation, of the new police. In a time when even Rowland Detrosier, a measured and self-taught Deist who impressed John Stuart Mill and helped organise Francis Place's campaign against 'extremists', could be blacklisted as a 'destructive', when English society seems sometimes to be grinding apart like some clumsy cast-iron mechanism, when in the pages of the 'pauper press' the very language sometimes seems to break down from sheer inadequacy of social communication, the growth in national coherence around a fierce class awareness was a natural climax.

The unity achieved was fragile and in the vivid and trenchant pages of Dorothy Thompson's volume, with her useful Chronology as guide, the reader can share the travail of building a popular movement through the rallies, the drilling, the Convention speeches, the 'sacred month', the shadowy vision of national insurrection, the confrontations at Newport and Llanidloes and Bradford, to the gritting of teeth and the Nelson slogan which accompanied the settling down to the long and arduous labour in the N.C.A. He may come away with a rather surprising sensation of optimism, with a perhaps wry but real appreciation of that ebullient Sunday School democrat:

> But yet the *dream*, which, when a boy,
> Was wont my musings to employ,
> Fast rolling years *shall not* destroy,
> With all their grief and pain.

Gwyn A. Williams

Editor's Note
Footnotes added by the Editor have been enclosed in square brackets so as to distinguish them from those belonging to the original documents.

Acknowledgements

I am indebted to the Earl of Harewood's estate for permission to reproduce the documents on pp. 194-5, 280-2, and 208-10 which come from the collection in Lord Harewood's possession which is lodged with the archives department of the Leeds City Library. Transcripts of Crown-copyright records in the Public Record Office (on pp. 187-92, 206-8, 211-17, 226-7, 241-8, 264-79, and 282-6) appear by permission of the Controller of H.M. Stationery Office.

I have received a great deal of help from the staff of many libraries which I have visited in search of Chartist material. In particular I should like to thank the staff and photographic departments of the Public Record Office, the Reading Room and Newspaper Library of the British Museum, the City of Birmingham Central Reference Library, the Archives Department of the Leeds City Library, Bury Public Library and the Special Collections Library at Columbia University, New York.

I should like to thank the Halifax Antiquarian Society and the chief librarian at the Central Library, Halifax, for permission to reproduce the letter which appears on the cover — a report from an informer to the Halifax magistrates in the winter of 1839-40.

D. K. G. T.

Introduction

The material presented in this collection has been selected with the aim of illustrating the sources from which our picture of the early years of Chartism has to be built up. No aspect of the movement is covered in any way comprehensively. This would require a series of volumes, each bigger than the present one. It may some day be possible to publish a full selection of Chartist pamphlets, selections from the Chartist press and a wide range of the very important material relating to Chartism in the Home Office Papers. None of these sources is at present easily available to students or general readers. All that can be done here, however, is to indicate the sort of material represented in these and other sources, and by so doing perhaps suggest the complexity of the task of assessing and elucidating the evidence relating to a movement which is of importance at so many differing levels of historical interpretation.

At one level, Chartism is one of the most richly self-documented subjects in English social history. Coming at a time when the press was comparatively free and cheap, and being essentially a movement of people to whom the printed word was important and accessible, Chartism has left behind an enormous number of printed documents, newspapers, journals, pamphlets, broadsides, handbills and posters. The extent to which these have survived depends partly on the obvious accidents of history. Journals survive better than pamphlets, both are more likely to have been bound and preserved than the more ephemeral broadside or poster, which may only have survived among the papers of a lord lieutenant or Home Secretary to whom it had been sent by an indignant or alarmed citizen. Handbills like those on pp. 193 and 195 are least likely to have survived, since their circulation enters an area of semi-legality or outright illegality, with all the precautions that that involves.

Apart from the publications of the Chartists themselves, there is a great volume of contemporary published material relating to Chartism. Parliamentary debates, newspaper reports, and descriptions and discussions by novelists, journalists and moralists abound all through the years in which the movement was a major political and social force in Britain. The value of this material as a source of information, both about Chartism and even more about the reactions to it of other classes in the country, is considerable.

The press in Britain was in a period of change and growth in the late 1830s. The provincial press was expanding rapidly, but not uniformly. Some papers were becoming genuine provincially based newspapers, produced in the local centres, and providing local news gathered by their own staff. Thus for some localities there is a coverage of Chartist activity which earlier radical movements outside London seldom received. Magistrates' hearings are reported in full (as in the case of the Bath Chartists on p. 251) and may be assessed separately from the editorial comment, which is, of course, usually hostile or derisory. Both the reporting and the comment are of value in obtaining a picture of the atmosphere in which provincial Chartism operated. But many provincial papers were still run on an older model, employing very small reporting staffs, and still concerned mainly to copy items of news and interest from the London and major provincial journals. The absence of reports of local Chartist activities from such newspapers does not mean the absence of such activity in the locality. Even in the case of areas served by more modern papers, hostility to Chartism could apparently show itself by the non-reporting of events as well as by hostile reports. In the rather rare cases of provincial papers such as the Tory 'Halifax Guardian' or the Liberal 'Birmingham Journal' which show some editorial sympathy towards the Chartists, this sympathy may itself dictate the aspects of the movement which get the widest coverage. The 'Guardian' was particularly sympathetic to the Oastlerite kind of social protest, and tended to give full reports of meetings and demonstrations in support of this end of the movement, in particular to anything discreditable to the non-conformist manufacturing interest, whilst the 'Journal', like some other early provincial papers, was of a strongly radical aspect, and tended to report favourably the local spokesmen who expressed the sort of political radicalism which brought Chartism nearest to the views of the local middle class. It would be wrong to assume from this bias in the reporting that other kinds of activity did not occur in the districts concerned.

The novels which concern themselves with Chartism, and there are a number of them, belong to a later period than that covered by this book. They are, in any case, fairly easily accessible; indeed, it may well be that the availability and readability of 'Alton Locke', 'Sybil' and 'Mary Barton', the three most frequently reprinted, have formed the main picture which existed of Chartism until it began to be studied seriously by historians. Their value as sources of evidence need not be considered here, except to suggest that the one thing which all the 'Chartist' novels have in common — whatever the motivation of their authors — is the acceptance of the fact that the Chartist case is an articulate one, and one which demands a reasoned reply.

An obvious source of information about any period is the memoirs of those who lived through it. Most published Chartist reminiscences are those of men who lived on until late in the century, and who had entered the movement late, during the forties rather than the thirties. The reason for this is probably that it was in the ambience of Gladstonian Liberalism that Chartism finally achieved an aura of respectability. In that period, Chartists could be viewed as Liberal reformers, ahead of their time. As Benjamin Wilson wrote in 1887:

> ... what they wanted was a voice in making the laws they were called upon to obey; they believed that taxation without representation was tyranny, and ought to be resisted; they took a leading part in agitating in favour of the ten hours question, the repeal of the taxes on knowledge, education, co-operation, civil and religious liberty and the land question, for they were the true pioneers of all the great movements of their time (1).

The Liberal 'Halifax Courier', which published Wilson's reminiscences, further accented the point when it reported on a meeting of old Chartists in 1885:

> At the time of the Chartist agitation they were all working men earning low wages, not the least interesting part of the speeches therefore was their account of the hardships the working classes had to endure within living memory, enabling young politicians to make a useful and instructive contrast. . . . (2)

But whatever the motives for the rediscovery of a tamed Chartism by late-century Liberals, the memoirs themselves sometimes break out of the frame of their premature Gladstonianism, as when Thomas Frost describes the various

3

communitarian experiments towards which he looked for a more satisfying way of life, or when Ben Wilson himself admits to having bought a gun and joined the 'physical force' Chartists, and recalls a friend who was moulding bullets in his cellar (3). Here a different, illiberal Chartism can be briefly glimpsed, a breadth of aspiration, a passion of protest and an intensity of resolve which had no place in the politics of Liberalism.

For the early years of the movement few coherent reminiscences exist. The outstanding exception is, of course, William Lovett's 'Life and Struggles'. Invaluable alike for its picture of the making of a radical artisan, and for its detailed documentation of the activities of the London Working Men's Association and of the first Chartist Convention, this book is now easily available in more than one edition. For this reason I have not for the most part included documents which Lovett reprinted. But London in the years 1838-40 is less important in Chartist history than many provincial centres, and indeed than London itself was to become in the later years of the movement (4). The mainsprings of action were outside the metropolis, and unfortunately no provincial centre had its Lovett, recording memories and preserving documents. The autobiography of Robert Lowery, soon to be republished, gives some picture of the making of a provincial Chartist, although it is written partly as a temperance tract, and bears some of the marks of this (5). John Frost never committed his memories to paper (6), and R. G. Gammage, whose personal experience illuminates part of his rather badly written history of the movement, did not become an active participant until after 1840. For personal memories of the first years we have to rely mainly on fragments, often produced to illustrate arguments in a quite different context, such as the letters of Matthew Fletcher, published in 1852, or Alexander Somerville and David Urquhart's apologias, also published in the fifties. An interesting series of letters on events in Newcastle in 1839 was published in 1889-90 in the 'Newcastle Weekly Chronicle'. These were occasioned by the publication of one of the few books which do contain personal reminiscences of this period. Thomas Ainge Devyr's 'Odd Book of the Nineteenth Century', published in New York in 1880. Perhaps because the general tone of Devyr is so different from the mellow Liberalism of most English ex-Chartists, his book has not generally been taken very seriously as a source of information. Allowing, however, for discrepancies of detail which might be expected after so many years (and

4

which are to be found equally in all the books of memoirs), the picture which he paints of Newcastle Chartism does fit in very well with that given by other sources, including the Home Office Papers. The discussions evoked by his book, and by his visits to Newcastle as an old man, suggest that his memory of events coincided with that of some of his surviving contemporaries of the days 'before the introduction of salad oil' (7).

Unpublished material about the early years of Chartism comes mainly from official sources. Lovett preserved the papers of the first Convention which are in the MSS room at the British Museum. Both the Place Collection in the British Museum and the Lovett Collection in Birmingham Central Reference Library contain a certain number of manuscript letters. But by far the richest sources of unpublished material are the Home Office and the Treasury Solicitor's Papers. The selection which has been given here from these sources is not intended to be in any way a 'typical' group of papers. Examples have been chosen of magistrates' letters, spies' reports, depositions, etc. which seem to throw light on aspects of Chartism. But since the material is so patchy, each must be taken to illustrate a limited area only. There was no uniformity in the police system during these years. The Rural Police Act was not passed until August 1839, and the reform in the boroughs was in its earliest stages. The main instruments of detection were still informers, and their use, and that of agents or spies, depended very much on the initiative of local magistrates. The extent to which even the most able and efficient magistrates were able to find out about the activities of the Chartists varies enormously from place to place. In Birmingham, where the magistrates included former members of the Political Union, and one of the original delegates to the Convention, and where police spies were regularly employed, it seems likely that the authorities were fairly well-informed about the local Chartists. But in most manufacturing districts the magistrates had little access to the activities and opinions of the labouring people, and their reports were based on hearsay and guesses. Letters to the Home Office, therefore, vary from the panic-stricken to the calm and self-confident, depending more on the personality of the writer than on the objective total situation. Since in most cases reports on a given locality came to the Home Office from only one source, it is clear that the assessments contained in them cannot be taken as objective. Even if the whole body of reports from magistrates, informers,

5

police, and the reports of the military commanders on special duty are taken together, they give only a fragmentary idea of what was going on. Working-class communities in the industrial townships which were the main centres of Chartism were opaque communities, rarely accessible to parson, policeman or magistrate. The authorities were on the whole ill-informed as well as excluded. For example, the report from Bradford of the encounter between Joseph North and the policeman gives the impression of being a quite straightforward incident. It is only when it is understood that North was probably a leading Chartist that the incident can be seen as a piece of covering-up by North of his son's indiscretion. There is no evidence that the policeman recognised this, however (8).

I am not attempting, in introducing this collection of material, to rewrite the history of Chartism. That a serious history has yet to be written is obvious. The lack of such a full-scale history must be my excuse for leaving open some of the unanswered questions about these early years. I have had to be content with indicating areas of controversy without suggesting answers, and in some cases with selecting documents which may be capable of contradictory interpretations.

The starting date for the series is 1838, since it is in that year that the name Chartism appears, and the movement assumes a national character. Nothing, however, would be further from the truth than to see Chartism as a sudden eruption into the political scene. Radicalism of the various kinds that came together in Chartism had been gathering momentum fairly steadily since the beginning of the decade. Most of the delegates to the first National Convention had taken part in the agitation for the Reform Bill of 1832, and many of them, like Peter Bussey of Bradford or Matthew Fletcher of Bury, had organised at the time of the passing of the Bill considerable campaigns for the extension of its terms. Bussey had collected six thousand signatures to a petition for manhood suffrage immediately after the passing of the Bill, and Fletcher had helped to sponsor a candidate in the first election after the Reform Bill who stood on the platform of universal suffrage and the ballot (9). In the years that followed, both men, and others like them all over the country, had emerged as town radicals, taking the lead in various radical campaigns, which increasingly appeared as campaigns of resistance to the actions of the Reformed Parliament. In 1834, Bussey is described as demanding of a parliamentary candidate, in front of a hustings crowd of five

6

thousand people, whether, if elected, he would vote for the abolition of tithes, the entire abolition of church rates, the abolition of punishment by death in all cases; for triennial parliaments, the abolition of flogging in the army, the reduction of the army estimates, the emancipation of the Jews so as to place them on the same footing as himself; for the ballot, for the throwing open of the universities to all classes of His Majesty's subjects of whatever sect; for corporate reform; for household suffrage; for the abolition of the stamp duty on newspapers; for the repeal of the corn laws; for a careful revision of the pension list; for the abolition of the taxes on industry and for the repeal of the game laws (10). This was the programme of working-class political radicalism, soon to be absorbed into the wider movement of Chartism. A few miles away, in Ripponden in the Ryburn Valley, another kind of organised radicalism was to be found. Here the Co-operative Society, founded in 1832 with a membership of 24, had, by 1834, reached a membership of 45. The fundamental principles of the society declared:

First.   — That labour is the source of all wealth; conse-
           quently the working classes have created all wealth.
Secondly. — That the working classes, although the producers
           of wealth, instead of being the richest, are the
           poorest of the community; hence, they cannot be
           receiving a just recompense for their labour (11).

Both Bradford and Ripponden were to become centres of Chartism. The movement brought together political radicals like Bussey and Fletcher with the Owenite weavers of the Calder Valley.

The years between 1834 and 1838 saw a continuous series of radical campaigns, in which groups from various backgrounds and various traditions were increasingly involved. The New Poor Law, introduced in the same year that saw the prosecution of the Dorchester Labourers, isolated in Parliament the handful of independent radical members who expressed in any degree whatever the opinions of the articulate working people in the country. William Cobbett opposed the new law in the short time that remained to him, whilst Thomas Wakley and Thomas Duncombe, members for Finsbury, and John Fielden, member for Oldham, always made it clear that they considered that they had a responsibility to represent the views of the working people as well as the views of those who had actually elected

7

them. In a famous speech in support of an amendment to the first speech from the throne of Queen Victoria in 1837, Thomas Wakley described himself as the representative of Labour in the House of Commons, whilst Fielden, in the election address at Oldham in 1833, declared that 'nothing but an anxious solicitude to see the people restored to their just rights, and especially the labouring portion of society greatly improved could have induced him' to enter Parliament (12). These three men remained strong supporters of the social programme of Chartism, as well as of its political points, throughout the first ten years of the agitation, and were to be the main spokesmen in Parliament for the Petitions and against the ill-treatment of imprisoned Chartists.

In the main, the Chartists received little support from the members of the House of Commons. Middle-class radicalism seemed in many cases to be acting against the interests of the working people in the years immediately following the 1832 Bill. Even the Municipal Reform Act of 1835, which on the face of it was an attempt to fulfil a long-standing Radical demand, the reform of the corrupt borough corporations, appeared in the event as simply a further strengthening of the powers of the middle class, a postscript to the 1832 Act. Thomas Cooper wrote of the 1835 Act:

... how the scale has turned, since the greater share of boroughs where the poor and labouring classes threw up their hats at 'municipal reform' — and now mutter discontent at the pride of upstarts become insolent oppressors — or openly curse, as in the poverty-stricken and hunger-bitten manufacturing districts, at the relentless and grinding tyrannies of the recreant middle classes whom municipal honours have drawn off from their hot-blooded radicalism, and converted into cold, unfeeling wielders of magisterial or other local power (13).

The prosecution of trade unionists which took place in the thirties was seen by working-class radicals as part of the same oppressive policy as the exclusion of working men from the franchise or the punishment of poverty by the proposals of the Poor Law Amendment Act. This interconnection of activity persisted throughout the Chartist period, although the emphasis laid on the achievement of the suffrage usually stressed its priority over other issues, as the primary means of obtaining

8

reform in other fields. But, as Challinor and Ripley have shown in their recent study of the Miners' Association (14), the Chartists were usually prepared to take any opportunity which presented itself to encourage the development of trade union organisation. Many of the leading Chartists, in the south as well as in the industrial north, had gained their first experience of radical activity as members of trade unions. William Cuffay for example, son of a West Indian slave, leading London Chartist, who was to end his days in Australia as a transported convict after the Orange Tree conspiracy of 1848, entered politics after he had taken part in the tailors' strike of 1834 (15). The London radicals who organised the great demonstration in support of the Dorchester Labourers on 21 April 1834 included the organisers of the co-operative societies, the unstamped press, the Owenite bazaars, as well as the National Union of the Working Classes and the Grand National Consolidated Trades Union. The prosecution and transportation of the Glasgow cotton-spinners in 1837 provoked a nation-wide campaign against the Whig government and in support of the convicted men. One of the men who took the lead in the collection of signatures and money to assist the convicted men was Lawrence Pitkeithly, of Huddersfield, local leader of radical politics, and in particular of the campaign against the Poor Law and of the movement for factory reform. Pitkeithly was later to become a leading West Riding Chartist (16). In Barnsley two of the leaders of the linen-weavers — both of whom were to become prominent Chartists — had been transported for their part in industrial disturbances in the twenties. In 1838, when Chartism began, one of them, William Ashton, had returned from Australia, his fare having been collected by a public subscription in Barnsley, and the other, Frank Mirfield, was awaiting repatriation (17). The concern with trade unionism was one of the issues which divided the Chartists from the middle-class radicals, many of whom, like Daniel O'Connell, were bitterly hostile to the idea of trade unionism.

Radicalism in the early 1830s had been given an increasingly national character by the activities of the cheap press. The unstamped press, produced in defiance of the government regulations, canalised metropolitan radicalism, and spread out into the provinces, where the sellers found themselves part of a national movement, taking part in a campaign of direct opposition to the law which won widespread respect and support among the lower orders of society. In spite of the

9

limited gains actually conceded by the act of 1836, it is impossible not to see the story of the 'unstamped' as one of a triumph for radicalism, a David-and-Goliath confrontation in which the honours went to the irreverent upstarts, giving them new confidence as well as the journalistic and organisational experience of producing newspapers (18). But the metropolitan papers produced after the 1836 newspaper act — the 'London Dispatch', the 'London Mercury', and the smaller sheets, including 'Bronterre's National Reformer', in which many of the ideas of the Chartists first appeared, did not meet the needs of the radical movement in the late thirties. It is with the foundation of the 'Northern Star' in Leeds in November 1837 that the new era of radical journalism begins (19). The Chartist period sustained a great number of journals and periodicals, but the 'Northern Star' was by far the most widely read. Its circulation waxed and waned with the movement. Its staff, editorial, reporting and distributing, included many of the ablest men in the movement. Its columns contained the widest reporting of radical activity ever made — covering a range which went beyond the Chartist movement itself. Feargus O'Connor, as owner of the 'Northern Star', was, of course, in a position of great strength to influence the readership. But his exercise of his power seems, in the main, to have been very reasonable. His editorial staff, who often had interests and emphases which differed from his own, were allowed a great deal of freedom, and the paper never became a purely personal vehicle — a fact which undoubtedly helps to account for its immense lead over all other Chartist and radical journals of the period (20). Of course the owner was the final arbiter, the 'Star' was the journal of the O'Connorites, if not of Feargus as an individual, and many Chartists were unfairly treated in its columns. It must never be used as the only source of information, particularly at periods of controversy. But it does provide a quite unequalled continuous record for the years of its publication of a kind which was never available for earlier radical movements. It also leads into a new kind of popular journalism which developed in the second half of the nineteenth century, for which the bridge with Chartism is the work of former Chartist journalists like G. W. M. Reynolds, Edward Lloyd and W. E. Adams. But this again belongs to a later period of the movement. Excerpts from the 'Northern Star' are included here to give an idea of the tone and subject matter of the paper in the early years (21).

The early numbers of the 'Northern Star', taken with the

'London Dispatch' of the same period, show some of the questions which were concerning radicals immediately before the beginning of the Chartist agitation. As well as the questions already mentioned, it is interesting to notice the intense interest which was taken in the revolution in Canada (22). Ireland was continually to the fore, although the hostility between O'Connor and O'Connell meant that many of the latter's working-class followers kept clear of Chartism (23). Not that O'Connor's differences with the Liberator were of a purely personal nature, as is sometimes suggested. As Devyr shows, there were always a number of Irishmen who were in agreement with the sophisticated radicalism of O'Connor, the descendant of United Irishmen, rather than with the popular Catholic nationalism of O'Connell (24). But the period in which there was the closest co-operation between the Irish repealers and the Chartists came after the death of O'Connell, in the later days of Chartism.

A question on which the working-class radicals found common cause with many middle-class reformers and even some Tories was the hostility to the Whig—Radical policies of centralisation. At its most hated this policy was attacked in the New Poor Law, but it was also fought in the debates about the Rural Police Bill. The twin dangers of the breakdown of traditional community responsibilities, and the setting up of a continental-type state administration were very widely feared. This fear accounts for a great deal of the division amongst the authorities, for the hesitancy of some magistrates in the face of insurrectionary threats, and above all for the intense hostility towards the metropolitan police when these were introduced into provincial centres. The Calthorpe Street affair, in which a jury of London tradesmen had returned a verdict of 'justifiable homicide' at the inquest on a policeman stabbed to death whilst helping to clear a radical meeting from a London street, had occurred as recently as 1833 (25). It is a paradox that Chartism, one of whose motive forces was the fear of the introduction of a centralised police system, should have helped substantially to clear the way for such a system by arousing in the respectable classes a fear of popular disturbance which overrode their suspicion of centralised administration (26).

Popular radicalism can thus be seen in the thirties as a diverse but increasingly coherent force. It was the response to changing social and economic conditions which were becoming felt over wider sections of the country. It was no new experience for large sections of the working people of Britain to feel hungry. What is of interest in the late thirties is why the British workers responded to hunger by forming a nation-wide movement around a political programme instead of by more traditional means of protest like food rioting, arson, begging, poaching or praying.

There would not be space in a collection of this sort to offer documentary illustration of the changes in the structure of industry which were among the causes of unrest. New methods and techniques of production, new relationships between employers, merchants and workers, the breakdown of traditional institutions and traditional relationships, the growing dependence on an increasing but fluctuating world market — all these were affecting the major industries of Britain, and affecting above all the many branches of her textile industries, still by far the most important manufacturing industries. Although there is still a great deal to be learnt about the occupational distribution of Chartism, and a great number of generalisations to be tested about the participation of different sectors of the labour force, nevertheless it is clear that the textile centres in general were strongholds of the movement throughout most of its active period. Chartism was the response to economic and social change of an urban working class, and it was in the manufacturing districts that it was always strongest. This is not, of course, to suggest that there were not important Chartist activities in the cities and in the villages. Local research seems to be providing an increasing number of illustrations of such activity. But it was above all in the groups of industrial townships which were the typical manufacturing centres of the nineteenth century, areas such as the West Riding of Yorkshire, Lancashire, Nottinghamshire, Staffordshire and South Wales, that the movement had most continuity, and that its tone was largely set. Within those areas it seems likely that the division which has sometimes been made between the factory workers and the domestic workers will not stand up to examination. Apart from the obvious fact that many factory operatives were women and children (27), the occupations of arrested Chartists would suggest that cotton-spinners, powerloom-overlookers and other male factory operatives were often amongst the active local leaders, even before the Plug Riots of 1842. That the handloom weavers in particular seem to stand out as local speakers and organisers may be due to the traditional participation of these men in the chapel and other social and cultural

12

activities of their communities, rather than to their numerical superiority in the movement as a whole (28). Biographies of rank-and-file Chartists are very difficult to obtain, by definition. The depositions from Sheffield which have been included here partly to provide such biographies cannot be taken as being in any way typical, since we do not have enough examples with which to compare them.

It is, however, an important part of the definition of Chartism to see it as the response of a literate and sophisticated working class. It is the response of a labour force faced not with the timeless custom of traditional work patterns and social structures, or with the vagaries of weather or harvest, but with a set of articulate postulations, the arguments of the philosophical radicals and the political economists. Much of the Chartist propaganda took the form of argument, a dialogue with the middle classes. Although clearly not all Chartists were able to read (classes at which members were taught appear in the programme of some localities) and although the level of literacy even amongst those who could nominally read and write must often have been low, nevertheless written and printed material was an essential part of the lives of them all. Newspapers and pamphlets were available in even very small communities, at beer-houses, inns, coffee-shops and at the homes of newsagents. In bigger centres the agents often provided both distribution centres for journals and collection points for money and signatures. Sometimes the local newsagent also ran a coffee-shop, as Thomas Cooper did for a time in Leicester, and here, and in each other's houses, journals were read and discussed, to an extent which represented a new dimension in radical politics. One writer reports that at Todmorden, on the day that the 'Northern Star' was due, the people used to line the roadside waiting for its arrival 'which was paramount to everything else for the time being' (29). The language of Chartism, in spite of the bitterness and hostility towards the ruling classes, both middle and upper, nevertheless contains a degree of rationality, even of optimism, which it would be difficult to define in earlier protest movements. The desperation which characterised the agricultural distrubances of the early thirties is very little in evidence. The machinery of the law and the constitution is invoked to resist the self-interest of the industrialist or the greed of the monopolist. Where force is invoked or threatened, it is the organised force of an excluded class, not the sporadic violence of desperate individuals or small groups. It will not do

13

to oversimplify this question, or to describe every aspect of Chartism as being entirely rational and articulate. But a comparison of surviving Luddite letters, or the letters from the 'Captain Swing' agitation (30), with the closing sentences of the appeal by the strikers at Ashton-under-Lyne against wage-cuts in 1842 will illustrate the point. The appeal ends:

> Whether we succeed or not, we shall have the satisfaction of knowing that we have asked for nothing unreasonable or unjust. We want a uniform price for the whole of the manufacturing districts, and it is in the interests of the masters to have it, in order that one man cannot undersell another in the market. Much is said about over production, and about the market being glutted. In order to obviate the past, let us all work ten hours per day, and we are sure it will lessen the amount of goods in the market. The home consumption will also be considerably increased by increasing the wages of the labourer.
>
> The operatives of Ashton-under-Lyne (31)

In the Chartist publications this element of rationality predominates. But obviously the motivation behind the actual movement operated at a different level. The impetus which sent people out in tens of thousands to demonstrate against the New Poor Law, or to take part in marches or listen to speeches, many of which were of a more violent tone altogether than was usually to be found in the published material, operated at another level of compulsion. Chartism was pervaded by a sense of class — both a positive sense of identification and a negative hostility to superior classes — which was stronger than perhaps existed at any other point in the nineteenth century. It has often been suggested that this class feeling was misdirected, and that the Chartists were badly misled in seeing their chief enemies as the manufacturing middle class. It has also been argued that they were used by upper-class interests, which also feared the increasing power of the middle classes, or even that the Chartists themselves were deferential towards the old land-owning ruling class, and therefore failed to see that their own interests were in reality bound up with those of the non-conformist manufacturers (32). The intense class bitterness, which it would be exceedingly difficult not to discern in almost every statement of the Chartists at all stages of the agitation, is seen as mistaken — mistaken in its main target, the manu-

14

facturing and employing class, or indeed in its whole tone. It is argued that the minority of leaders who, like Vincent and Lowery, turned away from the main stream of Chartism after 1840 and who were disavowed by most of their fellow Chartists were, in fact, pursuing the truest interests of the working class by helping to oppose monopoly and privilege in association with the radical part of the Liberal party, which they themselves helped to radicalise.

This is a serious argument which developed to some extent within Chartism itself in the later stages of the movement. There can be little doubt that the turning towards Liberal politics by former Chartists encouraged the development of popular Liberalism with its emphasis on parliamentary reform and muted opposition to imperialism. But in turning towards the Liberal party after the end of Chartism the former Chartists were to a large extent abandoning the social programme which had been such an essential part of the movement, and reverting to the political questions alone, which had not been essentially different from the Radical demands which had always had the support of a considerable group in Parliament. It was the social content of Chartism which had made co-operation with this group impossible, and it was not until the revival of independent working-class politics towards the end of the nineteenth century that this submerged social programme again became a part of British politics. The Liberal party did not in fact long survive the growth of this kind of radicalism, since it was not possible to contain both traditional nineteenth-century Liberalism and a dynamic policy of social reform within the same party. The Chartists certainly rejected the possibility of combining middle-class and working-class reform programmes within the same party; but to put the question in this way is to show its absurdity even in an academic sense in the years 1838-40, when the mutual hostility between the classes was at its height. The leaders of the Anti-Corn Law League may have wished to encourage working-class demonstrations against the Corn Laws, but they had no desire to see working men on the councils of the League, least of all leaders of the trade unions or Short Time Committees. Lord Ashley was for them less an object of hatred in his capacity as a Tory landowner than he was in that of a factory reformer. Amongst the working classes and the extreme radicals the actions of the Reformed Parliament had bred a suspicion against the middle classes and their upper-class allies which included the fear of a dramatic

15

increase in repressive government. Chartism in 1838-40 is pervaded by the possibility of a government terror, evident in the manifesto of the Convention as well as in the 'London Democrat'.

Chartism in its early years was held together by these various factors. First there was the breadth of the opposition of those who had been excluded from the franchise in 1832 to the activities of the government, secondly the strong sense of class engendered partly by the property definitions established by the 1832 Act, and partly by the increasing cohesion and stability of the merchant and employing classes in the industrial districts, thirdly the fear of strong government action, the establishment of a centralised state with a powerful punitive force at its disposal, and finally the example of 1832, in which determined political action backed by demonstrations and the threat of force in the country had succeeded in forcing a radical change on an unrepresentative legislature. These factors gave the movement a unity and a cohesion which it was never to achieve again after 1840, although the very divisions which existed in the later years sometimes made for the more sophisticated articulation of alternative programmes.

The unity of the movement centred around the programme of the collection of money and signatures to the first National Petition, and the organisation of the General Convention of the Industrious Classes which had been called for January 1839. The months of activity leading up to the Convention were informed with a sense of purpose and a discipline which is particularly surprising in areas such as the West Riding and East Lancashire with their recent history of violent opposition to the Poor Law. There was talk of violence, of arming, and of 'ulterior measures' to be adopted if the Petition should be rejected. But both the talk of violence and the actual arming were contained and controlled, and the enormous meetings which were held in preparation for the Convention took place without clashes with authority or the destruction of property.

A question which arises in these early months — the winter of 1838 and the early part of 1839 — is how far there was a genuine intention to resort to violence if peaceful methods failed to achieve the Charter. The whole question of Chartist violence in fact, must be examined from the very beginning.

Given that Chartism was a popular movement, rooted in the communities of the working people, an interesting phenomenon is the rarity of what might be called 'folk violence'. The

16

manifestations of violent protest which were most common in villages and townships — the pillorying of unpopular individuals by effigy-burning or rough music, sporadic outbreaks of arson, machine-breaking or cattle-houghing directed against unpopular employers or magistrates, were almost unknown amongst the Chartists. Although such occurrences were probably becoming rarer in the nineteenth century, they certainly occurred in this period in the agricultural districts, and recur again in popular demonstrations against the Cobdenite Liberals during the Crimean War and the 'pro-Boers' in the Boer war. In Chartist times, however, when tension was extremely high, there are almost no examples of their use by the Chartists. The few riots which did take place before the Newport outbreak did not follow the general pattern of popular rioting which had taken place even as recently as the Reform Bill crisis of 1831-2.

At Llanidloes, where the Chartists were provoked by the use of special constables from an unpopular neighbouring district, and where representatives of the hated metropolitan police were brought down to the district, the Chartists began by attacking the inn in which the policemen were lodged, but although doors and window-frames were torn out and furniture destroyed, the cellar was not invaded, and no ale or spirits were taken (33). In general, the extent to which discipline was maintained at a high level when thousands of people, many of them armed, were gathering regularly together, was novel and remarkable.

The movement against the Poor Law had contained a considerable element of lawlessness and direct action. Oastler believed that the Chartist movement had been deliberately started by London middle-class radicals to channel the violence and discontent in the manufacturing districts into the safe and predictable stream of an unrealisable political campaign. He was not alone in this view. Matthew Fletcher, a member of the Convention and a firm believer in universal suffrage, repeats the idea in his account of the origin of the Charter:

> When . . . honest and humane men of every political opinion which has regard for the ancient principles of the constitution, and for the ordinary rights of humanity, were banded in determined opposition to it; when the mandates of the commissioners were defied and their pretended authority set at nought; some of these people set to work to devise means of drawing off the attention of the 'masses' and depriving the anti-poor-law agitators of their support . . . after some quiet

17

but futile attempts to get up a movement, a negotiation was set on foot, in 1838, between the Working Men's Association of London and the Political Union of Birmingham. A great movement was decided upon; the radicals of the North of England and Scotland were communicated with, and all agreed to join it. In this neighbourhood we had our doubts, and they were not concealed, as to the source and motives of the agitation, but it was deemed most advisable to join it. We did so, and made it our own. It was obvious we were in earnest, and both the London and Birmingham men wished to back out of it. We would not let them, and for a time they were obliged 'to get into harness and do a little work' (34).

In its early days the anti-Poor Law men were amongst Chartism's most violent speakers. Fletcher, Stephens, Oastler and a host of local leaders had advocated opposition to the Law, and had carried out forms of direct action varying from mass meetings of protest and attacks on the commissioners in Huddersfield to the closing by the Fieldens of their factories in Todmorden and the throwing of all their employees simultaneously onto the poor rates. They brought the concept of the direct defiance of the law with them into the Chartist movement. Yet most of the prominent anti-Poor Law agitators were amongst the leaders who dropped out of the movement after 1840. The violence which developed within Chartism, and which came to a climax in the Newport rising and the events immediately following it, was of a different kind from that of the local resistance to the Poor Law (35).

One of the most difficult tasks in describing Chartism is to distinguish between the different kinds of violence within it, from the largely verbal bellicosity of Harney or O'Connor to the undoubtedly insurrectionary plans of Holberry or the Bradford Chartists. The attitude of the authorities varied from time to time, but on the whole they seemed to be fairly undisturbed by spoken or written threats by national figures until late in 1839, with the notable exception of the Stephens case (36). Before Newport a certain amount of threatening language appeared to be expected and tolerated. After the arrests of Frost, Williams and Jones the atmosphere changed, the violence became less generalised and more related to the circumstances of the trial and transportation of the Welsh leaders, and arrests for sedition increased dramatically.

Much of the violent language of the Chartist leaders was a

18

style of speech — a rhetorical device which both their followers and the authorities recognised to be a form of bluff. It was of two kinds, one provincial, coming from the anti-Poor Law movement and harking back as well to the armed demonstrations of the Reform Bill period. Certain phrases occur again and again in the speeches of the provincial leaders all over the country. The Whigs are reminded of their own bellicose posturings in the past, and Englishmen are reminded of their right and duty to defend the constitution. In Cornwall a clerical magistrate was horrified to hear Lowery declare that a musket was an essential article of furniture in every Englishman's home (37). But this expression was part of the stock-in-trade of most of the Chartist leaders. Thus Peter Bussey, replying to a toast at a dinner in his honour at Halifax in January 1839, is reported as saying:

> ... now he recommended that every man before him should be in possession of a musket, which was a necessary article that ought to provide part of the furniture of every man's house. And every man ought to know well the use of it, that he may use it effectively when the time arrives that requires him to put it into operation. . . . (38)

This type of rhetoric, summarised by the slogan 'Peaceably if we may, forcibly if we must', runs through almost all of the speeches made by Chartist leaders in the year before the Newport rising.

Rather different is the revolutionary vocabulary used by Harney and a small group of mainly London leaders, who took their expressions much more directly from the first French Revolution. It is in Harney's 'London Democrat' that 'the sacred right of insurrection' is appealed to, and a different kind of rhetoric appears. The 'Democrat', and Harney himself in many of his speeches suggest not a people arming to protect themselves against a violent and repressive government, but a revolutionary people, prepared to rise in support of their demands. Of the two kinds of rhetoric, the second is apparently the more revolutionary in tone, and has led some historians to suggest that Harney might have been expected to lead any rising that was being contemplated in these years (39). The Home Office was never very worried by either Harney or the 'London Democrat', however. The real threat to authority in these years was in the community-rooted organisations of the provincial

19

Chartists, less articulate though its leadership may have been than the French-inspired rhetoric of Harney or Taylor. When the two came together briefly in Newcastle and the north-east in the late summer of 1839, Harney's role was highly ambiguous. His speeches obviously appealed to the Tynesiders, and his popularity in Newcastle and district was obviously great. But how far he was in fact involved in insurrectionary activities — the manufacture of pikes, drilling, the collecting of arms and money — is not clear. It seems as though he was not in any way a leader of this kind of activity, which remained in the hands of the local people. Harney's recollections were only published in snippets in his later years, but one letter, published in the 'Newcastle Weekly Chronicle' in 1890, suggests that he was very much borne along by the tide of popular feeling at this time. Referring to the events of autumn 1839, he wrote:

One marked feature of the proceedings had been the concensus of opinion that force would have to be resorted to to obtain justice and the acknowledgement of right. This opinion has been placed to the account of certain names, at the head of which stands Feargus O'Connor; but I venture to affirm that, if any reader of these remarks has the opportunity to turn to the Newcastle papers of the time, he will find in their reports that it was not only Dr Taylor and others in unison with his views who referred to the probable employment of force, but also those who, at least later, acquired a character for moderation, who held the same view and expressed themselves in like terms. The opinion expressed and the terms of its expression may have been unwise; that I am not discussing; but the opinion was general. It was, so to speak 'in the air'. The fact is curious and suggestive of reflection. . . . (40)

Harney was quite correct in his recollection of the tone of Chartist speeches at the time. There is scarcely a single leader who remained prominent in 1838 and 1839 in whose speeches and writings there appears no suggestion of a recourse to arms. The May Manifesto of the Convention in 1839 was signed by William Lovett and Bailie Hugh Craig, one of the extremely moderate Scottish delegates, who withdrew soon afterwards from Chartist activity. It included among the eight questions put to the people 'Whether, according to their old constitutional right — a right which modern legislators would fain

20

annihilate — they have prepared themselves *with the arms of freemen to defend the laws and constitutional privileges their ancestors bequeathed to them*?' After the Birmingham Bull Ring affray, Lovett and Collins were arrested for seditious libel for attacking the behaviour of the magistrates and police, and Henry Hetherington, always on the moderate constitutional wing of the movement, announced that he would henceforth advocate going armed to meetings (41). The line between the advocacy of violence and the expectation of provocative violence by the authorities was always very fine. Advocates of the 'Sacred Month' — the general strike for the Charter — included some who, like Thomas Attwood, believed it to be a totally peaceful method of persuasion, and others who, like Bronterre O'Brien, considered that once it was embarked upon it would amount to a declaration of war against authority which must inevitably lead to a violent confrontation.

Since most of the Chartist leaders in the early months used to some extent the rhetoric of violence, it is difficult to assess which of them might have been expected to put themselves at the head of an insurrectionary movement after the rejection of the Charter. In the event the only national leader to find himself on trial for his life for levying arms against the Queen was John Frost. Frost was a middle-aged man, a life-long radical whose activity in politics had mostly been in the local government of the borough of Newport, Monmouthshire, where he was a magistrate and a respected local leader. He was removed from the bench as the result of his Chartist activity, but continued to speak and to write for the Chartist press. Although his radicalism went back to the days of the English Jacobins, he was very much in the main stream of British provincial radicals, and was never of the Harney or O'Brien type of revolutionary. He belonged to the category of men like Fletcher, Richardson and Bussey, who tended to drop out of activity after 1840. The logic of Frost's position as a leader of the Welsh radicals forced him to the head of the columns which marched on Newport on the night of 4 November 1839. Had the revolt succeeded, and had it been followed by other outbreaks at this time, it is almost certainly men of his sort throughout the country, men who had strong and long-standing links with their local communities, who would have been at the head of them.

The evidence for the widespread belief that the Newport events were only a part of a wider national conspiracy has not yet been fully assembled and examined. The difficulties in

21

assessing it now are, of course, very considerable. Had the Newport rising itself never taken place, it seems highly unlikely from the information which survives in official sources that the scale of the arming and preparation which must have gone into it would ever have been guessed at. There is no real suggestion in the reports from south Wales that in the month or so before the rising the arming and drilling being carried on in the locality was more than sporadic. The Home Office had no more reason from the information available to it to suspect an outbreak there than in Lancashire, the West Riding or Newcastle. On the other hand, there was obviously a very widespread belief that a conspiracy was in existence. Napier certainly believed it (42), and later evidence exists from the pens of Dr Taylor, William Ashton, Thomas Devyr and other Chartists, as well as from possibly more suspect witnesses such as David Urquhart and Alexander Somerville (43). Certain stories, such as the story of the defection of Peter Bussey, who should have led the West Riding outbreak, appear in different forms in the writings of contemporaries. The details may vary, and make reliance on their absolute veracity impossible, but the fact that both Benjamin Wilson and Frank Peel (44), who were personally acquainted with many of the leading West Riding Chartists, repeat versions of the story of Bussey's defection, makes it seem likely that there was some basis for it. In general, however, the ferreting out of the details of the 'underground' Chartist organisation is bound to be a complicated task. Information has been obscured by so many factors. At the time both fear of government action and the desire to justify flight — as in the case of Devyr — may have led to a denial or an exaggeration of the conspiracy. Later the record will have been obscured by the motives of men who had become active in different kinds of politics. The very fact that the death sentences on the Welsh leaders were commuted, and that the government terror did not materialise on the scale which it threatened, led many ex-Chartists to regret their adhesion to the idea of forcible resistance, and to suppress this part of their past. So that one of the most fascinating questions about the early years of Chartism remains, by definition, the least well documented (45).

A straightforward military rising aimed at the overthrow of the government and the taking-over of the strategic points throughout the country was not, however, the most likely way for a clash to have occurred between the Chartists and the authorities. In such a confrontation, even had the Chartists had better organisation and better weather than the Newport contingent, it is impossible to imagine that the military and tactical advantages could ever have been other than with the government. Two other main possibilities were present in the situation. One, which has not been taken very seriously by later historians, was that the proposed 'national holiday' should have been called in August 1839. It is quite impossible to predict how such an action might have developed, but it is at least possible that the tensions which were undoubtedly present throughout the manufacturing districts might have been increased to the point of civil war by strike action on a large scale, as Harney indeed prophesied would happen. In the atmosphere of 1839 such action would have had a different effect from the strikes of 1842. The national holiday was, however, rejected by the committee of the Convention which was set up to examine the question, and this possible collision was averted. The other, and in some ways the most likely, way in which hostilities might have broken out, was by the use of force against a Chartist demonstration. Such provocative action was always anticipated by the Chartists, and a Peterloo-type action by the military forces would have certainly sparked off a reaction throughout the country.

The fear of repressive action against the movement was, as has already been said, present throughout the first two years of the movement. The Manifesto of the Convention already referred to makes continual reference to the possibility of such attacks:

> ... The mask of *constitutional liberty* is thrown aside, and the form of *despotism* stands hideously before us. Shall it be said, fellow-countrymen, that four millions of men, capable of bearing arms, and defending their country against every foreign assailant, allowed a few domestic oppressors to enslave and degrade them? ... If you longer continue passive slaves, *the fate of unhappy Ireland will soon by yours*, and that of Ireland more degraded still ... we trust you will not *commence* the conflict. We have resolved to obtain our rights, 'peaceably if we may, forcibly if we must'; but woe to those who begin the warfare with the millions, or who forcibly restrain their peaceful agitation for justice — at one signal they will be enlightened to their error, and in one brief contest their power will be destroyed. ...

But the authorities did not provoke a clash during the vital period. The only armed confrontation was initiated at Newport, by the Chartists themselves.

The avoidance of provocation was obviously an important part of the policy of Lord John Russell, who as Home Secretary had the main responsibility of dealing with the Chartist crisis. It was also an essential element in the plans of Sir Charles Napier, who was appointed in February 1839 to command the army in the north. In the circumstances the appointment of Napier was a brilliant one, although it was by no means universally approved (46). He had been without an appointment for eight years, partly no doubt because of his well-known radical views. Both he and his brother William, to whom he wrote many of the letters which give a picture of his work in the Chartist period, had made no secret of their political views. William had, indeed, been invited by the Chartists of Bath to be their delegate to the National Convention, and had declined for two reasons, one the republicanism of some of the local Chartists, and the other the currency theories of Thomas Attwood, which he could not support, being himself a staunch supporter of the views of William Cobbett (47). Charles Napier shared his views, although he subsequently declared that 'Conscience should not wear a red coat. When I undertook the command of the Northern District under Lord John Russell, I put all my Radical opinions in my blue coat-pocket, and locked the coat in a portmanteau which I left behind me. I told Lord John this when I went to see him on taking the command' (48). His journal and his letters to William show, however, that he retained a considerable degree of sympathy for the aspirations of the Chartists.

They also show that he made more than one attempt to propose political measures, in the form of major concessions to the demands of the Chartists, as well as the enforcement of order (49). He had, as the result of his experiences in Ireland during the rebellion of the United Irishmen (50), a horror of civil war, and a particular sensitivity to the position of a military commander who, as his father had done in that period, had sympathies with both sides in the conflict. The extracts from his journal and the letters which were published in 'The Life and Opinions of General Sir Charles James Napier', edited by his brother William in 1857, reveal various changes in his attitudes and his views of the activities of the Chartists in the north during 1839. But all through is a constant determination

24

to prevent bloodshed, and above all to restrain the magistrates, whose hasty invocation of armed force might at any time have sparked off a conflict. 'At Manchester', he wrote to William in July, 'I found the magistrates reasonable, yet several were for stopping the meeting by force, and would have done so without any encouragement; but I swore if they attempted it not a soldier should quit the barracks till both constables' and magistrates' heads were broken. This was bravado, for I dare not refuse to obey their orders . . .' (51). Before the Kersall Moor meeting earlier in the year, he is reported as having called a secret meeting of Chartist leaders and told them: 'I understand you are to have a great meeting on Kersall Moor, with a view to laying your grievances before parliament: You are quite right to do so and I will take care that neither soldier or policeman shall be within sight to disturb you. But meet peaceably, for if there is the least disturbance I shall be amongst you and at the sacrifice of my life, if necessary, do my duty. Now go and do yours!' (52)

He attended the meeting himself, and reported to one of his officers that there were 'twenty-five thousand very innocent people, and ten thousand women and children' present. 'The remainder might have been Chartists, expressing orderly, legal political opinions, pretty much — don't tell this! very like my own . . .' (53). His radical sympathies were not merely political, but were informed by a very deep humanity which shows continually amongst the military and political comments in his journal. He wrote from Nottingham in September: 'There is among the manufacturing poor a stern look of discontent, of hatred to all who are rich, a total absence of merry faces: a sallow tinge and dirty skins tell of suffering and brooding over change. Yet often have I talked with scowling-visaged fellows till the ruffian went from their faces, making them smile and at ease: this tells me their looks of sad and deep thought are not natural. Poor fellows!' (54) His concern to prevent a clash with the Chartists, and his abhorrence of civil war did not prevent an occasional flash of sympathy in his journal even for the physical force Chartists. On 8 April 1840 he summed up the position in the northern district:

This meeting of delegates has not produced any sensation, the physical force heroes are cowed for the present: they started too sharply and are obliged to pull up: they had zeal, good-will and arms, but were deficient in arrangement, in

25

union, in leaders, in money, all of which are necessaries of
life to a rebellion! (55)

In July 1841 Napier relinquished the northern command to
take up an appointment in India. His brother, writing his
memoir in 1857, briefly summarised the subsequent history of
the movement, ending with the opinion 'Chartism is, however
not dead, it only sleeps to awaken with an improved judgement'
(56).

During the summer of 1839, particularly in the months after
the rejection of the Petition, there were undoubtedly widespread preparations amongst the Chartists for insurrection, and
a continual fear of government attack and the provocation of
open conflict. That such conflict did not occur was due to the
discipline and restraint which existed among the Chartists, to
the policy of the Home Secretary in restraining local action by
the authorities, other than the precautionary swearing-in of
special constables, and to the determination of Napier and his
juniors to avoid provocative action. The two major clashes
which did occur in those months, at Birmingham and
Llanidloes, although they roused very great local feeling, and
resulted in heavy punishment for some of those arrested,
nevertheless remained local incidents. They may have
strengthened the Chartist conviction that a clash with the
government was inevitable, but they neither of them occurred
in a context in which they sparked off other incidents. The
Newport rising of 4 November was the occasion chosen by the
Chartists themselves for the challenging of the authority of the
government.

The reasons for the failure of the Newport attempt have been
discussed many times, and will be discussed again (57). Apart
from the local misfortunes and failures of organisation, the
basic reasons why an insurrection had little chance of success are
clear enough. The British government was secure in the support
of the upper and middle classes, the army was loyal, no foreign
forces threatened — even Ireland was able to spare troops for
the English manufacturing districts in 1839 and 1840 (58). But,
although Chartism as an alternative government was not a
possibility, it may well have been possible that skirmishes and
outbreaks could have occurred which would have changed the
pattern of development of British politics in the later years of
the century. One event which might have led to further outbreaks and to a heightening of class feeling, which could well
26

have embittered the political atmosphere for decades, would have been the execution of the Welsh Chartist leaders. John Frost in particular was not simply a local leader. He was a chairman of the Convention, a hero to the whole movement since his public exchange of letters with Lord John Russell (59), and was respected by all sections of the Chartist movement. Whilst he and Zephenia Williams and William Jones were under sentence of death, there was considerable talk of risings, rescue attempts and retaliatory action of all kinds. Had the executions taken place, they might well have been the first of many. The legal query on which Frost's appeal was based allowed time for a slight cooling of the atmosphere on the side of the authorities, and for a nation-wide campaign by the Chartists in support of the three leaders (60). The commutation of the sentences almost certainly prevented many outbreaks of violence, although there were in fact some abortive risings in January 1840, notably in Yorkshire, in the period between the trial and the commutation of the sentences (61). The decision not to execute the Welsh leaders was undoubtedly, as Napier noted in his journal (62), a very wise one politically, and prevented much bitterness in the later development of working-class politics.

The radicals of the older kind who had stayed with Chartism after the end of the first Convention mostly seemed to have dropped out after the Newport rising. The atmosphere had changed, and the government, having avoided a policy of terror, was able to pursue a policy of repression with the maximum of support from the respectable classes. For the radicals of the Jacobin type, who had seen Chartism as an extension of the movement for political reform which had achieved a partial success in 1832, with its threats of armed action being essentially a tactic, Newport was a watershed. They saw here a face of radicalism which they neither understood nor approved. For Matthew Fletcher, the leaders of the movement 'had contrived almost to bury the term radical, which had begun to find much favour in the political world, and conjured up a terrible 'raw head and bloody bones' called chartism, associated in the minds of old ladies with nothing but 'treasons, stratagems and spoils', and which soon died a natural death . . .' (63). Chartism was to remain an important political force for another ten years, but it was an almost entirely working-class movement in these years. It was carried on, as Fletcher said sneeringly, by 'miserable knots of a dozen or two in each town, meeting generally in some beer-shop, and calling themselves branches of

27

the National Charter Association' (64).

It was, nevertheless, these 'knots of a dozen or two' who argued out, and attempted to implement, programmes of working-class activity. The National Charter Association was founded in July 1840. It was a nation-wide organisation — its actual organisational details had to be modified to meet the legal limitations of the law against Corresponding Societies — but it was in effect a national political body, with elected officers, locally and nationally. O'Connor himself was an elected member of the national executive, and submitted to annual re-election with the other members. This was certainly a decisive break with the past, with the tradition by which popular leaders declared their policies and relied on a 'following' amongst the common people. The idea of, for example, Cobbett or Hunt submitting themselves for election to the leadership of a popular movement illustrates the great change that Chartism had made in the tradition of popular radicalism. O'Connor undoubtedly had many of the qualities of an old-fashioned mass leader — the messianic as well as the oratorical gifts which aroused enthusiasm and devotion in his followers. But he was also leader of a movement in which democratic control was an essential element — he had to be prepared to debate his actions and his policies with other leaders, and to submit them to the membership for final judgement.

In the years following 1840 the Chartists debated the most effective way of achieving their aims. Their publications contain discussions of socialism, republicanism and nearly all possible variations of democratic government. In practical terms they carried out experiments ranging from the presentation of working men candidates at the hustings to the establishment of Chartist land colonies. Many of the ideas which were touched on in the early years were examined and developed at greater depth in the later years of the movement. But in the years covered here certain essential definitions were established. Above all, the national scale of Chartism was something quite new in popular politics. It is not the differences in the movement in the regions which are surprising — they were to be expected, given the great regional variations in the country's industry in these years — but the very great similiarity of political and social response. Essentially a provincial movement, Chartism arose at a time when the workers engaged in industry and crafts had achieved a sense of class identity, and were able to respond to a national programme and a national press, but lived still in small and closed enough communities to sustain an organisation with the minimum of finance and very few paid officials. The desperation of dying trades and the expansive prospects of the newer industries were contained for a time within the same movement, just as the pessimism of those who feared political reaction and the optimism of those who believed in the possibility of a breakthrough into a new phase of political democracy combined to forge a movement which seemed for a time to gain its strength from an equilibrium of threat and promise and a controlled tension between discipline and despair.

I have included at the beginning of the selection of documents a chronological list of the important events which relate to the Chartist movement during the years covered by the documents. Those who wish to do so may relate these events to the indices of trade and of bread prices. That there is a connection between large-scale protest or political action by the working people and the state of trade and the price of provisions is clear. But the correlation should not be over-simplified, nor should it be assumed that such a correlation effectively 'explains' any movement even of the complexity of a bread riot. Chartism was not, in fact, always at its strongest in areas of the greatest deprivation (65), and it was certainly not the programme of the most deprived and oppressed sections of society. The Chartist critique of contemporary industrial society found the greatest support in the areas of Britain's key industries — textiles, mining, iron-working and light metal-working. It was here that the working man who had hitherto been able to provide for his family by practising his trade appeared to be threatened. Here the changes associated with the Industrial Revolution were beginning to be felt on a large scale during the Chartist period. They did not necessarily involve an absolute lowering of the family's standard of living, but they often seemed to involve the removal of control and decision-making from the home to a wider social context. There was, therefore, every reason to look for political solutions to problems. Hunger, exploitation and oppression might each or in combination lead a working man to react against society. To some extent the working population of Britain were constantly aware of all three, and local recessions in particular trades must often have accentuated the insecurity of working-class life without necessarily provoking a political or even a turbulent or

29

riotous reaction. But the Chartist solutions to the three questions evoked the enormous response which they did because they appeared to be both rational and possible of achievement. Hunger and deprivation resulting from bad trade could be remedied by enlightened taxation, and by a humane system of out-relief. The extremes of exploitation could be prevented by the legal restraint of some employers by the limitation of hours of work and the protection of young children, and oppression by the defence of the rights of publication, assembly and free speech, all of which had been recently challenged and successfully defended. The working class had before them the example of the successful campaign by the middle classes for political recognition. The 1832 Bill and the subsequent Whig government had shown that it was not necessary to change the class of the representatives to have a House of Commons and a government that was sensitive to the requirements of a wider electorate. Not only were the political demands of the Chartists encouraged by the success of the middle-class campaign of a few years earlier, but they were made essential by that very success. The measures which had been passed in the interests of the middle-class voters seemed in many cases, as has been suggested earlier, to be directed against the working class.

The great interest of Chartism was that it was so much more than a movement of protest. It gave to the British working class a self-awareness and a self-confidence which, for all the short-term failure of the movement, were carried into varied forms of activity, social and political, in Britain and in other countries overseas. The working class was established as an essential and articulate force in British politics, whose effect was to be felt increasingly throughout the second half of the century, in both local and national affairs.

1. Benjamin Wilson, 'The Struggles of an Old Chartist' (Halifax, 1887).
2. 'Halifax Courier', quoted in Wilson, op. cit. p. 39.
3. Wilson, 'Struggles of an Old Chartist'.
4. For discussion of the importance of London as a Chartist centre, see: D. J. Rowe, 'The failure of London Chartism', in 'Historical Journal', xi 3 (1968); I. Prothero, 'Chartism in London', in 'Past and Present', no. 44 (Aug 1969).
5. Originally published between 12 April 1856 and 30 May 1857, in the 'Weekly Record of the Temperance Movement'

(not, as William Lovett mistakenly states in ch. vii of his 'Life and Struggles', in the 'Temperance Weekly Record').

6. See the letter from Frost in W. E. Adams, 'Memoirs of a Social Atom' (1903) i 201.

7. A phrase attributed to Frederick Engels, describing the Chartist period, by Belfort Bax, 'Justice', 24 Aug 1895. The reliability of Devyr's account of Newcastle Chartism in 1839 is discussed briefly in Adams, 'Memoirs of a Social Atom'. Adams knew Devyr later, and heard him tell the story again. He comments, 'Such is the story of my Irish friend Thomas Ainge Devyr. It is a story I have heard old Chartists dispute, and other old Chartists say they believe.'

8. p. 210.

9. Short biographical notices of delegates to the National Convention appeared weekly in 'The Charter', while the Convention was sitting. Fletcher's appeared in the issue of 31 March 1839, and Bussey's 5 May 1839.

10. 'Pen and Pencil Pictures of Old Bradford', by W. Scruton (Bradford, 1889).

11. J. H. Priestley, 'The History of the Ripponden Cooperative Society' (Halifax, 1932).

12. J. Holden, 'Short History of Todmorden' (1929).

13. Thomas Cooper, 'Wise Saws and Modern Instances' (1845) xi 23-4. Cooper goes on to describe the only Radical alderman in the old Lincoln corporation, who became a councillor and later the mayor under the new: 'The abhorrent enactments of the New Poor Law, — how he hated them! — and how staggered he felt in his reforming faith, when the 'liberal' administration urged the passing of the strange Malthusian measure! 'I cannot understand it' he would exclaim, in the hearing of the numerous participants in his English hospitality; 'I never thought that Reform was to make the poor more miserable and the poorest of the poor most miserable. It is a mystery to me! Surely it is a mistake in Lord Grey and Lord Brougham!' '

14. Raymond Challinor and Brian Ripley, 'The Miners Association, a Trade Union in the Age of the Chartists' (1968).

15. 'Reynolds Political Instructor', 13 April 1850.

16. 'Northern Star', 16 Nov 1839. An interesting short account of Pitkeithly is given in a series of articles on Chartism by Lloyd Jones, the Owenite Socialist, in the 'Newcastle Weekly Chronicle' in 1879 ('NWC', 27 Sept 1879).

17. 'Northern Star', 12 Jan 1839.

18. For a full account of the unstamped press agitation, see: Joel Wiener, 'The War of the Unstamped: The Movement to Repeal the British Newspaper Tax, 1830-1836' (New York, 1969); Patricia Hollis, 'The Pauper Press' (1970). See also P. Hollis's introduction to the Merlin Press reprint of 'The Poor Man's Guardian' (1969).

19. For the 'Northern Star', see Eric Glasgow, 'The establishment of the Northern Star newspaper', in 'History', n.s. xxxix (1954), Donald Read, 'Press and People' (1962) and Read and Glasgow, 'Feargus O'Connor, Irishman and Chartist' (1961). For a general description of the radical and Chartist press, see my 'La Presse de la Classe Ouvrière Anglaise 1836-1848', in 'La Presse Ouvrière 1819-1850', ed. Jacques Godechot (Paris, 1966).

20. Thus, Harney wrote to Engels, 30 March 1846, 'I must do O'C. the justice to say that he never interferes with what I write in the paper nor does he know what I write until he sees the paper': 'The Harney Papers', ed. Frank Gees Black and R. M. Black (1969) p. 241.

21. See below, pp. 128, 139, 177-84, 196, 218.

22. An interesting footnote to the radical support for the Canadian rebels is provided by an article by Michael Brook, 'Lawrence Pitkeithly, Dr Smyles and Canadian revolutionaries in the United States, 1842', in 'Ontario History', lvii (1965). See also W. H. Maehl, 'Augustus Hardin Beaumont, Anglo-American Radical, 1798-1838,' in 'International Review of Social History', xiv (1969).

23. For some of the points at issue between O'Connor and Daniel O'Connell see 'Letters from Feargus O'Connor to Daniel O'Connell' (1836).

24. For example, an item in the 'Northern Star', 30 Jan 1840: 12s is contributed to the Forst defence fund from Barnsley, from 'A few Bandon [Ireland] men to shew the traitor O'Connell falsified the character of Irishmen when he said the Irish in England were opposed to the Radicals.'

25. For a rather unsatisfactory account of the affair, see Gavin Thurston, 'The Clerkenwell Riot' (1967).

26. For an account of the passing of the Rural Police Act, and a discussion of its significance, see L. Radzinowicz, 'A History of English Criminal Law', iv (1968). For the view that the Chartist threat as a stimulus to police innovation has been overstated, see E. C. Midwinter, 'Law and Order in Early Victorian Lancashire' (York, 1968).

27. In Ashton-under-Lyne, one of the most active Chartist localities throughout the whole of the Chartist period, and where the very great majority of the working population were cotton factory operatives, not only was there a large Chartist organisation, but there were both juvenile and female Chartist groups ('Northern Star', 16 Nov 1839, 4 Dec 1841, and passim).

28. For a brief examination of the numerical strength of the cotton handloom weavers in the main Chartist centres, see Duncan Bythell, 'The Handloom Weavers' (1969).

29. 'Autobiography of Samuel Fielden', in 'Knights of Labour' (Chicago 1887).

30. For Luddite letters, see E. P. Thompson, 'Making of the English Working Class' (1963) ch. xiv. See also the interesting group of such letters in W. B. Crump (ed.), 'The Leeds Woollen Industry' (1930) ch. 111. For Captain Swing letters, see Eric Hobsbawm and George Rudé, 'Captain Swing' (1969).

31. 'The Trial of Feargus O'Connor and Fifty-eight others at Lancaster' (1843).

32. Brian Harrison and Patricia Hollis, 'Chartism, Liberalism and the life of Robert Lowery', in 'English Historical Review', lxxxii, and R. Soffer, 'Attitudes and allegiances in the unskilled North', in 'International Review of Social History', iii (1965).

33. T. E. Marsh to Viscount Clive, 1 May 1839, and Thomas Hayward to Viscount Clive, 4 May 1839, in 'National Library of Wales Calendar of Letters and Documents relating to the Chartist Riots in Montgomeryshire in the possession of the Earl of Powis' (1935).

34. 'Letters to the Inhabitants of Bury', by Matthew Fletcher (Bury, 1852). For an earlier expression of this view by Fletcher, see 'Northern Star', 19 Oct 1839.

35. Among those who withdrew their support after the events at Newport was Frances Trollope, the second volume of whose novel 'Michael Armstrong' was to have described the hero's participation in legitimate radical agitation, but 'when those in whose behalf she hoped to move the sympathy of their country are found busy in scenes of outrage and lawless violence ... the author feels that it would be alike acting in violation of her own principles, and doing injury to the cause she wishes to serve, were she to ... hold up as objects of public sympathy men who have stained their righteous cause with deeds of violence and blood ...': preface to 'Michael Armstrong' (1840).

36. Rev. Joseph Rayner Stephens was arrested in

Ashton-under-Lyne in Dec 1838, and charged with attending an unlawful assembly and with inciting the people to unlawful acts. He was tried in Aug 1839, and sentenced to eighteen months' imprisonment.

37. p. 189.

38. 'Northern Star', 19 Jan 1839.

39. A. R. Schoyen, 'The Chartist Challenge' (1958), examines in some detail Harney's connection with the insurrectionary side of Chartism.

40. 'Newcastle Weekly Chronicle', 5 Jan 1890. This letter is one of a series of reminiscent letters about 1839 in the Newcastle area. Taylor was almost certainly more deeply implicated in the plans for the north-east than Harney. See letter, John Grey of Millfield to Lord Howick, and the enclosure — a letter addressed to John Taylor by 'M.L.', and intercepted by Grey, in the Papers of the 3rd Earl Grey, Prior's Kitchen, Durham Cathedral.

41. 'Northern Star', 13 July 1839.

42. But by the end of Dec 1839, although he issued a warning to local commanders in the north of the persistent rumours of a general outbreak 'in favour of Mr Frost', he adds 'That such a general rising should take place the Major-General deems to be so wild a scheme that he does not place much belief in the truth of the report . . .': W. Napier, 'The Life and Opinions of General Sir Charles James Napier' (1857).

43. For Urquhart's account, see 'Sheffield Free Press' (1856). For Somerville's, see his 'Cobdenic Policy, the Internal enemy of England' (1854).

44. Wilson, 'Struggles of an Old Chartist'. Frank Peel, 'The Rising of the Luddites, Chartists and Plug Drawers' (1880).

45. The extent to which the commutation of the death sentences on the Welsh leaders 'de-fused' Chartism of its potential violence will remain a question of debate. Devyr reports that, when the death sentences were first announced, 'there were those on the sidewalk in front of our office who gave a bound of delight, with 'Thank God! the Government has just pronounced its own death sentence. That on John Frost will never be executed!' ' ('Odd Book', 1880).

46. Hobhouse to Lord John Russell: '. . . we have no particular reason for being anxious to place a Napier in high command, quite the contrary . . .': 'Later Correspondence of Lord John Russell' i 274.

47. 'Life of General Sir William Napier, K.C.B.', ed. H. A.

Bruce, M.P. (1864) pp. 297, 346 and passim.

48. Lord Broughton (J. C. Hobhouse), 'Recollections of a Long Life', ed. Lady Dorchester (1909).

49. Napier so far forgot the principles he had expounded to Hobhouse as to write to the commander-in-chief in 1839, saying he could see no way to meet the evils of the situation 'but to concede to the people their just rights, while the principle of order is at the same time vigorously upheld'. The reply was uncompromising: 'Lord Hill desires me to point out your observations and to suggest that you avoid all remarks having allusion to political questions; and I am to say without entering into the merits of the question, that neither he, as C-in-C, nor you as Major-General commanding the Northern District, can have anything to do with the matter; it is therefore better that you should confine yourselves to what is strictly your province as military men': Butler, 'Sir Charles Napier' (1890), and Napier, 'Life and Opinions of Sir Charles Napier'.

50. The Napiers were first cousins to Lord Edward Fitzgerald, who died of his wounds whilst under arrest for his part as a leader of the United Irishmen in 1798.

51. Napier, 'Life and Opinions of Sir Charles Napier', ii 53.

52. Ibid., ii 40.

53. Ibid., ii 39.

54. Ibid., ii 77.

55. Ibid., ii 122.

56. Ibid., ii 154.

57. See in particular Schoyen, 'The Chartist Challenge', and David Williams, 'John Frost' (1939).

58. Napier, 'Life and Opinions of Sir Charles Napier', ii 60.

59. Reprinted in full in the 'Annual Register' (1839).

60. In Aberdeen, the news of the death sentence arrived on Sunday. By Monday morning the petition for a pardon was ready. It was dispatched by 3 p.m. on Wednesday, with 15,000 signatures: 'John Mitchell, Aberdeen Chartist', in 'Aberdeen Peoples Journal', 24 Feb 1887. This is one example, which could be matched from many other centres, of the speed and scale of the response.

61. In a recent publication, 'Bradford Chartism 1838-40' (York, 1969), A. J. Peacock for the first time examines the evidence for and the reports of the attempted risings which took place *after* Newport. He shows that much of the contradictory evidence relating to a national conspiracy arises from the confusion between activity before and at the time of

Newport, and activity in Dec 1839 and Jan 1840.

62. Napier, 'Life and Opinions of Sir Charles Napier', pp. 125-6.

63. Fletcher, 'Letters to the Inhabitants of Bury', letter iv. Fletcher also speaks of the dropping out of the Convention of the 'timid — I should perhaps say prudent' members, soon after its beginning, and their replacement by 'what Feargus O'Connor called 'new blood' . . . it was after the new blood had begun to show itself that an excellent friend of mine, an Unitarian minister, suggested we had better go home while we yet had a character . . .'. Fletcher himself, however, stayed in the movement until after Newport.

64. Ibid., letter v.

65. See, for example, Home Office reports relating to the Newcastle area (H.O. 40). W. H. Maehl, 'Chartism in Northeastern England', in 'International Review of Social History', viii (1963), discusses the comparative prosperity of many of the Chartists in the area, and quotes pitmen of Whitridge as saying, in Aug 1839, that 'it was for their political rights they were struggling, and quite unconnected with the question of wages, respecting which they had no complaints to make . . .'. See also letter from the Bradford (Yorkshire) magistrates to the Lord Lieutenant, 18 April 1838, reporting that muskets, pikes and pistols were being bought by 'parties of the very lowest grade. . . . This state of things is more to be regretted as there is plenty of Employment for the working classes. . . .' (Harewood Papers).

Chronology

Some of the important dates in the first years of Chartism.

Before 1836

June 1832   Passing of the Reform Bill.

13 May 1833 Calthorpe Street Affair. Meeting called to propose the holding of a National Convention was declared illegal by the Home Secretary, and when it was nevertheless held, an attempt was made by the metropolitan police to disperse it forcibly. A policeman was stabbed to death, and a jury of London tradesmen returned a famous verdict of 'justifiable homicide'.

March 1834   Sentence of seven years' transportation passed on six agricultural labourers from Tolpuddle, near Dorchester, for administering an illegal oath, in the process of organising a local branch of the Grand National Consolidated Trades Union.

July 1834   Poor Law Amendment Act passed.

Sept 1835   Municipal Corporations Act passed.

1836

March   Newspaper Act passed, reducing stamp duty on newspapers to 1*d* per issue.

June   London Working Men's Association formed.

August   National Radical Association of Scotland formed.

November   'The Rotten House of Commons' published by the L.W.M.A. O'Brien's translation of Buonarotti's 'History of Babeuf's Conspiracy for Equality' published.

1837

January   East London Democratic Association formed.

28 February Meeting of Radicals called by the L.W.M.A. at the Crown and Anchor tavern in the Strand. Petition to the House of Commons adopted.

March	First L.W.M.A. missionary sent to the provinces (Cleave).
Throughout the year	Anti-Poor Law Associations formed in Yorkshire and Lancashire. Demonstrations and meetings addressed by O'Connor, Oastler, Stephens, etc.
April	Glasgow Cotton Spinners strike.
18 April	Proposal to revive Birmingham Political Union.
19 June	Meeting summoned by B.P.U. decided to petition Parliament for currency reform and universal suffrage.
31 May and 7 June	Conference between members of the L.W.M.A. and a group of radical M.P.s. A committee appointed to draw up a bill embodying the six points for presentation to Parliament.
November	Rebellions in Upper and Lower Canada.
November	First issue of the 'Northern Star' in Leeds.
7 November	B.P.U. decided to abandon currency reform as its programme and concentrate on universal suffrage.
December	Prosecution of leaders of Glasgow Cotton Spinners Union on charges of conspiracy, arson, assault and murder. Found guilty and sentenced to seven years' transportation.
December	Government, at O'Connell's suggestion, set up an official inquiry into trade unions. The trade unions set up their own committee to watch this, including three nominees from the L.W.M.A.

1838

8 May	'People's Charter' published in London.
June	Great Northern Union formed at Leeds.
June	Northern Political Union founded at Newcastle.

Mass meetings to present the Charter and to elect delegates to the proposed National Convention were held throughout the late spring and summer, including:

21 May	Glasgow meeting. Speakers from B.P.U., L.W.M.A. and Glasgow Cotton Spinners (150,000 claimed present).

27 June	Mass Meeting on Town Moor, Newcastle-upon-Tyne.
1 August	Mass meeting at Nottingham.
6 August	Meeting at Newhall Hill, Birmingham (200,000 claimed present).
September	Lord John Russell, Home Secretary, in a speech at Liverpool, reiterated his belief in the right of peaceable meetings in the open air.
17 September	Meeting at Palace Yard, Westminster, to elect London delegates (30,000 present).
24 September	Meeting at Kersall Moor, Manchester, John Fielden M.P. in the chair (250,000 claimed present).
14 November	J. R. Stephens addressed open air meeting at Hyde, for which he was later arrested.
8 December	Meeting at Calton Hill, Edinburgh, at which resolutions against the use of physical force were passed (5000 present).

1839

January	Examination of Stephens before the magistrates and his committal for trial.
4 February	General Convention of the Industrious Classes assembled at the British Hotel, Cockspur Street, Charing Cross. After two days, meeting place was transferred to Bolt Court, Fleet Street.
February	John Frost removed by the Home Secretary from the Commission of the Peace.
March	Anti-Corn Law League founded.
April	Major-General Sir Charles Napier appointed to command of the northern district.
April-May	Llanidloes riots.
7 May	Petition, with 1,280,000 signatures, given to Attwood and Fielden.
13 May	Convention moved to Birmingham.
May	Convention Manifesto issued, asking for consideration of eight forms of 'ulterior measures' to be undertaken in the event of rejection of the Petition.
Whitsun	Huge demonstrations in the major centres of Chartism.
14 June	Petition presented to Parliament by Attwood and Fielden.

8 and 15 July	Birmingham Bull Ring Riots.
9 July	Placard condemning behaviour of police issued by Convention, signed by Lovett and Collins. Lovett and Collins arrested.
12 July	Division in House of Commons on motion that the petitioners be heard at the bar of the House. Defeated by 235 to 46.
22 July	'Battle of the Spittal' (Newcastle): meeting attacked by troops and police.
21 July	'Address to the Middle Classes' issued by the Northern Political Union. Publisher arrested.
15 July	Convention called for the 'Sacred Month' — i.e. general strike — to begin on 12 August.
6 August	Resolution calling off the Sacred Month.
July-August	Rural Police Act debated and passed.
6 September	Convention dissolved.
3 November	March of Welsh Chartists on Newport.
4 November	Attack on Westgate Hotel, Newport.
November — December	Many Chartist leaders, local and national, arrested, mainly on charges of sedition.
10 December	Special commission at Monmouth to examine charges against Welsh Chartist leaders.
31 December	Trial of John Frost on charge of high treason begun.

1840

9 January	Verdict of 'guilty' on Frost.
11-12 January	Abortive rising in Sheffield. Samuel Holberry and others arrested.
16 January	Arrest of armed Chartists in Bethnal Green, London.
19 January	Death sentence passed on Frost, Williams and Jones.
26-27 January	Abortive rising in Bradford. Arrest soon after of Peddie and others.
1 February	Sentences on Welsh leaders commuted to transportation for life.
29 February	Chartist trials at Liverpool begin — Richardson, O'Brien, etc.
March	Trials of Chartists at York: Holbery and Sheffield Chartists for conspiracy; Bradford Chartists for riot and conspiracy; Barnsley

	Chartists for conspiracy; Feargus O'Connor for seditious libel. Sentences passed of from 18 months to four years.
March	Bath Chartists tried at Taunton for sedition. Sentences of from 6 to 18 months.
January	Small Convention met in London.
March	Convention in Manchester.
April	Convention in Nottingham.
April	Revival of Northern Political Union at Newcastle.
20 July	Delegate meeting at Griffin Inn, Great Ancoats Street, Manchester, to set up the National Charter Association.
24 July	Lovett and Collins released from Warwick Gaol.
August	McDouall released.

Other prisoners were released during the autumn and winter, providing opportunities for large welcoming demonstrations and the revival of activity.

PART I

Origins, Motives and Components of Chartism

The story of the social movements which became absorbed into Chartism has already been partly told (1). The documents in this section illustrate to some extent the way in which the different elements were united into one movement.

Richard Oastler, with his passionate defence of the poor and of the factory children, recalls in many of his political attitudes and arguments a social structure which belongs more to the eighteenth than to the nineteenth century. He believed in an essentially paternalist structure, in which the rich and the powerful acknowledged a duty to support the poor and the weak, and in which, moreover, the poor were entitled to demonstrate if they had genuine grievances which their rulers ignored. His direct action tactics in the opposition to the New Poor Law recall in some ways those of an eighteenth-century food riot. It may well be that he himself never realised how far he had moved from his paternalist preconceptions when he took part in the Fixby Hall Compact, by which he agreed to co-operate with the organisations of the working people in the West Riding. He did not consider that political emancipation would gain the working class any benefits, and he therefore never supported the Charter. But most of the men with whom he worked in the earlier movements became Chartists, and he retained their friendship and confidence, although he considered that they had taken a wrong path. Since the social rights, which were to him all-important, never ceased to be prominent in the Chartist agitation, he did not, in fact, find himself in active conflict with the movement at any time, although he continued to believe, as he suggests in the excerpt published here from the 'Fleet Papers', that the people had been deliberately misled by the supporters of Malthus, who wanted to prevent the poor from marrying and reproducing, and of free trade, who wanted cheap labour and an end to the influence of the landowning aristocracy.

The rules of the two organisations of London radical working men, both of which were established in the years immediately

43

preceding the publication of the Charter, show some of the attitudes which existed among metropolitan radicals. These attitudes had been partly defined in the agitation against the newspaper taxes in the early thirties.

O'Brien's account of the Crown and Anchor meeting early in 1837 is a good illustration of the sense which was abroad from that year onwards of a coming-together of the various strands of radical agitation into a single movement. In Halifax a similar process can be seen amongst the radicals — the supporters of the extension of the suffrage sharing the platform with the leaders of the handloom weavers, prominent in their opposition to the Poor Law Amendment Act. Both meetings took place before the actual publication of the People's Charter.

The appeal from Bolton from the W.M.A. to the trade societies was published later. It was a placard, published after the main sessions of the Convention, at a time when the question of a possible general strike was in the air. It shows a recognition of the importance and the power of the trade unions, and the desire which the Chartists felt to have organisational links as well as the more informal links which undoubtedly existed in most areas owing to the overlapping membership of the two organisations.

The placard from Bury might perhaps have been included in a later section, but it has been put here to illustrate the way in which various preoccupations at a local level could overlap. All of the incidents in the summer of 1839 which led to clashes with the authorities — at Llanidloes, in the Bull Ring at Birmingham, and this smaller affair at Bury — were sparked off by a clash with a section of metropolitan police. The hatred which these men invoked, and the fear which the proposals for the establishment of rural police forces aroused are illustrated by Fletcher's appeal. The events at Bury were fairly simple. A squad of metropolitan police had been applied for by the local magistrates, some of whom were millowners who feared for the safety of their property. The house in which the police were billeted was surrounded by a hostile crowd, and when three of the police, in plain clothes, who had been walking in the town, returned and tried to get in, the crowd surrounded them and refused to let them pass. They were eventually rescued by a sally of their comrades from within the house, using truncheons and firing without effect over the crowd's heads. After their return to the house, the crowd continued to throw stones through the windows, and one of the policemen, fearing that

44

the doors would not hold, fired a pistol from an upper window. The ball went through the leg of a young mechanic in the crowd. After the crowd had finally dispersed, the magistrates sent to Manchester for troops. It is significant that here, as in Birmingham and Llanidloes, the leading Chartists did their utmost to restrain their followers from violent action. They were very much afraid that police provocation would be used to provoke an outbreak on the authorities' own terms, which could be used to suppress the Chartists violently. The leading Chartist in Bury, John Rawson, was addressing a meeting of a large number of the local Chartists in a hall in the town — at which Bronterre O'Brien was the main speaker. The news arrived that a boy had been shot by the police, and there was a rush to the doors. These were immediately closed, and Rawson and O'Brien, in the words of the former, 'reasoned with [the Chartists] on the folly of being led into an outbreak by the machinations of villains, who panted for an opportunity of shedding their blood; we happily succeeded in quieting the people who, if they had got out of the hall, would have taken summary vengeance on the murderous police and the vagabonds who brought them into the town . . .' (2).

The last document in this section is the story of the discovery of Chartism by an individual working man. This was published in the 'Christian Socialist' in an incomplete autobiography by an anonymous ex-Chartist. There is a slight doubt about the dating of the events described, which the author says took place in February 1838. Since this was before the publication of the Charter, and the word 'Chartist' is used, this may well be a misprint, but whether for 1839 or 1848 is not clear from the narrative. However, it is such a good, and rare, example of the experience of a rank-and-file Chartist, and of the way in which the attitudes towards his poverty of his social superiors led him into radicalism, that I have reproduced it in spite of the doubt, since it represents a type of working-class experience which could have taken place at any time in the Chartist years.

1. See particularly Cecil Driver, 'Tory Radical' (1946), J. T. Ward, 'The Factory Movement', and M. Rose, 'The anti-poor-law movement in the north of England', in 'Northern History', (no. 1 (1966); also L. Radzinowicz, 'History of English Criminal Law', iv (1968).
2. 'Northern Star', 15 June 1839.

1 Richard Oastler on the Origins of Chartism

From the 'Fleet Papers', 20 March 1841

... It is because 'the multitude of the people' is believed to be too great, that measures hostile to nature are attempted to be enforced; it is because the Bible is thus declared to be a Lie — that religion is set at naught. It is *that* war against nature, which bewilders our mistaken governors, and forces them to acts, of which no other Government was ever guilty. They are all at sea, having thrown overboard the compass — which is Christianity; — they do not attempt to legislate *for* the people — their only aim is to *diminish* them! Hence they have persuaded you, the landlords, that if you do not send your 'surplus' population to be worked-up in their Factories, or to be poisoned in the Union Workhouses, they will eat up your estates! whilst at the same time they persuade the Factory population, if they are not allowed to feed on foreign corn, they will be pined to death! They have in great measure succeeded by the New Poor Law in separating the poor from any connection with the soil; they have, by deluding the people, nearly succeeded in forcing them to prefer the prosperity of foreign agriculture to our own!

Would that I could convince you of your danger, whilst listening to such ignorant 'school masters', whilst following such blind guides! There is nothing English, nothing Christian, nothing 'Home' in their plans.

Shall I tell you a secret, Sir?* If 'your order' will read it, and believe it, and take a hint, mayhap you may save yourselves. I know that what I am about to state is true. *If the New Poor Law be continued it is out of the power of man to prevent the entire repeal of the Corn Laws.* I shall not argue the question of whether it is better to encourage the growth of English corn, or the spinning of American cotton? whether it is wiser to force the population to inhale the impure fumes of the Factories, or to breathe the refreshing breezes of nature? to work by the light of gas or that of the sun? to be crippled in childhood by

[* The 'Fleet Papers' took the form of a series of letters addressed by Oastler, while in the Fleet Prison for debt, to his former employer, Thornhill of Fixby Hall.]

46

excessive labour, and instead of being, in manhood, strong and able defenders of their country, to become a dead weight upon her charities? or whether 'England would be no poorer if she were never to grow another ear of corn?' Sir, on this occasion, I will trouble you with none of these questions — but I will tell you a fact, which it will be well for you, landlords, to consider, remembering always, that that enthusiastic friend of the New Poor Law, Earl Fitzwilliam has said — 'If the Corn Laws are not repealed, the New Poor Law is an unjust measure.'

You must remember, Mr. Thornhill, that about the time when you discharged me, I was engaged, with others, in a powerful movement in Yorkshire and Lancashire, against the New Poor Law. You know that your attempt to stay my proceedings failed, and that, in consequence, you discharged me. You will remember also that, by some means the movement against the New Poor Law was suddenly silenced. I will tell you how that was effected. The knowledge of that fact ought to open the eyes of the 'country gentlemen' to the delusions practised upon them by the Malthusians. Nothing is more clear, than if there are too many of us we must seek food from our neighbours. Do you not see that, Mr Thornhill? To hope for relief, from such an evil, from emigration, is absolute madness! You will learn by the fact I am about to state, how this great nation is governed!

It so happens, that there are in London, two men, who, in a private way, manage the domestic affairs of the Government. One of them is an M.P., the other was formerly an important and influential M.P. manufacturer. If it were needful, I could mention their names.

These two men are *avowed* Infidels and Malthusians; they profess to be Radicals, Chartists, or Republicans, or any thing which, for the time, will best catch the ear of the disaffected. They keep up a regular communication with the Government, and also with a few honest men, who have much influence with the working people. These honest men, believe the two Malthusians to be as honest as themselves, and consequently they act with confidence on their suggestions.

Now, sir, it so happened that at the time when we in the north, were busily employed in attending meetings against the New Poor Law, the Government, finding it absolutely impossible to silence us by London Police, Spies, Russell Magistrates, or Troops — nay, after they found that the soldiers disliked to be employed on such service; and that, every where,

47

our meetings were immensely numerous, highly respectable, unanimous and peaceable: and perceiving that it was impossible for any law, which was so steadily and constitionally opposed, long to remain on the statute book — what trick, Sir, do you think the Government played, to please the landed interest, and to put down the cry against the New Poor Law? I will tell you, Sir. — They communed with their two friends, to whom I have above alluded. With them, a bargain was struck to this effect: 'If *you* will put down the movement against the New Poor Law, *we* will agree to the repeal of the Corn Laws!' Do not start, Sir, what I tell you is the truth. The two Malthusians set to work immediately; they excited the hopes of the honest but mistaken friends of the working classes. The *Charter* was immediately urged upon the attention of the masses - the cry for the repeal of the New Poor Law was abandoned, and, at the instance of the Government, to gratify the country gentlemen, and to serve a Malthusian purpose, the agitation of the *Charter*, was substituted for that of the repeal of the New Poor Law! The prisons are now filled with Government *Chartist* victims: and the two Malthusians are, at this moment, (backed by the 'anti-Corn Law league') demanding of the Government 'the pound of flesh' in the shape of 'the repeal of the Corn Laws'! To serve the 'country gentleman' the Government employed the Chartists, and thus retained the New Poor Law! To please the Malthusian cotton-gentry, the Government are now required to repeal the Corn Laws! and the Chartists, hoping to advance their own favourite question, have swamped the Metropolitan Anti-Poor Law meeting, and have insulted the chairman, Mr Walter, whose disinterested and noble efforts for the poor have endeared him to all but their enemies. Thus have the Chartists, while intending to serve the poor, delighted and strengthened the 'man-without-a-heart', and all those who are determined to uphold the system of oppression under which the working classes now groan. The reward for the services thus rendered by the Chartists, is the transportation and imprisonment of their leaders and the establishment of the Rural Police! The Chartist may well say: 'Call you this backing your friends.'

Sir, I am not romancing; what I have herein stated is *true*. It is high time that this *Farce* of governing was ended. See the mischief that it has already engendered. Every institution, from the Church downwards, is shaken and threatened. Every party is divided by rancorous jealousy. There is no union or combination of interest; all is disjointed and unsettled. The very *pets* of the system themselves — the cotton Lords and *millionaires* — dream of ruin and confiscation, even in *their* camp, doubt and uncertainty prevail, and each distrusts his neighbour. It is not safe that a great nation should any longer, by thus wafting in mid air, like a balloon, driven about by every breeze, having neither anchor, nor compass. That this is a true picture of England, facts innumerable prove — Government is no longer a science, — it is a trick, a swindle. The most cunning, not the most wise, is admired. How long this state of things will continue, no one can tell; though all know, assuredly, that very long it cannot last.

Do you not think, Sir, that it would be better to legislate upon some settled principle? I do — All this confusion, and fraud, and oppression, and injustice, arise from the adoption, by the Government of the insane notions, that there is no natural tie between the soil and the people — that property has no duties — that man has no natural *rights* — that there are too few acres and too many men!

Until we can humble ourselves to obey Nature's laws, and to believe Bible truths, we shall go on blundering and floundering, until our institutions will be destroyed, and anarchy or despotism will be our inevitable fate! It is well worth the while of those persons who are possessed of large estates, seriously to resolve that these evils shall be averted.

If the facts which I have stated, should have the effect of inducing the aristocracy to 'consider their ways', to see the danger which they are in by uniting with the Malthusians to rob and oppress the poor, this letter will not have been written in vain.

Surely I have already satisfied you that, unless the nobles will unite with the people, their 'order' will soon be extinct.

The object of the Malthusians is to transform this country into one great workshop, therein to work the poor to death, and thus to enrich the immense capitalists, — levelling every rank between. The object of a wise Government would be to encourage agriculture, to unite the owners, occupiers and tillers of the soil in one bond of interest and union — to restore, as much as possible, the domestic system of manufacture, and repress that infernal system of competition, which enables a very large capitalist to ruin a whole neighbourhood, and *millionize* himself, by schemes and plots as immoral and disgraceful as murder, robbery and fraud!

. . . I am, your Prisoner, RICHARD OASTLER

2 Address and Rules of the Working Men's Association* : Brochure to Members Issued June 1836

Copy in Lovett Collection, Birmingham

(E PLURIBUS OMNIUM)

Let us apply with hearts sincere as Truth
Our mental might to this ennobling work —
The Mind's regeneration — and become
Messiahs in the cause of Liberty
Nor cease, until from out of the book of life
We blot the name of Tyrant and of Slave.

Charles Cole

ADDRESS

Fellow Labourers in the pursuit of knowledge and liberty

We are anxious to express our grateful acknowledgements thus publicly, to those associations who have addressed us in the spirit of fraternity, and especially to those individuals who have so kindly assisted our missionaries in their exertions to form other associations.

It is a pleasing evidence of the progressive knowledge of those great principles of democracy which we are contending for, to find kindred minds prepared to appreciate, and noble hearts seeking their practical development in the remotest parts of the kingdom.

But we would respectfully caution our brethren in other societies strictly to adhere to a judicious selection of their members — on this more than on any other of their exertions harmony and success will depend. Let us, friends, seek to make the principles of democracy as respectable in practice as they are just in theory, by excluding the druken and immoral from our ranks, and in uniting in close compact with the honest, sober, moral, and thinking portion of our brethern.

[* The L.W.M.A. was formed on 16 June 1836.]

Doubtless, by such selections our numbers in many instances will be few compared with the vicious many, but these few will be more efficient for the political and social emancipation of mankind than an indiscriminate union of thousands, where the veteran drunkard contaminates by his example, and the profligate railer at abuses saps by his private conduct the cause he has espoused.

In forming Working Men's Associations, we seek not a mere exhibition of numbers unless, indeed, they possess the attributes and character of *men!* and little worthy of the name are those who have no aspirations beyond mere sensual enjoyments, who, forgetful of their duties as fathers, husbands, and brothers, muddle their understandings and drown their intellect amid the drunken revelry of the pot-house — whose profligacy makes them the ready tools and victims of corruption or slaves of unprincipled governors, who connive at their folly and smile while they forge for themselves the fetters of liberty by their love of drink.

We doubt not that the excessive toil and misery to which the sons of labour are subject, in the absence of that knowledge and mental recreation which all just governments should seek to diffuse, are mainly instrumental in generating that intemperance, the debasing influence of which we perceive and deplore. But, friends, though we possess not the political power to begin our reformation at the source of the evil, we cannot doubt the efficacy of our exertions to check by precept and example this politically-debasing, soul-subduing vice.

Fellow-countrymen, *when we contend for an equality of political rights*, it is not in order to lop off an unjust tax or useless pension, or to get a transfer of wealth, power, or influence, for a party; *but to be able to probe our social evils to their source, and to apply effective remedies to prevent, instead of unjust laws to punish.* We shall meet with obstacles, disappointments, and it may be with persecutions, in our pursuit; but with our united exertions and perseverance, we must and will succeed.

And if the teachers of temperance and preachers of morality would unite like us, and direct their attention to *the source* of the evil, instead of nibbling at the effects, and seldom speaking of the cause; then, indeed, instead of splendid palaces of intemperance daily erected, as if in mockery of their exertions — built on the ruins of happy home, despairing minds, and sickened hearts — we should soon have a sober, honest, and reflecting

51

people.

In the pursuit, therefore, of our religious object, it will be necessary to be prudent in our choice of members; we should also avoid by every possible means, holding our meetings at public-houses; habits and associations are too often formed at those places which mar the domestic happiness, and destroy the political usefulness of the millions. Let us, then, in the absence of means to hire a better place of meeting – meet at each others' houses. Let us be punctual in our attendance, as best contributing to our union and improvement; and, as an essential requisite, seek to obtain a select library of books, choosing those at first which will best inform of our political and social rights. Let us blend, as far as our means will enable us, study with recreation, and share in any rational amusement (unassociated with the means of intoxication) calculated to soothe our anxieties and alleviate our toils.

And, as our object is universal, so (consistent with justice) ought to be our means to compass it; and we know not of any means more efficient, than to enlist the sympathies and quicken the intellects of our wives and children to a knowledge of their rights and duties; for, as in the absence of knowledge, they are the most formidable obstacles to a man's patriotic exertions, so when imbued with it will they prove his greatest auxiliaries. Read, therefore, talk, and politically and morally instruct your wives and children; let them, as far as possible, share in your pleasures, as they must in your cares; and they will soon learn to appreciate your exertions, and be inspired with your own feelings against the enemies of their country. Thus instructed your wives will spurn instead of promoting you to accept, the base election bribe – your sons will scorn to wear the livery of tyrants – and your daughters be doubly fortified against the thousand ills to which the children of poverty are exposed.

Who can foretell the great political and social advantages that must accrue from the wide extension of societies of this description acting up to their principles? Imagine the honest, sober and reflecting portion of every town and village in the kingdom linked together as a band of brothers, honestly resolved to investigate all subjects connected with their interests, and to prepare their minds to combat with the errors and enemies of society – setting an example of propriety to their neighbours, and enjoying even in poverty a happy home. And in proportion as home is made pleasant, by a cheerful and intelligent partner, by dutiful children, and by means of comfort, which their

52

knowledge has enabled them to snatch from the ale-house, so are the bitters of life sweetened with happiness.

Think you a corrupt Government could perpetuate its exclusive and demoralizing influence amid a people thus united and instructed? Could a vicious aristocracy find its servile slaves to render homage to idleness and idolatry to the wealth too often fraudulently exacted from industry? Could the present gambling influences of money perpetuate the slavery of the millions, for the gains or dissipation of the few? Could corruption sit in the judgment seat — empty-headed importance in the senate-house — money-getting hypocrisy in the pulpit — and debauchery, fanaticism, poverty, and crime stalk triumphantly through the land — if the millions were educated in a knowledge of their rights? No, no, friends; and hence the efforts of the exclusive few to keep the people ignorant and divided. Be ours the task, then, to unite and instruct them; for be assured the good that is to be must be begun by ourselves.

OBJECTS OF THE ASSOCIATION

1. To draw into one bond of *unity* the *intelligent* and *influential* portion of the working classes in town and country.

2. To seek by every legal means to place all classes of society in possession of their equal political and social rights.

3. To devise every possible means, and to use every exertion, to remove those cruel laws that prevent the free circulation of thought through the medium of a *cheap and honest press*.

4. To promote, by all available means, the education of the rising generation, and the extirpation of those systems which tend to future slavery.

5. To collect every kind of information appertaining to the interests of the working classes in particular and society in general, especially statistics regarding the wages of labour, the habits and condition of the labourer, and all those causes that mainly contribute to the present state of things.

6. To meet and communicate with each other for the purpose of digesting the information required, and to mature such plans as they believe will conduce in practice to the well-being of the working classes.

7. To publish their views and sentiments in such form and manner as shall best serve to create a moral, reflecting, yet energetic public opinion; so as eventually to lead to a gradual

improvement in the condition of the working classes, without violence or commotion.

8. To form a library of reference and useful information; to maintain a place where they can associate for mental improvement, and where their brethren from the country can meet with kindred minds actuated by one great motive — that of benefiting politically, socially, and morally, the useful classes. Though the persons forming this Association will be at all times disposed to co-operate with all those who seek to promote the happiness of the multitude, yet being convinced from experience that the division of interests in the various classes, in the present state of things, is too often destructive of that union of sentiment which is essential to the prosecution of any great object, they have resolved to confine their members as far as practicable to the working classes. But as there are great differences of opinion as to where the line should be drawn which separates the working classes from the other portions of society, they leave to the Members themselves to determine whether the candidate proposed is eligible to become a Member.

3 Prospectus of the East London Democratic Association issued January 1837

Copy in Lovett Collection, Birmingham

Prospectus of the East London Democratic Association,
No. 19, Swan Street, Minories.
Established January, 1837

The object of this Association is to promote the Moral and Political condition of the Working Classes by disseminating the principles propagated by that great philosopher and redeemer of mankind, the Immortal 'THOMAS PAINE'.

The subscription of a penny per week constitutes a member (subject to the approval of a majority of the members at any meeting). Which subscription can be paid Weekly or Monthly as convenient.

That the annual meeting of the Association be held on the 29th January, being the anniversary of the death of that great Man, whose character and principles we duly appreciate, by a social and convivial supper on that occasion.

That all members entering on or before the first Sunday in May, shall be entitled to a double ticket of admission to the supper, in commemoration of the birth of Thomas Paine, which will admit a Lady and a Gentleman; all persons entering on or before the first Sunday in August, will be entitled to a single ticket. Persons entering after that time will be entitled to the same by paying up the arrears from the first Sunday in August, and to a double Ticket by paying 1/- extra.

That the members of the Association meet the first Sunday in every month, at Six o'Clock in the Evening, to enroll names, to discuss the principles of cheap and honest Government, and to adopt such means as may seem expedient to carry out the five grand principles of Radical Reform, viz: 'Universal Suffrage, Vote by Ballot, Annual Parliaments, No Property Qualification, and Equal Representation.'

That we agree to discuss, to agitate, and petition until those just demands be conceded.

55

For Freedom's battle once begun
Bequeathed by bleeding sire to son,
Though baffled oft, is ever won.

Committee

Mr A. Davenport
  „ S. Yarham
  „ W. Edmonds
  „ J. Harvey
  „ G. J. Harney

Mr C. Needham
  „ G. H. Hedger Senr
  „ G. Hedger Jun.
  „ T. Biggs
  „ A. Milcham

E. Harvey, Treasurer pro tem.
J. Harper, Secretary pro tem.

4 Bronterre O'Brien's Account of the Radical Meeting at the Crown and Anchor, 28 February 1837

From the 'London Mercury', 4 March 1837

To all my Brother Radicals in town and Country

Lift up your democratic heads, my friends! Look proud and be merry. I was at a meeting on Tuesday night which does one's heart good to think on: a meeting which forbids that the sons of Radicalism should ever again indulge in blue devils. I have seen many public assemblies in my time; I have been present at all sorts of political meetings, Whig, Tory and Radical, but never was it my good fortune to witness so brilliant a display of democracy as that which shone forth at the Crown and Anchor on Tuesday night. I often despaired of Radicalism before; I will never despair again after what I witnessed on that occasion.

Four thousand democrats, at least, were present at the meeting. The immense room of the Crown and Anchor was crowded to overflowing, several hundreds stood outside on the corridor and the stairs, or went away for want of accommodation. The platform was equally crammed as the body of the room, and notwithstanding the great pressure and the great excitement that prevailed, the most perfect order characterised the whole of the proceedings from beginning to end.

The meeting (as will be seen by our report elsewhere) was convened by the Working Men's Association, to petition for a reform of Parliament, based on the five cardinal points of Radicalism, viz: UNIVERSAL SUFFRAGE, EQUAL REPRE-SENTATION, ANNUAL PARLIAMENTS, VOTE BY BALLOT, and NO PROPERTY QUALIFICATION FOR MEMBERS. The arrangements of the committee were in every respect complete, and of the true democratic stamp. A working man was appointed to preside. The resolutions and petitions were severally proposed and seconded by working men. The principal speakers who supported them were working men. The petition itself, which is one of the very best of the kind ever submitted to Parliament, was drawn up by working men. In short, the whole proceedings were originated, conducted, and

57

concluded by working men, and that in a style which would have done credit to any assembly in the world.

The chairman, who is a compositor,* opened the business by a masculine speech, in which he energetically but temperately set forth the objects of the meeting. He was followed by Mr Lovett, who in one of the most eloquent addresses I ever heard, gave a philosophic and historic analysis of despotism, in which he showed its invariable object in all climes and ages to have been the protection of unduly-acquired wealth and power in the hands of small monopolizing fractions of each community, and exhibited the various phases and modifications it assumes, according to the varying degrees of civilization it has to deal with. Here was opened a wide field to the orator: — kingcraft, privileged castes, superstition and priestcraft, military glory, scenic representations, corrupting and brutalising spectacles, restraints on the freedom of speech and writing, literary prostitution, standing armies, juggling money-systems, fiscal exactions etc. etc. etc; each and all of these passed in rapid but brilliant review before the meeting. The manner in which despotism brought each sinister appliance to bear on its purpose was beautifully shewn, while the speaker never lost sight of the great moral to be inculcated, which was, that the end and object of all despotism being to uphold monopolies, there can be no escape from it, so long as the *exclusive power of law-making shall be* suffered to abide with the monopolists. To the destruction of that parent of all monopolies, tended the speech and resolution proposed by Mr Lovett.

The next speaker was Mr Vincent, a young and very ardent republican of the 'out and out' school. — Vincent is, I believe, a great favourite among his brother operatives; at any rate, he is one of their most effective speakers, and well deserving the applause so frequently and liberally bestowed upon him. I had heard him on a few previous occasions, but the meeting on Tuesday called forth the full extent of his powers. He spoke with boldness, fluency and a perfect command of his subject; Paine is evidently a great favourite with him, for not only does he delight in recommending that writer, but he has all his best maxims and arguments at his fingers' ends. Amongst many other good things, he gave a masterly exposition of the 'rotten House of Commons', and a `capital spicy hash of Paine's exposure of Blackstone's old humbug about the checks of our

[* I.e. Robert Hartwell, who remained a leading London Radical for nearly the whole of the nineteenth century.]

58

'nicely balanced Constitution'. Sir Bobby Peel also came in for a lash or two, in consequence of his late audacious harangue at Glasgow in which he described the American system of government as the despotism of a majority, and laid down the doctrine, that if a similar government were to be instituted in this country, the aristocratic minority (of which Peel is one) would have a right to rebel against and overthrow it. On the whole, Mr Vincent promises to prove a very valuable member of his order, as a public man. Mr Vincent was followed by two speakers named Hoare,* who moved and seconded the second resolution, with great spirit and effect. The first, in particular, drew repeated applause by the manly and animated strain in which he dwelt (with conscious, honest pride) on the merits and capabilities of his 'order' — 'The aristocracy' said Mr Hoare 'call us an ignorant mob, and affect to justify our disenfranchisement on such pretended grounds of ignorance. But, in what are the aristocracy our superiors? Not, assuredly, in knowledge, for if they know some things which we do not, we know many other and better things of which they are totally ignorant.' etc. Here Mr. Hoare instituted a comparison between the relative knowledge of the aristocracy, middle, and working classes, in which he showed with unanswerable truth that with all their pretended superiority, the two former classes are, after all, vastly inferior to the working classes in all those departments of knowledge which society most needs, and without which it could not exist an hour. 'The aristocrats' quoth Mr H. 'can make a more graceful bow, and do the like gentilities better than we operatives can. The middle classes, too, can lie and cheat and chicane in trade better than we can, but what does the aristocrat or shopocrat know of husbandry or ship-building or any other of the useful arts?' I should like to know what the aristocrat and profit-monger have to say to that — For my own part, I agree implicitly with Mr Hoare, that excepting the knowledge of words and ceremonials, or the still baser knowledge which consists in the art of chicanery, and swindling other peoples' earnings into their own possession, the upper and middle classes are in every respect, the inferiors in knowledge of the class they affect to despise. 'They pretend' said one of the speakers 'that our ignorance is the sole cause of their excluding us — odious hypocrisy! It is our knowledge, not our ignorance they fear. If we were really ignorant, they would give us the franchise, as

[* Actually the second was called Moore (possibly Richard Moore of Finsbury).]

they did to the poor 40/- freeholders in Ireland — expecting that while *we* had it in name and appearance, they themselves would possess the substance and reality!' The other speakers who followed Mr Hoare, spoke with equal force and fervour, though not perhaps with equal eloquence. Great diversity of style and manner was observable: but a single soul appeared to animate the whole. This singleness of purpose was, perhaps, the most striking, as it was certainly the most encouraging feature of the proceedings. Hitherto our Radical meetings had presented but too lamentable evidences of a contrary character. Discrepancy, divisions and irresolution were our predominant characteristics. One leader pulled one section of the audience this way, another pulled a second section that way; a third leader excercised a similar influence with a third party, and so on — Nothing of the kind was visible at the meeting on Tuesday — we had neither Toryism nor Whiggery, nor sham-radicalism. I verily believe there was not a single mock-liberal in the room — the spirit of humbug was completely gone — there was but one creed, and that was *Universal Suffrage and no Compromise*! Every man of the assembled thousands, was for going the 'whole hog' and for going it speedily. — No tergiversations — no shuffling — no mental reservations — 'All that are not with us are against us' was the predominant, indeed, the all-pervading feeling.

I have many reasons to feel proud of this meeting. I am proud of it on personal as well as public grounds. For six years have I laboured in obscurity, and almost alone, to inculcate certain great principles to serve as a never-failing test, by which the millions might be enabled to distinguish their *true* from their *sham* friends. During the greater part of that time, I had not (excepting Mr Bell) a single coadjutor in the press, nor did I witness a single public meeting in favour of my views. If I wrote to show the uselessness of repealing the Corn Laws, or the mischievousness of establishing the ballot without a previous enfranchisement of the working people, I found no echo anywhere to my sentiments. That misfortune I have no longer to regret. The meeting on Tuesday has given its sanction to every principle I proclaimed, and gone with me even in those dubious points in which the majority are still against me. Witness the frequent allusions to the Ballot, the Corn-Laws and the Property-qualification. Witness also the repeated declarations of the principal speakers, that all other reforms, whether organic or remedial, are useless to the working classes without the

60

franchise. I remember, when I first attacked O'Connell, what a hue and cry was raised against me. A publication which I then edited fell one thousand in sale in one week in consequence. Did that make me retreat? On the contrary, I redoubled my blows at him, and kept hammering away ever since, till almost everybody is of my opinion now. In like manner, when *'Reform of the Lords.'* was broached, and when every mercenary print, stamped and unstamped, was taking part in the crusade — I denounced the project as a vile cheat — as a decoy to lure off our attention from the House of Commons, which I knew, and know still, to be the real seat of the mischief. I said at the time that O'Connell's object in starting 'reform of the Lords' was to break up the working-class associations, and especially the trades unions. What was the fact? In three weeks after I made my prediction, O'Connell induced the trades of Dublin to suspend their sittings for twelve months, lest, forsooth, 'they *might embarrass Lord Mulgrave's government*!' Many other instances might I adduce to which I could prove positive losses to myself in consequence of my being in advance of public opinion. But reckless of consequences I still persevered; and now I have had the glorious satisfaction of seeing a meeting of 4,000 Radicals applaud all my principles, and determined to trust no individual or party who is not in favour of similar principles. Have I met my reward here?

One word as to the petition adopted at the meeting. I hope my friends that you will make known the facts contained in it to every working man within reach of you. It will supply excellent material for similar petitions all over the country. The meeting on Tuesday night ought not to pass unheeded. It has set an example to the country which the Radicals of England will be traitors to themselves if they do not imitate. Now is the time to strike a blow for universal suffrage.

Yours affectionately etc.
Bronterre

5 Petition Adopted at the Crown and Anchor Meeting

From 'The Life and Struggles of William Lovett' (1876)

To the Honourable the Commons of Great Britian and Ireland. The Petition of the undersigned Members of the Working Men's Association and others sheweth —

That the only *rational use* of the institutions and laws of society is justly to protect, encourage, and support all that can be made to contribute *to the happiness of all the people*.

That, as the object to be obtained is mutual benefit, so ought the enactment of laws to be by mutual consent.

That obedience to laws can only be *justly enforced* on the certainty that those who are called on to obey them have had, either personally or by their representatives, the power to enact, amend, or repeal them.

That all those who are excluded from this share of political power are not justly included within the operation of the laws; to them the laws are only despotic enactments, and the legislative assembly from whom they emanate can only be considered parties to an unholy compact, devising plans and schemes for taxing and subjecting the many.

That the universal political right of every' human being is superior and stands apart from all customs, forms, or ancient usage; a fundamental right not in the power of man to confer, or justly to deprive him of.

That to take away this sacred right from the *person* and to vest it in *property*, is a wilful perversion of justice and common sense, as the creation and security of property *are the consequences of society* — the great object of which is human happiness.

That any constitution or code of laws, formed in violation of men's political and social rights, are not rendered sacred by time nor sanctified by custom.

That the ignorance which originated, or permits their operation, forms no excuse for perpetuating the injustice; nor can aught but force or fraud sustain them, when any considerable number of the people perceive and feel their degradation.

That the intent and object of your petitioners are to present such facts before your Honourable House as will serve to convince you and the country at large that you do not represent the people of these realms; and to appeal to your sense of right and justice as well as to every principle of honour, for directly making such legislative enactments as shall cause the mass of the people to be represented; with the view of securing *the greatest amount of happiness to all classes of society*.

Your Petitioners find, by returns ordered by your Honourable House, that the whole people of Great Britain and Ireland are about 24 millions, and that the males above 21 years of age are 6,023,752, who, in the opinion of your petitioners, are justly entitled to the elective right.

That according to S. Wortley's return (ordered by your Honourable House) the number of registered electors, who have the power to vote for members of Parliament, are only 839,519, and of this number only 8½ in 12 give their votes.

That on an analysis of the constituency of the United Kingdom, your petitioners find that 331 members (being a *majority* of your Honourable House) are returned by *one hundred and fifty-one thousand four hundred and ninety-two registered electors!*

That comparing the whole of the male population above the age of 21 with the 151,492 electors, it appears that 1-40 of them, or 1-160 of the entire population, have the power of passing all the laws in your Honourable House.

And your petitioners further find on investigation, that this majority of 331 members are composed of 163 Tories or Conservatives, 134 Whigs and Liberals, and only 34 who call themselves Radicals; and out of this limited number it is questionable whether 10 can be found who are truly the representatives of the wants and wishes of the producing classes.

Your petitioners also find that 15 members of your Honourable House are returned by electors under 200; 55 under 300; 99 under 400; 121 under 500; 150 under 600; 196 under 700; 214 under 800; 240 under 900; and 256 under 1,000; and that many of these constituencies are divided between two members.

They also find that your Honourable House, which is said to be exclusively the people's or the Commons House, contain *two hundred and five persons who are immediately or remotely related to the Peers of the Realm*.

Also that your Honourable House contains 1 marquess, 7 earls 19 viscounts, 32 lords, 25 right honourables, 52 honour-

63

ables, 63 baronets, 13 knights, 3 admirals 7 lord-lieutenants, 42 deputy and vice-lieutenants, 1 general, 5 lieutenant-generals, 9 major-generals, 32 colonels, 33 lieutenant-colonels, 10 majors, 49 captains in army and navy, 10 lieutenants, 2 cornets, 58 barristers, 3 solicitors, 40 bankers, 33 East India proprietors, 13 West India proprietors, 52 place-men, 114 patrons of church livings having the patronage of 274 livings between them; the names of whom your petitioners can furnish at the request of your Honourable House.

Your petitioners therefore respectfully submit to your Honourable House that these facts afford abundant proofs that you do not represent the numbers or the interests of the millions; but that the persons composing it have interests for the most part foreign or directly opposed to the true interests of the great body of the people.

That perceiving the tremendous power you possess over the lives, liberty and labour of the unrepresented millions — perceiving the *military* and *civil forces* at your command — *the revenue* at your disposal — the *relief of the poor* in your hands — the *public press* in your power, by enactments expressly excluding the working classes alone — moreover, the power of delegating to others the whole control of the *monetary arrangements* of the Kingdom, by which the labouring classes may be silently plundered or suddenly suspended from employment — seeing all these elements of power wielded by your Honourable House as at present constituted, and fearing the consequences that may result if a thorough reform is not speedily had recourse to, your petitioners earnestly pray your Honourable House *to enact the following as the law of these realms*, with such other essential details as your Honourable House shall deem necessary:-

A LAW FOR EQUALLY REPRESENTING THE PEOPLE OF GREAT BRITAIN AND IRELAND

EQUAL REPRESENTATION

That the United Kingdom be divided into 200 electoral districts; dividing, as nearly as possible, an equal number of inhabitants; and that each district do send a representative to Parliament.

UNIVERSAL SUFFRAGE

That every person producing proof of his being 21 years of age, to the clerk of the parish in which he has resided six months, shall be entitled to have his name registered as a voter. That the time for registering in each year be from the 1st of January to the 1st of March.

ANNUAL PARLIAMENTS

That a general election do take place on the 24th of June in each year, and that each vacancy be filled up a fortnight after it occurs. That the hours for voting be from six o'clock in the morning till six o'clock in the evening.

NO PROPERTY QUALIFICATIONS

That there shall be no property qualification for members; but on requisition, signed by 200 voters, in favour of any candidate being presented to the clerk of the parish in which they reside, such candidate shall be put in nomination. And the list of all the candidates nominated throughout the district shall be stuck on the church door in every parish, to enable voters to judge of their qualification.

VOTE BY BALLOT

That each voter must vote in the parish in which he resides. That each parish provide as many balloting boxes as there are candidates proposed in the district; and that a temporary place be fitted up in each parish church for the purpose of *secret voting*. And, on the day of election, as each voter passes orderly on to the ballot, he shall have given to him, by the officer in attendance, a balloting ball, which he shall drop into the box of his favourite candidate. At the close of the day the votes shall be counted, by the proper officers and the numbers stuck on the church doors. The following day the clerk of the district and two examiners shall collect the votes of all the parishes throughout the district, and cause the name of the successful candidate to be posted in every parish of the district.

SITTINGS AND PAYMENTS TO MEMBERS

That the members do take their seats in Parliament on the first Monday in October next after the election, and continue their sittings every day (Sundays excepted) till the business of the sitting is terminated, but not later than the 1st of September. They shall meet every day (during the Session) for business at 10 o'clock in the morning, and adjourn at 4. And every member shall be paid quarterly out of the public treasury £400 a year. That all electoral officers shall be elected by universal suffrage.

By passing the foregoing as the law of the land, you will confer a great blessing on the people of England; and your petitioners, as in duty bound, will ever pray.

6 Account of Public Meeting of Radicals in Halifax, 22 January 1838

From the 'Halifax Guardian', 23 January 1838

Yesterday, a public meeting of the Radicals of this town was held in the Old Assembly Room, and, by adjournment, in the Talbot Inn Yard.

The object of the meeting was to take into consideration the propriety of petitioning Parliament in favour of the Ballot, Universal Suffrage, Annual Parliaments, Equal Representation and No Property Qualification; after the discussion of which the subject of the New Poor Law was to be taken into consideration. The meeting was announced for twelve o'clock, shortly after which time the business commenced.

On the motion of Mr Robert Wilkinson, seconded by Mr Benjamin Rushton.

Mr William Thorburn was called to the chair. He commenced by reading the placard calling the meeting. He said he was proud of the honour of being called to preside over a meeting of this nature. The principles noted in the placard were the principles he had ever advocated through life. He considered every man who entered into the social compact had a right to a voice in the representation. As one who loved his neighbour as himself he denied that, though he himself had a voice in the representation, he had a separate right over his neighbour. He considered that annual parliaments were essential to the just administration of the country. Commercial men took their stocks every year at the time when members of Parliament were sent home to spend their Christmas holidays, and he thought that that ought to be the time for annual elections to take place. As to the vote by ballot, he cared very little about it as an individual. He would have conceded along with it universal suffrage, but not without it. (Cheers) As to equal representation, he proposed that the country should be divided into equal districts and that householders should have the vote. He (the chairman) wished that Earl Grey had given them that in the Reform Bill. As to the property qualification, he wished England to be placed on the same footing as Scotland, which country could send a man to

Parliament even if he were without a coat. In conclusion he thanked them for the patient hearing they had given him. (cheers).

Mr Robert Sutcliffe rose to address the meeting. He spoke with disapprobation of the English Aristocracy and the mode in which England had been governed, by which so much taxation had been inflicted upon them. If they had been fairly represented this would not have been the case. He condemned the Whigs for passing the Irish Coercion Bill, and while Daniel O'Connell was stating that the Radicals of England had no sympathy for Ireland, he would assure him that they felt as keenly for their Irish brethren as for their own sufferings. He was no orator, he spoke plain home-spun stuff (laughter).

Mr B. Rushton* seconded the resolution. Until they had universal suffrage, the Aristocracy would continue to rob them. Taxation without representation was no better than robbing a man on the highway. If they got universal suffrage they would then get all they wanted.

After some further observations interlarded with the set phrases of 'moneyocracy' and 'shopocracy' etc., he concluded.

Mr. Abraham Hanson,† of Elland, proposed the next resolution. No man had a right to tax them without the consent of their deputies, for taxation was tyranny. Did the law require electors to be grammarians or classical scholars, or even honest men? No, but it asked 'Do you pay £10 rent?' Instead of being based upon intellect, the qualification was based upon pounds shillings and pence. Let not their children say 'behold these vile chains which are the legacy of our dastardly forefathers;' but let them have to say 'behold these monuments erected to the men who broke our chains of slavery, and interested themselves in our welfare when we did not exist.' (Cheers)

Mr Robert Wilkinson seconded the resolution in a speech of some length.

Mr. John Crossland proposed the next resolution, which was that a petition be presented to Parliament which he read to the meeting.

Mr. Thomas Cliffe seconded the adoption of the petition. He commenced by addressing the meeting as 'Gentlemen Radicals' which excited some laughter. He was aware that they had

[* Benjamin Rushton, handloom weaver, later treasurer of the West Riding National Charter Association.]

[† Abraham Hanson, Methodist local preacher, later expelled from the Methodists for the language of his Chartist oratory.]

petitioned Parliament so long to little effect that they would have no confidence in the success of the present petition. Nevertheless it was the only constitutional mode — remonstrance the house would not have. The reporters from the press could not say that there was any violent language in their speeches to excite their judgement with (cries of ' 'Express' will'). As for the 'Express', it would still continue to go at a 'small gallop' and do no harm. (Laughter) He knew that as soon as the petition was received into the house, it would be just read and thrust under the table. He had more confidence in the labouring classes than at any former period. Edward Baines esq.* told the people in 1832 to come forward in their thousands and hundreds of thousands in order to carry the Whigs into office, so that they might do something for the people. The people did so, thinking to obtain a realisation of the expectations held out to them. In 1836, however, when the people met at Peep Green, in order to save themselves from being imprisoned in Bastilles, the same *gentleman* declared it was unbecoming and improper in people meeting in large masses. This was the inconsistency of Whiggery. He cordially seconded the resolution.

Thanks were voted to the chairman, who, in returning thanks said he hoped the meeting had been conducted in a satisfactory manner. On all occasions when he could be of service in promoting the interests of his fellow-men and in advancing the cause of human happiness, his person and his pocket would be with them. (Loud cheers).

This part of the business being finished, the subject of the new poor law was then brought before the meeting, previous to which, however, a fresh chairman was chosen, in the person of Mr B. Rushton, who introduced the question by observing that they were going to kill two birds with one stone. The object of this part of the meeting was to petition for the total repeal of the new poor law, which was calculated to drive the good but destitute paupers into the poor-house, and the youth of our country to the gallows. He had now been a common labourer thirty-three years, and after having toiled fifty or sixty years, he had the consolation of knowing that he might retire into a bastille and finish his existence upon fifteen pence halfpenny a week. They who produced the necessaries of life had a right to

[* Edward Baines, editor of the 'Leeds Times', opponent of the Factory Reform movement and supporter of the New Poor Law. He had been an ardent reformer in 1832, but opposed the further extension of the suffrage.]

live, and if any person ought to suffer it was the idler.

The meeting was afterwards addressed by Mr Thornton and others and did not terminate till a late hour of the day, which necessarily precludes us from furnishing more than a hasty and imperfect sketch of it.

7 Appeal to the Trade Societies of Bolton from the Bolton Working Men's Association, 29 July 1839

Printed placard, copy in H.O. 40/43

Fellow Operatives

We now make to you an appeal, trusting that ere this, you have seen the necessity of losing no time in allying yourselves to the present movement of the working classes. What you have so sedulously for years, we have been also pursuing, but on a more extended scale; what you have devised for the benefit of your own particular trade we now ask for the whole Family of Man. There are numbers of your patriotic members who have joined our ranks in the struggle for freedom, and we greatly acknowledge our conviction (from experience) that we have scarcely an enemy amongst you. Yet, at a time so pregnant with good or evil, your Delegation of Adhesion in Bodies, — as has been done at Birmingham, Newcastle, Manchester, Oldham, Bury, and other places of importance — to the great principles we advocate, is absolutely necessary, the adoption of which can alone rid you of the vexations and tyrannical interference at the hands of your Petty Oppressors, or of unprincipled legislators: you must be aware that the newly projected measures of the Government are aimed at yourselves in common with us. We put to you the question — How long should your Societies be allowed to hold together, should the 'FINALITY LORD' succeed in introducing his RURAL POLICE FORCE? a force professedly intended to put down 'Trade Strikes'. What hope, we ask again, have you that your organisation can outlive this crusade of

MIGHT AGAINST RIGHT?

The Present Movement of the Government, as a child may see, is a campaign against the 'RIGHTS OF LABOUR'. In it you are most deeply concerned; by it your commanding position is sought to be underminded. What, then, remains for you to do? Why, to shake off your dreams of security, and as in the last session of Parliament, under the guidance of the 'PATRIOT

LOVETT' hurl back upon the corruptionists this base attempt to destroy you.

We therefore request that you will lose no time in calling meetings of your different Trades, and electing Delegates to confer with the Committee of the WORKING MEN'S ASSOCI-ATION, at their room, MILLWELL — LANE, Deansgate, at eight o'clock on the Evenings of TUESDAY and WEDNESDAY, the sixth and seventh days of August next. As this course will entail no expense on your Societies, we impress upon you the necessity of giving this business your immediate attention.

Yours, in brotherhood,
the Committee of the Bolton
WORKING MEN'S ASSOCIATION

Bolton, July 29th, 1839.

8 Address to the People of Bury by Matthew Fletcher

Printed placard, copy in H.O. 40/43

My Friends

I have already, in a Letter which I doubt not has been read at some of your Meetings, briefly conveyed to you my feelings and opinions on the scandalous proceedings by which the Peace of our town has lately been disturbed. But considering a rigid adherence to truth of the utmost importance in all political discussions, and especially when the character of individuals is implicated, I have waited to be put fully in possession of the facts previous to the publication of any remarks on the conduct of the ruffianly upstarts who have been guilty of the gross outrage of introducing into a peaceful and orderly town a band of hired bludgeon men to insult and abuse the unoffending people.

If anything could add to the baseness and audacity of this proceeding, it is the well known abhorrence of anything in the shape of a Police Establishment which is entertained by all classes of the Inhabitants of Bury; except indeed that class which lives on extortion, fraud and oppression. If these men could have entertained any hopes that this feeling had declined, they had a convincing proof to the contrary in the fate of the tricksy attempt to smuggle the provision of a Police Act, into a bill for regulating the Market; that paltry job dictated by the low and insatiable cupidity of the Earl of Derby. Foiled in their cunningly devised scheme to get up a hole and corner meeting, under the guise of a Public town's meeting, the open scorn with which an assemblage of both the working and middling classes met the clumsy sophistry of the brazen renegade, who had been bribed by the promise of a share of Public Plunder under the corrupt working of their bill to become its advocate; — the miserable minority in which they were left — the exposure and defeat of their subsequent trick of a meeting of 'the most influential inhabitants' — the fact that the occupiers of two of the most respectable Inns refused to incur the odium of allowing these conspirators to meet in their houses; — These

73

facts occurring not more than six months ago, must have convinced them that amongst all the reputable classes in the town, the detestation of a police force under any modification is unabated.

It is just seven years since I first called your attention to the obvious intention of the whig Government to establish an armed police on the model of the French Gendarmerie in this country. Since that time I have let slip no fitting opportunity to excite your abhorrence of such a treasonable design, or to warn you to be prepared to resist it. I have been accused of pressing this most important subject on your attention 'out of season as well as in season'. But you have never appeared to entertain such an opinion, and the crisis has come before those who did so anticipated it. It behoves us now to show that all we have said of our determination to resist this desperate expedient of the weak and unprincipled men who are called the government, to destroy all that remains of constitutional rights in England has not been mere empty bravado. Let us remember what we have done, that we may have no misgivings as to what we still have the power to do. The battle against the New Poor Law began in Bury, in the presence of the very men who have been made or who have voluntarily become the agents of this fresh outrage on ENGLISH RIGHTS and English Feelings. I said to the tramping commissioner POWER, 'we will not have it,' the men of Bury responded 'we will not have it'. Let these slaves ask themselves whether the men of Bury have made good their promise? I tell them we will not have an armed police, we have told them so already. Yes, Lord JOHN RUSSELL knows of the shout of defiance which rang through the People's Hall, on the night when we first received an official intimation of the intention of the ministry, to carry into effect their long-hatched plot. I defy Lord John Russell and his gang, as contemptuously as I defy the Mill owners and their servants the magistrates, to bend the 'stuborn English Zeal' of the men of Bury to so degrading a yoke. But let us not get into a passion about this matter, it was not in that way we brought the knaves to admit that it would 'not be safe to attempt to carry the New Poor Law into effect' in our town. The little row you have had has done no harm thus far. It has brought the matter fairly before the country, and though there was a little boyish folly, which I trust will not be repeated, in collecting together for the purpose of hissing and hooting the mill-owners' bludgeon-men, the illegal violence evidently began with these vagabonds, and the

74

responsibility must rest with them and the men who brought them. But let me entreat the people of Bury of all ages and conditions, not to assemble again for such a purpose, and to be especially careful that their political meetings shall not be disturbed or the slightest character of illegality given to them, by any disorderly conduct excited by the presence of these fellows. Such conduct is what our enemies wish to produce, and I know that you need only to be warned of this to prevent the most thoughtless amongst you from falling into the snare. If it will gratify you to hiss either the bludgeon-men or the other ruffians, on any other public occasions, I can see no harm in it, it is a kind of prescriptive right of the people of England to express their disgust for dishonesty in this way; and there never was an occasion more calculated to excite the feeling. But be careful that no violence is offered to any one, except in resistance to violence. I have repeatedly explained to you my feelings as to the right of the people, not only the natural but the legal right, to resist any violence to their persons by men employed as peace officers. I shall repeat the advice I have before given you on this point at the conclusion of my address, and I am the more convinced of the legal correctness of my views, inasmuch as the 'Morning Chronicle' did a few weeks ago, when I stated to the Convention the advice I had given to you, my townsmen, consider the matter of sufficient importance to be made the subject of a leading article, in which the Editor was not sparing of personal abuse. The report of what I had said was palpably garbled for the purpose of evading the legal justification of my recommendation to resist violence by violence; and when the editor was challenged to a fair discussion on the legality of my remarks, we heard no more from him on the subject, notwithstanding the dangerous tendency, in his opinion, of the doctrines I had promulgated. And dangerous they undoubtedly are to the system which the 'Chronicle' has to support. The editor, who I believe is really a learned man, would therefore undoubtedly have exposed to just contempt, these 'dangerous' doctrines if they had been wild and unfounded as he had insinuated. I put them forth again, too, with the greater confidence that I shall lead you into no errors, inasmuch as we know that a number of those who are implicated in the infamous transactions now under our consideration, are very zealous and active in the 'diffusion of useful knowledge'; and however lamentably deficient they may themselves be in knowledge of the legal rights of the people or even of those corrupt laws under which they, and such as they, insult and oppress the people, yet they have the means of buying information, and as they have spent a little at times in taking advice as to the possibility of imprisoning, transporting, or even hanging me for my 'wicked instigation', to resistance of their self-assumed authority, as they have spent no small sum for this laudable and charitable purpose, these diffusers of useful knowledge will doubtless not grudge a small outlay in guarding the people against my mishievous suggestions, by proving to them the legal obligation under which the people of this country lie, to submit to being cudgelled by policemen. They will convince you that I am wrong in asserting that no constable has a legal right to offer the slightest violence, except he be resisted in the discharge of his duty, and that it is no part of that duty to meddle with the people who have been guilty of no offence. They will point out to you the statutes which give such rights, or which make it any more an offence to knock down a constable who has tried to knock you down, than it is to knock down any other person under the same circumstances. They will perhaps at the same time condescend to explain to the 'ignorant rabble' under what existing law a committee of millowners are authorised to take into their pay a gang of bludgeon-men, and send them out among the industrious inhabitants of a town, noted for its peace and good order, to jostle and otherwise insult honest and decent people in the street.

When, public curiosity being excited by the presence of a considerable number of strangers thus conducting themselves, and having no ostensible means of earning a livelihood, a few curious people gather together to ascertain if they can, what can have brought so unusual an assemblage of well-dressed vagrants into the town; the knowledge diffusers will perhaps enlighten the misled people by explaining the legal right of their hired bludgeon-men to command the crowd to disperse on pain of being shot, and the mandate being disregarded, to proceed to bludgeon and shoot them.

I am still ignorant enough to imagine that even constables, legally appointed constables, have no right to disperse an assemblage of the people by force, till the riot act has been read by a magistrate, and therefore maintain, that the people were right in using either stones or any other weapons which chance threw in their way in repelling the brutal attack which was made upon them. I maintain that the fact of the people having hissed these fellows did not in the slightest degree justify the attack, and that the firing of the pistol by which a youth was wounded was a capital offence for which, if the ruffian who did the act can be identified, and brought to trial, and if anything like justice remains in England, he will be hanged. I make these assertions not merely on the strength of my own opinions of the still existing constitutional checks, on the abuse of the privileges and authority of peace officers. We have not forgotten that, in the Calthorpe-Street affair, the verdicts of two honest juries decided that an attack, made by a posse of policemen, acting in their own district, and under the eye of a secretary of state, was illegal, the riot act not having been read. It was also decided that the killing of one of these policemen, not the knocking out of his brains with a stone picked up on the spot — but the killing him with a weapon which had obviously been carried to the meeting for defence against any such attack, was justifiable.

In the present case another important question presents itself: have these bludgeon-men under the existing laws, a right to act as constables in Bury? I have said they were brought under Secretary of State's law. I am not ignorant that there is a thing which they call an act of Parliament, which authorises the Secretary for the Home Department to send out squads of London policemen to a certain distance, I think two hundred miles, from the metropolis. This act of parliament, as it is called, I treat with the most thorough contempt. If it had been fairly passed through parliament, I should have considered it a thing which ought in every judicious way to be resisted, because it is an invasion of that right of local self-government which you, the people of Bury consider as one of the most valuable portions of our ancient privileges. But this act never was passed by the two houses of parliament. It was introduced into the commons by one of Lord John's journeymen, at midnight, when the few honest and all the indifferent members had retired, and when only a small knot of ministerial toad-eaters who had no doubt been warned of the job, remained. It was smuggled through the different stages in the same rascally manner, and afterwards by a similar process, shuffled through the Lords. — And this piece of political swindling is called a law, and if any man had assaulted or had killed one of the men acting under it in the ordinary course of a constable's duty, but in a district where he was a perfect stranger, though the provocation under the common law of England would have justified the assault or the killing, this 'act', if it must be recognised as

77

law, would have made the assault a serious misdemeanour, and the killing a murder, the 'act' being at the same time so profound a secret, except to the few who read all the enormous mass of trumpery statutes which issue ever session; that two of the most attentive members of the House of Commons declared their ignorance of it a year after it was placed on the Statute book. Of course, we do not expect Lord John Russell and his squad to be impeached for this contempt of the two houses, and treason against the people; but the subserviency and corruption of parliament which renders this act of justice hopeless, does not alter the fact that such conduct is a high crime and misdemeanour, and that the act thus surreptitiously placed on the statute book, ought to be treated with contempt. But villainous as the thing is, so villainous that Lord John Russel was evidently hopeless of getting it through such a House of Commons even as the present, it does not authorise the hiring of bludgeon-men by a 'committee of millowners', by men without official character, and representing the class who are the most notorious of any set of men in the country, not only for oppression, extortion and barefaced fraud in their own establishments, but for the most open, reckless defiance of law when it crosses their own corrupt interests. It is presumed too, that if men are to be sent perfect strangers into a district to act with the authority of constables, they must at least wear the LIVERY of the body to which they belong, and I believe even in London, though they do the spy part of their business in plain clothes, the bludgeoning is performed in livery. In every respect therefore, the proceedings in our town have been so calculated to set every principle of law, and every feeling of decency at defiance, that it would appear that Lord John Russel has taken advantage of the application which we are informed by Mr W. Walker was made for troops to protect the lives and property of the White Slave dealers. That, considering the applicants brutally ignorant enough to be made the instruments of the most shameless defiance of those laws which it is his object to destroy, but the responsibility for destroying which it has been his obvious policy to shuffle on others, he has tricked these pig-headed ruffians into this open violation of law, in order to make an experiment on the forbearance and prudence of the people at the expense of the characters of these boobies, which, if there were no other consideration at stake, no one need feel much compunction in destroying. The plot has been as clumsily got up, as those best acquainted with the parties could have anticipated. The disturbances at Heywood will have a light thrown upon them, which will not be very creditable to millowners, or to the magistrates who were on such cordial terms with the principal instigator, but it is too glaring to plead this partial riot in Heywood as a reason for quartering policemen in Bury, after all tendency to distrubance had ceased, and the parties who excited it, having sunk into contempt with the people, had been openly rewarded for their services by their employers. The attempts to burn the mill, in which Mr Walker is a partner further used as an apology for an arrangement, which according to his statement had been previously made. I congratulate him on the good fortune of detecting those repeated attempts just in the mark of time to prevent mischief. The incendiary must certainly be a most ingenious as well as a most determined rascal to have repeated his offence so often and always escaped detection. But if his mill has really been set fire to, what besotted fools Mr W. Walker and the rest of the millowners' committee must be to exasperate the people under such circumstances. If one of Mr Walker's workmen can fire the mill two or three times without detection, is Mr Walker stupid enough to suppose that a dozen policemen quartered half a mile from this mill can prevent the repetition of the offence. He will not have forgotten my telling Commissioner Power that it would come to this at last; I have not forgotten, and hundreds of the people of Bury have not forgotten, the ghastly stare with which Mr Walker heard my assertion that the people could burn their mills, if they had a policeman in every one of them. But I trust it is not come to this; should this crime become common in the manufacturing as in the agricultural districts, society will be utterly disorganised, and in a way, too, that can only lead to hopeless anarchy. Always maintaining boldly, and in defiance of all the cant about moral force, which means, in the mouths of many, passive submission: always maintaining that if they come to butchering the people with artillery and Congreve rockets, fire will be the people's irresistible weapon, I do most sincerely declare my destestation of secret incendiarism. I implore the people to withstand the temptation which the cruel insults and oppressions of these petty despots furnishes, to this ready means of revenge. It is for their own sakes, and in the hope of a speedy triumph of our good cause that I implore them. As to the brutal and besotted ruffians who conscious that they are tottering on the verge of insolvency, are driven to this desperate attempt to

79

break down the spirit of the people into submission to fresh acts of extortion; who, determined to support the corrupt system by which they are all but ruined, see no hope of escape but reducing the wages of their work-people to a pittance which will barely afford them strength to perform the labour assigned to them, and when that is past, to die in ditches; who for this end have consented to aid the factions in enforcing those monstrous laws which even many of themselves formerly denounced. I charge these ignorant and heartless ruffians to ask themselves what *they* would do if they and their families were reduced to this extremity of wretchedness by men whom they were toiling to support in luxury and extravagance. I tell them that if they do bring the mass of honest and industrious people of England, as the people of Ireland have already been brought, to die in ditches it shall be my endeavour, as it will be the endeavour of better and abler men to bring about such a state of things as shall either amend the system, or cause them to die in ditches also.

We have now only to consider what it is advisable that the people should do under the present circumstances. I thank my townsmen most sincerely for the spirit and good sense which they have evinced. I trust that they will not condescend to hold any further communication with the millowners' committee. It was well to get out of the fools the important admissions which they have made; but, if there were no other objection, the impertinence of these impudent upstarts, in keeping a deputation of rate-payers who had condescended to wait on them, dancing in attendance, as I understand they did; this alone ought to be a bar to any further communication with them.

I shall have another opportunity of discussing with you the mode of communicating if it should be considered necessary to communicate with the proper authorities; and also of considering under what circumstances we may be disposed to pay a rate, when we can, by paying, cause these people more embarrassment than by refusing. For my part I will never pay a rate, except for the purpose of qualifying myself to take part in some IMPORTANT meeting, while anything in the shape of a police force exists in Bury.

The proper mode of dealing with the bludgeon-men is to take no notice of them while they do not interfere with you; to pay no attention to any impertinent orders they may assume the right to give; if they jostle you, as it appears they have done,

80

jostle them; if they strike you, strike again — and strike hard — and let it be the fashion to carry a good thick Walking Stick, for the protection of your lives and property, which I conceive fully as legal, as the mill-owners hiring bludgeon-men to protect theirs.

Fear not the result — this battle is one we can fight in our own town — thank God, the base traitors cannot 'carry out' their plan of centralisation without first carrying the war into our respective parishes. There are a few which have a sufficient spirit and honesty left to be single-handed more than a match for the whole power of government — we have beaten them once and we will beat them again if the people of Bury will only have the good sense, as they have hitherto had, to manage their own local affairs for themselves and allow from no quarter impertinent and mischievous interference.

    I am —
      always Your Friend and Servant,
        MATTHEW FLETCHER
Greenwich
June 20th 1839

9 The Autobiography of One of the Chartist Rebels of 1848

From the 'Christian Socialist', vol. ii, no. 59, 13 December 1851

CHAPTER X

HOW I BECAME A REBEL.

DEDICATED TO MY LORD JOHN RUSSELL.

(Continued.)

The next day I became a Rebel, and this was how it was, 'Lord John,' — all facts, without a comment. Going up Holborn on Friday morning, I met a man carrying a board with bills on it, having words to the following effect: — 'Give no money to beggars, — food, work, and clothing, are given away to them by applying to the Mendicity Society, Red Lion Square.' What, food, work, clothing, given away! O! here's good news! Let them give me work though, and I'll find food and clothing myself. — 'I say, governor,' to the man with the board, 'what's all that mean?' 'What's all what mean?' said as comical a looking figure-head as any Great Exhibition directed by phrenologists could well produce. 'That bill.' 'Vy, dos'ent yer know?' 'No' 'Vell you *is* raw, and no flies.' Now what this distinguished agent of the Association meant by *raw*, I did not then comprehend, and what flies had to do with his reply is also a mystery which future enlightened generations must unravel; for he did'nt tell, and I did'nt ask him. I wanted just then to get at something else. 'Do, my good fellow,' said I, 'pray do tell me if I really *can* get food, work, and clothing, and how.' 'Is yer a beggar?' 'No — yes.' 'Now none of yer lies, 'cos if yer is'nt a beggar, the gemmen vont giv yer not nuffin.' 'I am, I am, my friend.' 'Vell then, you must get a ticket.' 'A ticket?' 'Yes, or it's not no account I tells yer.' 'And how am I to get a ticket?' 'Vy go to Russell Square, or any o' them air grand cribs, and axxe the first gemman you meets.' 'Shall I say you sent me?' 'O no, yer fool; jist axxe, I tells yer, for a ticket for the Mendickety Siety, and they'll give it yer, and then take it to the place what's directed, and then (with a leer — such a leer!) you'll see what you *will* see.' I thanked him, and started for Russell Square, full of wonderment. Sure enought, I *did* get a ticket, of the third person I asked. Here was fortune! — food, work, clothing, by just applying for it; and I had not known of it before; well, I *was* a fool, as the man just told me. Food, work, clothing! and with joy and boldness I knocked at the office door in Red Lion Square. 'What do you want,' said the opener. 'Here's a ticket, sir,' (showing it for fear he wouldn't believe me) 'I want to see the gentlemen inside.' 'O, go round the corner; that's *your* way,' and he slammed the door in my face. Ah! stop till I see the gentlemen, *they'll* not speak to me so, thought I, as I went round the corner, and down some dirty steps. And then such a scene presented itself to me as never can be effaced from my memory! — a hundred — fully a hundred, of the most emaciated, desolate, yet hardened, brutal-looking creatures, were congregated together in the kitchen, the majority of them munching, like so many dogs, hunks of bread and cheese. I was told to pass on, and then another hundred daguerreotype likenesses of the first hundred met my bewildered gaze, waiting to pass a wooden bar one by one. Of course I had to stay my turn; and not knowing how to be 'jolly' with them — for even these neglected miserable wretches were jolly — I got finely chaffed. I dare not attempt to write their filthy remarks; — one man, however, in all that Devil's crowd, took pity on the 'green one,' and I began to tell him all about the food-work-and-clothing idea, which still kept wandering about my brain, though it seemed trying to find an outlet as if tired of stopping there. I shall never forget how heartily he laughed, as I related to him my affair with the board-man, — Bill Somebody, of the 'Dials,' whom he appeared to know very well. After informing him how long I had begged, and pretty well all my circumstances, he said to me, 'I tells you what, old flick, you've been deceived, — its all lies, — they'll only give you a bit of bread and cheese, and you must be up to snuff to get *that*, — not one in a hundred gets more. Clothing's all my eye. And them as gets work, it's to break stones at six bob a-week — its all lies I tell you.' Now by this time I scarcely knew who to believe — the gentlemen who advertised such good things, or the poor beggar who had branded them as liars. But in about an hour longer, I found out. — It was my turn to pass the barrier — I was ushered into a room by a beadle, and stood behind

83

another bar like a criminal; and on the other side sat six gentlemen, as people call bears that are dressed well; when the
following dialogue, nearly word for word, took place, between
me and the chairman: — 'Well, what do *you* want?' I fumbled
for my *prize* ticket, and said, 'Here's a ticket, sir, — a gentleman
gave me in Russell Square.' 'Well, well, what do you want, I
say?' 'If you please sir, I met this morning a man carrying a
board on which was stated that I could get food, work, and
clothing, — but I only want work, sir.' 'Are you a beggar?' 'Yes,
sir.' 'How long?' 'Eight days.' 'Only eight days, — are you sure
of that?' (with a cunning infidel leer). 'Yes, sir, that is all.' 'Are
you married?' 'Yes, sir.' 'Ah I thought so. How many children
have you got?' 'One, sir.' 'O, I wonder you did'nt say a dozen —
most beggars say a dozen. How do you beg?' 'I sing hymns, sir.'
'O, one of the pious chanters,' — with a grin at the *gentlemen*,
Who grinn'd too, at his brilliant wit. 'Have you applied to your
parish?' 'No, sir.' *That* did it, — that *truth*, — if I had told a lie,
the wrath of his worship the Chairman might in time have been
assuaged, but telling the truth proved I was not *'up to snuff,'*
for in a loud, angry voice he called the officer, and thus
addressed him, — 'Officer, you see that fellow — you'll know
him again — he goes about singing hymns; he says only eight
days, — is that a truth?' 'O dear no,' said the lying scamp, 'I've
known him for years!' 'Ah, now, mark him well, watch for him,
and directly you catch him, lock him up, and send for me. We'll
have this gentleman before a magistrate, and he shall sing hymns
on the treadmill.' — Now its some time before I break loose, but
when I do, I never stay at a half-way-house — all the way there
and no stoppages, — is my motto; so I retaliated, as every
honest man ought to do when he's insulted and belied by a
thing that feeds on him according to law. I retaliated, I say,
with equal warmth, calling him a liar (a scriptural phrase by-
the-bye) point-blank, and all the *gentlemen* too; — 'you adver-
tise lies, said I, wholesale, now lock me up, and I'll show the
magistrate and the world that *you* are the impostors, and obtain
money under false pretences from the benevolent.' Well to be
sure, I expected to be collared every moment. — Yet I fired
away, bang, bang, till I was more than a match for the Chairman, who at last listened staring, without saying a word, but
just a grunt now and then, like a pig as he was. One of the
gentlemen at length said — 'Give him some bread and cheese,
and let him go,' (I was hungry enough, for not a bit of anything
had I tasted since eight in the morning, and then it was late in

84

the afternoon). Well, they gave me another *prize* (!) ticket, entitling me to half-a-pound of bread and a piece of cheese, and I went back into the kitchen to get it, pocketed it, and was about to sheer off, when the beadle stopped me and ordered me to eat it there. 'I shall not,' said I. 'You must.' 'I won't.' 'Then give it back.' 'I won't do that either.' 'Then come along with me,' and I was again before the immortal six. 'Sir, he won't eat his bread and cheese.' 'O, then, let him give it back.' 'He won't do that, sir.' 'You must, sir,' said the Chairman to me. 'I won't.' 'You must, I tell you, it's the rule, and you must obey it.' 'I don't care about your *rules*, I want to share it with those I love, who are as hungry as I am, and if you are a Devil with no natural feelings, I am not. Get out of the way, beadle,' and out I rushed, like one mad, through the crowd of astonished beggars, right into the street, without one stopping me.

After I had got home, and told them of my adventures, (I had told them of my *singing propensities* a day or two before), I went downstairs to the landlord to pay him a week's rent out of the four I owed him, and the good fellow said, 'Never mind, if you haven't yet got any work, I don't take any till you do, I'm sure you'll pay me — how long have you been out of work?' 'Near seven months,' I said, with a sigh, thinking more of the dogs I had encountered in the day than anything else. 'Ah,' says he, 'there'll be no good done in this country till the *Charter* becomes the law of the land.' 'The Charter?' 'Yes, I'm a Chartist — they meet to-night at Lunt's Coffee House on the Green — will you come?' 'Yes.' It was only a 'Locality' meeting, but there were about sixty people present, and as one after another got up, oh, how I sucked in all they said! 'Why should one man be a slave to another? Why should the many starve, while the few roll in luxuries? Who'll join us, and be free?' 'I will,' cried I, jumping up in the midst. 'I will, and be the most zealous among you — give me a card and let me enrol.' And *so*, Lord John, I became a Rebel; — that is to say: — Hungry in a land of plenty, I began seriously for the first time in my life to enquire WHY, WHY — a dangerous question, Lord John, is'nt it, for a poor man to ask? leading to anarchy and confusion.

Well, but it wasn't my fault, you know. When *you* are out of *a place*, you are about the first one to cry there's something wrong. — Now I was out of *a place*, and so I cried the same. Politics, my Lord, was with me just then, a bread-and-cheese-question. Let me not, however, be mistaken; — I ever loved the idea of freedom, — glorious freedom, and its inevitable consequences, — and not only for what it will fetch, but the *holy principle*; — a democrat in my Sunday School — everywhere — and whether the sun shines on my future pathway, or the clouds look black as they have ever done, neither sun nor cloud shall alter my fixed principle.

> A boy I *dreamt* of liberty;
> A youth — I said, but I am free;
> A man — I felt that slavery
> Had bound me in her chain.
> But yet the *dream*, which, when a boy,
> Was wont my musings to employ,
> Fast rolling years *shall not* destroy,
> With all their grief and pain.

PART II

Chartist Propaganda

Most of the material in this section is self-explanatory. From the vast amount of printed material, this small selection of pamphlets and addresses gives a fairly representative idea of the tone of the printed material which the Chartists issued in the early years. The tone is reasonable and measured, though not without passion and not without humour.

The two items relating to women are of considerable interest. In most of the main centres of Chartist activity, female Chartist sections were formed. Activities such as exclusive dealing relied very much on the co-operation of the women, while it is clear that the semi-legal and illegal activities must have relied heavily at least on the acquiescence, if not on the active co-operation, of the women. Two things mark the difference between the Chartist women and the originators of the movement for women's emancipation which was to begin soon afterwards, mainly amongst the middle classes. Although many Chartists believed in the vote for women, it was never part of the programme of the movement. But the women themselves, as the Newcastle document shows, saw their enemy as the same as that of their husbands. There is no suggestion that they considered themselves oppressed within their own families, and there is no record of 'anti-men' agitation amongst the female Chartists. In the same way, they are not concerned with the right to work — they are in the main more concerned with the right to stay at home and care for their children. Whereas the middle-class women were soon to be seeking ways in which they could obtain training and entry into the professions and into rewarding paid employment, the women of the working classes are still concerned that their husbands should earn enough to support them and their children at home.

The author of 'The Rights of Women', R. J. Richardson, was the delegate from Manchester and Salford to the National Convention. A master joiner from Salford, who also kept a bookshop, he had made his first public appearance in 1826, at the age of twenty-three, during the riots caused by the setting up of powerlooms. He had been a leading radical during the Reform Bill agitation, representing the section of the radicals who were pressing for universal suffrage. He founded the South Lancashire Anti-Poor Law Association in 1837, and had taken the lead in all forms of radical activity. It is interesting that Lloyd Jones, the Owenite missionary, writing in 1879, remembers Richardson as being 'almost uncouth by his rude provincialism of speech and awkwardness of manner' (1) when debating the New Poor Law at Salford. Richardson was well known locally as a debater, and a successful one. He was, as this pamphlet shows, a man of considerable education — he had had more than the usual education as a child and had remained an avid reader all his life. Lloyd Jones's comment is one of the rare examples of an occasion in which the demotic speech of a leading Chartist seems to have prevented communication. In general it is remarkable how readily leading figures managed to make themselves understood and felt in different parts of the country, at a time when regional variations of speech were considerable.

The Female Chartists of Newcastle upon Tyne were one of the most active groups of which we have record. At the initial meeting to found the group, women were admitted free, and men charged twopence per head. The chair was taken by a man, James Ayr, whose introductory remarks had a somewhat middle-class air about them: 'Women', he said, 'had been much neglected — the education of sons was attended to, but that of daughters was overlooked. Balls dresses and finery fitted them out for the market — it was thought enough to make them domestic slaves, but this state of things should not be allowed to continue. . . .'(2)

The 'Appeal to the Middle Classes' was written, according to his recollections in 'The Odd Book', mainly by Thomas Ainge Devyr. For writing it he was arrested, and skipped his bail to escape to the United States. It is a splendid piece of polemical writing, and was reprinted as a placard and a broadside in many parts of the country.

The editorial on 'Constitutional Arming', also from the pen of Devyr, is an example of the sophistication with which radicals were able to treat the arguments of their opponents, Tory as well as Liberal.

1. 'Newcastle Weekly Chronicle', 27 Sept 1879.
2. 'Northern Liberator', 5 Jan 1839.

10 The Question 'What is a Chartist?' Answered

Tract issued by the Finsbury Tract Society, 1839

Mr Doubtful. Good morning to you, friend; I understand you profess Chartist principles, and as I confess, in common with many others, my ignorance of what Chartism means, I should be obliged by your informing me what is the meaning of the term 'Chartist.'

Radical. It is one who is an advocate for the People's Charter.

Mr D. The People's Charter, pray what is that?

Rad. It is the outline of an act of parliament, drawn up by a committee of the London Working Men's Association, and six members of parliament; and embraces the six cardinal points of Radical Reform.

Mr D. What are these points?

Rad. They are as follows: 1. *Universal suffrage* — 2. *Annual Parliaments* — 3. *Vote by Ballot* — 4. *Equal Representation* — 5. *Payment of Members* — 6. *No Property Qualification*.

Mr D. Do you mean by *Universal Suffrage*, that men, women, and children should vote?

Rad. No, we do not: it is often difficult to find a term which shall clearly express what you mean, and perhaps universal adult male suffrage would have been a more near approach to our meaning; but we mean by the term that every man twenty-one years of age, unconvicted of crime and of sound mind, should have a vote in the election of the representatives who are to make the laws he is called upon to obey, and who lay on the taxes he is required to pay.

Mr D. Do you think this essential to obtain and secure good government?

Rad. I do, for the following reasons: first, because the possession of the franchise is the only difference between a freeman and the Russian serf, who is sold with the land and the cattle, as part of the farm stock; or the slave of South Carolina, where it is punishable to teach a slave to read: it is the only security against bad laws and for good government, and while the exclusive few have a profitable interest in bad laws, there will be no barrier to tyranny and corruption, but the fear of resistance on the part of the enslaved many.

Mr D. Why do you prefer *Annual Parliaments* to septennial, as at present?

Rad. Because we should be enabled by this means to get rid of a bad servant at the end of one year, instead of being fixed with him for seven, as at present.

Mr D. But would a man be able in one year to obtain an insight into the forms of parliament? and would it be prudent to dismiss a man as soon as he became useful?

Rad. This is begging the question; we should not dismiss an honest and capable man, and the sooner a dishonest or incapable one was dismissed, the better. With respect to obtaining an acquaintance with the forms of parliament, every man must at his first entrance be ignorant of the practice of the house; and the knowledge he would acquire in the first year would enhance his value, and, provided he was honest and capable, would ensure *his re*-election.

Mr D. By *Voting by Ballot* of course you mean secret voting: what benefit is expected from that?

Rad. The prevention of bribery or intimidation at elections; or the influencing a man to vote against his own will or judgment.

Mr D. Oh, but consider how un-English it is in character, and what lying and deception it will occasion.

Rad. I am not so bigoted an admirer of English customs as to refuse to adopt the regulations of other countries, where they are proved to be beneficial; besides, the practice is not so un-English as you seem to think; those very consistent and independent gentlemen who profess so much care for the morals of the electors, and such a horror of the ballot, constantly make use of it for the protection of themselves, in the election of the members in their clubs. With regard to the deception, it is admitted that the ballot is merely a remedy for a disease; and if it can be proved (which I believe it can to demonstration,) that the evil the ballot will remove is so enormous compared with any it can possibly inflict, that the question resolves itself into a balance of evils, and of course the lesser evil is preferable to the greater.

Mr D. Pray, what it meant by *Equal Representation?*

Rad. It means that the country should be divided into equal electoral districts (say 300) each containing, as nearly as conveniently may be, an equal number of inhabitants, each district to send one representative to parliament.

Mr D. Is it not divided into electoral districts at present?

Rad. It is, but not equal; for instance: — Harwich sends two members to parliament, and numbers 156 electors, while Westminster, with 13,268 electors, sends no more; so that, if it is right that Harwich should send two members, Westminster should send 170! nor is this a solitary instance. There are ten boroughs sending twenty members, the total of whose electors amount to 2411, while ten other boroughs, also sending twenty members, number 86,072 electors; so if it be right that the ten small boroughs should send twenty members, the ten large boroughs should send about 700!!

Mr D. What proportion do the electors bear to the whole male population above twenty-one years of age?

Rad. About one to seven and a half: the total number of registered electors being 839,519; and the number of males above twenty-one years of age is 6,023,752.

Mr D. We will now come, if you please, to the next point of your Charter, which I think is *Payment of Members*; do you not think, if men capable of the duty can be found to execute it for nothing, it would save money?

Rad. I doubt much whether it would save money. If I gave a servant no wages, and he paid for his place as servants in hotels and members of parliament do at present, I should suppose he expected to make more by it than he could fairly ask as wages.

Mr D. But it seems to me a sort of degradation that a member of parliament should receive wages like a servant.

Rad. You have no good grounds to think so. Does any one consider the great officers of state, the judges, &c. &c. degraded by receiving the salaries they do? If a man devotes his time and talents, he is fairly entitled to remuneration; and it is proposed by the Charter to give each member 500*l*. per annum. Besides, there is nothing new in this: members of parliament used to receive wages, and this mode was in practice for several ages; and there is an account in a not very ancient chronicle, of a member of parliament who was also recorder of the borough, who agreed upon condition of being re-elected to forego his wages: we may imagine, that like the modern members, he discovered there were pickings in parliament which would enable him to work for nothing and pay for his place.

Mr D. The last is — *No Property Qualification*. Pray what is meant by that?

Rad. We mean, that the choice of the electors shall be the

91

only qualification necessary.

Mr D. But would you send men to parliament not worth a shilling?

Rad. I doubt whether a man without a shilling would be elected: but the present property qualification is a fraud: if a man has money or interest enough to get into parliament, he can purchase a sham qualification for £25. But why should not a poor man, if he have ability sufficient, and a majority of the electors have confidence in him, be elected? If none but rich men are sent to parliament, the feelings and wants of the poor cannot be fairly represented. In Norway, the peasant farmer in his grey, homespun doublet sits in the house of deputies beside the noble; and there the laws are just and equal, while here, because the law makers are the few, the laws are unequal and oppressive.

Mr D. But where is the clause for the distribution of property? have you forgotten that?

Rad. That is a base and slanderous calumny, which those who profit by things as they are have forged to damage our cause. There never was the slightest foundation for such a charge, although judges on the bench and parsons in the pulpit have not scrupled to give currency to the falsehood.

Mr D. What are the benefits you anticipate from the adoption of the Charter?

Rad. The repeal of bad laws and the making of good laws in their stead; a reduction of taxation, by which the productive industry of the nation would be increased; the abolition of the enormous abuses of the civil and criminal law, which amount in most cases to an utter denial of justice to the poor; a liberal and general system of national education, without reference to sect or creed, which would tend at once to diminish crime, by striking at its root. The cost of the civil and criminal justice in this country is above two millions, while only 30,000*l.* is devoted to national education. Would it not be far better to diminish the former amount by increasing the latter?

Mr D. Why this certainly appears reasonable: are there any other benefits you expect?

Rad. Yes, certainly; more than I can now enumerate. There is the expense of the state, the civil list as it is called, amounting to about 1,000,000*l.* sterling, while the United States' civil list is not 20,000*l.*; I think we might be as well or better governed for less money *by half* than we pay at present.

Mr D. Oh, but consider: the expenditure of this money

makes good for trade — what should we do without it?

Rad. That is a mistaken notion; if the money were left in the pockets of the people, they would spend it in comforts for themselves, and thereby make better for trade than if it were spent in luxury by idle and useless placemen and unworthy pensioners.

Mr D. Well, your objects seem more reasonable than I expected, so I wish you success. Good morning to you.

Price 1s. 6d. per hundred, or five for a 1d.

Persons or Societies anxious to distribute this useful Tract will be dealt with on the most liberal terms.

11 The Just Claims of the Working Classes

Pamphlet issued by the Kettering Radical Association, 1839

Be just and fear not.

Kettering: printed and sold by Joseph Toller;
London: published by H. Hetherington, Strand, and Cleave, Shoe Lane.
Price fourpence
To the Reader
In consequence of the occurrence of two incendiary fires in this town, on the 23rd of Febuary last, the Kettering Radical Association published a handbill, for the purpose of vindicating its members from the aspersion which their opponents had thought proper to cast upon them; and entreating the gentlemen of Kettering and its vicinity to consider 'whether their general hostility to the just claims of the Working-Classes, was not assisting to sever the ligaments of society, and thereby originating a state of things which it is fearful to contemplate.' On the reception of a copy of this handbill, Mr Madge addressed a note to our chairman, enquiring what were 'the just claims' to which we had adverted. In answer to this enquiry the letter now in the hand of the reader was written. We intended that this Introduction should contain a copy of Mr M's note; but after it was in type he forbade our printing it; although he had previously granted what we understood to be full liberty of doing so. He has also sent us a long reply to the following statement of our claims. That, in our opinion, his production is a failure, may be inferred from the fact that we have offered to publish it at our own cost, provided Mr M. would take one hundred and fifty copies. This offer he has declined.

Kettering, May 10th, 1839

A LETTER, &c.

Kettering, March 19, 1839

REV. SIR

The proceedings of our Association having generally been treated with contempt, it was with considerable pleasure that we received your communication to the chairman of our last meeting; especially as it confirms us in the belief that the time is approaching in which it will be impossible longer to despise us.

As we are unwilling to suspect you of affectation, you must allow us to express our surprise that one whose sacred office requires him to explain the rights and duties of his hearers, should have yet to learn, what *are* the rights to which they are justly entitled. Had not your note been laid before us, we could not have believed, that you could have needed an assemblage of unlettered operatives to remind you that the just claims of any class of men can be neither a figment of their fancy, nor a secret concealed so deeply in their bosoms, as to be discernible only by the curious gaze of the inquisitive; but that they must, in every case, be clearly written in the book of reason, and deducible from the unequivocal statements of the book of God. If, in this reply, we advance a single claim bearing any other stamp than this, present us with proof to that effect, and we will forthwith erase it from the list of our demands.

Is it possible, Sir, that although 'the People's Charter' has been circulated through the length and breadth of the land, and the 'National Petition' signed by an unprecedented number of the population, you have been so unobservant of the 'signs of the times,' as to have yet to ascertain the claims which those documents set forth? Can it be true that a public meeting for the purpose of adopting the National Petition, was held at noon-day, on the market-place of our town, and that the individual whose special duty it is to watch over its inhabitants, that he may by all practicable means, promote their temporal and spiritual well-being, has permitted seven months to pass away, without taking the trouble to enquire into the nature of the claims which so large a portion of his parishioners thus publicly avowed to be their own? If the only effect of our handbill had been to arouse you from this indifference, we should rejoice to think that we had not published it in vain.

When you stated that you had 'no hostility whatever to the working classes,' had you not misread this handbill, as though it

95

charged the gentlemen of Kettering, and consequently yourself, with that which you disclaim? That there may be hostility to our claims, where there is none to our persons, is a distinction we thought easy of perception.

But though we have thus freely animadverted on your communication, be assured that few things could be more welcome to us than your request to be informed what are 'the just claims,' referred to in the placard which you have received: inasmuch as we hope never to entertain principles, which we are not ready, to the best of our ability, to state and justify. As, however, we have not had the happiness of participating in the literary advantages which you have been privileged to enjoy, we trust you will not criticise the mode of expression we may adopt, but accept our reply as the candid statement of men who deem themselves to have become acquainted with their rights, and are determined never to forego them.

First; *We claim to have a voice in the making of the laws under which we live*. This being a claim of paramount importance, we shall devote a considerable part of this reply to its exposition and enforcement.

A learned bishop of your church ventured to affirm that 'the people have nothing to do with the laws but to obey them.' How far the inculcation of such a doctrine, forms part of an university education, we have not the means of judging; but you must permit us to express our belief that it has never yet been taught in the school of common sense. As men, we deem ourselves entitled to our native rights. As members, of that great society which is called 'the Nation,' we claim to be considered such. As partakers of a common nature, we do not think ourselves one whit inferior to those of our neighbours, who are invested with the elective franchise: we therefore claim to possess it too. The blood which flows in *our* veins is as pure and as warm as theirs; their sense of injury is not more acute than ours; nor do we think that as a body we have cause to shrink from a comparison of our *intelligence* with that of the men whom we have been accustomed to see present themselves at the hustings as electors.

Were the value of the right of suffrage as imaginary as it is real, we think we ought not to be deprived of it without our own consent; inasmuch as it is often far from easy to bear the loss of even an *imaginary* good. But the privation of the right now claimed, is an infliction of *real* and *enormous* evil. Those who take upon themselves to govern us, often enact laws which

96

are at variance with our interests, — not unfrequently in violation of the first principles of equity — and should we break those laws, they would fine, imprison, transport or hang us at their pleasure! The losses we sustain, and the punishments in which some of our brethren have been innocently involved, are no *imaginary* evils.

We believe, Sir, that you, in common with ourselves, are deprived of your right to exercise the elective franchise; but the injury which *you* thereby sustain, is comparatively small. to *us*, (although we are far from supposing that the realization of this, or any other of our claims, will transform the earth into a paradise, or attain for us all that is expected from it) its possession or non-possession constitutes no small proportion of the momentous difference between moderate and excessive toil, competence and penury, and possibly, of even life and death.

Not a few who are opposed to our possession of this right, professedly found their opposition on the ground that the claim is novel, and the experiment untried. We are not concerned to reply to so frivolous an objection; for it is evident that railroads and canals, sickles and plough-shares, with all the various conveniences of life, must originally have been novel and untried. In point of fact, however, the *existing* system is the innovation. The truly great Algernon Sidney, the learned Selden, and the celebrated Rapin, unite in assuring us that the government of our Saxon ancestors, was conducted on the principle of universal suffrage, a testimony which is confirmed by the account given by Tacitus, of the customs of the country whence those ancestors emigrated to the British shores. Until historians of superior note shall venture to affirm the contrary, we *might* enforce our claims upon the ground of ancient right. But we have no need to search for arguments, amidst the dust and cobwebs of antiquity. We believe that every generation has both the capacity and the right of acting for itself — that the Supreme Ruler holds it responsible for its *own* proceedings — and that when any given mode of conduct is propounded, the enquiry suggested by true wisdom is not how far does it accord with the customs of our ancestors, but how far is it in accordance with justice, and sound policy.

That the existing system is both impolitic and unjust may be easily demonstrated. The population of Great Britain and Ireland is about twenty five millions, of whom between six and seven millions are males above twenty one years of age. The number of electors is 839,519: but even this limited proportion is, in a great measure, only nominal; many persons being registered as electors in two or more places. The real number of electors is about 600,000: or less than one tenth of those who on every principle of reason and justice are entitled to the franchise! Nine persons out of every ten are thus defrauded of their birthright! And the plea advanced in defence of this injustice, serves but to aggravate the wrong. An authority which our oppressors profess to regard has said, 'Rob not the poor *because* he is poor;' yet on this ground, *and on no other*, does the law deprive us of our rights! Although we were the veriest dolts on whose countenance stupidity is engraven, or were our morals baser than any which have yet disgraced the name of man, we should be readily allowed a voice in the election of the national legislators, *provided we had property*: but because we are poor, and only because we are poor, that right is stolen from us! And the cruelty of this is equal to its injustice. Our opponents have enacted laws, the tendency of which is to make us poor, and to keep us so; and then because we have quietly allowed the State to rob us of the produce of our toil, we are told that justice requires that we should also be deprived of our birthright!

Nor can we refrain from complaining of the *ingratitude* of this. When the fields are to be ploughed, or the harvest gathered in, — when clothing is to be fabricated or fuel procured, — when dwelling-houses are to be erected or roads stand in need of repair, — it is by the working-classes that these, and all similar services are rendered. When the property of our more favoured neighbours is on fire, our aid is eagerly sought and cheerfully afforded, for the quenching of the flames. Should riots unhappily disturb the nation, or a foreign foe invade its shores, we should be compelled to assist in quelling the disturbance, or repelling the invasion. Yet, after having thus contributed our labour and hazarded our persons for the advantage of our superiors in station, they recompence our services by depriving us of the rights of our common humanity! When our *duties* are enforced upon us, we are invariably addressed as *men*; but the moment we turn our attention to the contemplation of our *rights*, we find ourselves degraded to the level of *things* — mere goods and chattels; for should we require the overseer to enrol our names in the list of voters for members of parliament, a similar claim advanced on behalf of the chairs and tables of our cottages would meet with as much favour from the revising barrister, as that made on our own behalf! After we have enriched the nation by the skilful application of our labour, and

98

to the best of our knowledge performed the duties of our station; yea, after we have, for the sake of public tranquillity, patiently submitted to impositions which we might justly have resisted; we are excluded from the privileges of citizenship, and placed on a level with the hammers we lift, or the shuttles we throw! Such is the gratitude of those whom we daily supply with the necessaries, the comforts, and the luxuries of life. Are we not well entitled to complain?

It is thought by some that the granting of universal suffrage would endanger the safety of property; inasmuch as we should probably return such representatives as would make laws to enrich us at the cost of others. Permit us to ask if those who cherish this anticipation do not measure us by their own standard? Be assured, Sir, that though the rights of industry may be easily plundered from their owners, property will always find means of ensuring its own protection. The suspicion is enormously cruel and unfounded, that those who have so long patiently endured the injustice and insults which have been heaped upon them, will abuse their rights when they have the good fortune to acquire them. This objection is, in fact, only a repetition of the abundantly falsified predictions formerly advanced by the interested abettors of Colonial Slavery.

The pretext that property would be endangered by the universal extension of the franchise, we regard as the offspring of either ignorance or hypocrisy; and consider it to be, more-over, a highly mischievous calumny upon the working classes. Treat men as dishonest, and you assist to make them so. Favour property at the expense of labour, and you teach the operative to regard it as his foe. On the contrary, let the holders of property always act upon the principle that its rights are so closely connected with those of industry that neither can be disregarded without the other being proportionably endangered, and they will then have no reason to fear its spoliation. The working-classes, in general are not ignorant of this mutual dependence. They are well aware that if capital without the aid of labour, would fail to realize profit, labour, in the absence of capital, would often fail to find employment.

That it would be unsafe to grant us the suffrage we utterly deny: let the recent fears of some around us answer us when we ask if there is no danger in refusing it? On this side, fear is far from being unreasonable. It is impossible that an enlightened nation can enjoy permanent internal tranquility, so long as the elective constituency comprises less that one-fortieth part of the population. But the constituency of the United Kingdom is, in effect, far more restricted than this; for 331 members (that is, more than the majority) of the House of Commons are returned by 151,492 electors; 165th of the entire community, and less than one in forty of the adult males! Were the base of the noble steeple which ornaments our town, to be narrowed in a like proportion, he might be a bold man, but could not be a wise one, who should repair to it for shelter when the earth was trembling beneath the raging storm.

We have said that property will always find means of ensuring its own protection: but to this general truth there is one exception, namely, when the owners of property persist in witholding the rights of those who are less fortunate than themselves. Should this unhappily continue to be the case in our beloved country, crimes more atrocious than any which have yet occurred, will, we fear, disgrace the land — reward after reward may be offered for the discovery of the offender, yet still he will escape detection — the number of watchmen may be increased tenfold, and a rural police palmed upon the country — yet all these safeguards will fail to procure more than the sleep of the robber, who, though surrounded by swords, pistols, and daggers, finds himself scared by the visions of the night. Be assured, Sir, that the only certain way of safety, is the path of righteousness. Such is the state of things which we anticipate. We leave it to you to say how far 'it is fearful to contemplate.'

And are these anticipations the offspring of our wishes? Assuredly not; although such is the base assertion of our slanderers: — nay, some who ought to be ashamed of their uncharitableness, have more than insinuated that the incendiary fires which have recently disgraced our town originated with us. Were we inclined to imitate an example so unchristian, we also could easily insinuate that these atrocious crimes were perpetrated by parties, who are neither radicals nor operatives; but, knowing ourselves to be guiltless, we have no wish to traduce the character of others. The motto on our flag — the pole-star of our hearts — is 'JUSTICE TO ALL;' which it is needless to say forbids *injustice* to any.

But you cannot be ignorant that there are men who are neither with *us*, nor with *you*, — men, in fact, who are too low to have any rational principles, religious, or political, — who will eagerly avail themselves of a time of general agitation to perpetrate the most flagrant crimes. By men of this description, Bristol was a few years ago, to a great extent, reduced to ashes.

100

Whether a similar desolation awaits other towns and cities of the kingdom, in our opinion, rests with those who, if they are wise, will, by timely homage to the claims of justice prevent 'the severance of the ligaments of society.'

Secondly; *We claim that all votes for Members of Parliament shall be taken by Ballot*. That we are neither ashamed of our political opinions, nor afraid to maintain them, the existence and prosperous state of our Association sufficiently attests. Some of us, moreover, have the happiness to serve employers whose sense of justice would prevent their interference with our rights, or are so independent that we could publicly record our votes for members of the legislature, without the slightest hazard. But such is not the case with all. And we need scarcely add that there are hundreds of thousands in the country, to whom the elective franchise, unprotected by the ballot, would be a curse and not a blessing. That this is the case with a large proportion of the present constituency is abundantly notorious. Some of us have seen clergymen conducting groups of voters to the polling-booth, and watching them as carefully as the cat watches the mouse, lest she should fail to secure it as her prey. We have seen upon the countenances of these voters an expression which betrayed the struggles of the soul, and belied the utterance of the tongue. The real opinions of some of these persons we know to be in accordance with our own, yet at the hustings they have recorded their votes for candidates of a totally opposite description; and if they had not done so, the resentment of those on whom they are dependent would have been poured upon them. Is it reasonable to expect the good of a nation to be promoted, when the mass of its electors vote for men whose political principles they in their consciences, believe to be inimical to the national prosperity? On the highest of all considerations we hold that it would be infinitely preferable that the elective franchises of the constituency should be by law transferred to the landowners and clergy of the kingdom, than thus to ensnare the consciences and souls of men. Every elector is responsible to his Maker for the vote he gives, and therefore ought in every case to give a conscientious one; but we hold that the State is bound to afford him the greatest possible protection in so doing. Therefore, Sir, we claim the Ballot.

Thirdly; *We claim the abolition of all property qualifications for the legislative office*. When men are assailed by dangerous sickness, or are about to engage in important litigation, they do not enquire for the *richest* physician, or attorney, but for one

101

whose advice is likely to be most skilful and judicious. If the man would be justly reckoned foolish who should, in either of these cases, prefer wealth to wisdom, what terms can adequately describe the folly of a nation which restricts itself from choosing the most competent individuals for the management of its affairs? For so comparatively narrow is the circle within which candidates for the representative trust must at present be sought, that the probability always is that the wisest and best men are on the outside of it. To this cause we mainly ascribe the slovenly manner in which our laws are usually enacted, — the incessant amendment and re-amendment of even recent acts of parliament, — and especially the habitual conducting of the national business in opposition to the most indisputable principles of political economy, and even to the plainest dictates of common sense.

Thus far the community at large is injured by the existing system. On this ground, therefore, we claim that the several constituencies shall be allowed to return such individuals to parliament as they deem best qualified for that important trust.

But, in addition to this general consideration, there is another in which we, as working-men, are more directly interested. So long as human nature retains its known propensities, members of parliament, however chosen, will be sure to legislate, at least in part, for the peculiar benefit of the class to which they belong. The fifty pound tenancy clause — the privilege of franking letters — the corn-laws — the game-laws — the new poor-law — and a long list of other enactments, might be cited in proof of this remark. Thus it has been; and thus it will ever be. From which it follows that so long as our legislators are required to be men of property, this exclusive legislation will always be *against* the working-classes, never in their favour.

A regulation which should require members of parliament to be not less than six feet high, would be sufficiently absurd, and injurious enough to the public interests; but *we* should have no *peculiar* reason to complain of it, for these *great* men would probably be found in *all* classes of society. The existing regulation, while it is scarcely less absurd than the one now supposed, is far more inimical to us.

Fourthly; *We claim that every member of parliament shall receive a salary out of the public treasury.* 'The labourer is worthy of his hire:' and he who is not paid will be sometimes tempted to think himself excusable if he neglects to labour. Gratuitous services are, it is true, in some cases more efficient

102

than any which pecuniary emolument could procure; but human nature is not such as to warrant the hope that such cases will be of frequent occurrence: and where a servant is likely to have ample opportunity of preferring his own interest to that of his employer, his offer to serve without reward is evidently open to suspicion. How far suspicion of this sort is just, in reference to members of the legislature, is shewn by the pension list, the army list, the navy list, the list of sinecures, and the numberless holders and expectants of emoluments derived from the patronage of government. We do not hope to be able altogether to prevent this; but to render it, in future, inexcusable, and as far as possible, to cover it with deserved infamy, we claim that the full value of the services rendered by our legislators shall be paid out of the exchequer.

It is scarcely necessary to add that we claim this on another ground. There are many working-men whose talents and character are so justly appreciated by their fellow-citizens, as that, were no property qualification required, they would be certainly returned to parliament; but as they are destitute of private property, it is evident that they could not serve their country without remuneration.

Fifthly; *We claim that parliaments shall be elected annually.* The trouble and expence of an election would then be far less than what is now incurred: but even were it greater, the cost would be more than counterbalanced by the gain. 'Short reckonings make long friends.' A representative who had acted well would seldom find any difficulty in securing his re-election; and surely it would be better that one who had betrayed his trust, should pay the penalty at the end of one year, than that he should, in defiance of his constituents, hold his seat for seven years. In fact, however, there would be very much less of this betrayal, than is now experienced. Acts granting an enormous civil list, acts of coercion, and of gross injustice, and, in general, measures embodying that upper class legislation to which we have adverted, are passed when the Members of the House of Commons have the prospect of retaining their seats, for six or seven years: while those which have any features of good about them, are usually adopted in the *last* session of a parliament. We therefore claim that a parliament shall have no other session than its last.

Sixthly; *We claim that the country shall be divided into equal electoral districts.* We have said that a majority of the House of Commons is at present returned by about 150,000 electors.

This is owing to the inequality of the present electoral districts. That such inequality exists, is well known; but it is not generally understood to what a degree this is the case. West Yorkshire,* for instance, with about 2500 electors returns two members; Harwich with 156 electors, also returns two members! The Tower Hamlets with a population of 302,519, Dublin with 265,316, Edinburgh with 265,263, Marylebone with 234,294, Finsbury with 224,839, Glasgow with 202,426, and Westminster with 202,080, return two members each; Evesham with a population of 3991, Guildford with 3813, Buckingham with 3610, Honiton with 3509, Thetford with 3462, Totness with 3442, Bodmin with 3375, and Wareham with 2325, collectively return *fifteen* members; so that *less than twenty eight thousand persons can in the legislative machine, cause nearly seventeen hundred thousand to kick the beam!* These are extreme cases, but they are not solitary ones. Fifteen members are returned by constituencies, comprising less than 200 electors each: fifty-five by constituencies under 300; one hundred and twenty one, under 500; one hundred and ninety six, under 700!

It may be thought that the evil of this is more apparent than real; for that the choice made by one small constituency may be expected to counterbalance the choice made by another. So far as the peculiar interests of the rival aristocratic factions are concerned, this may be true; but in reference to the *general* good the fact is notoriously otherwise; for these small constituencies are, almost without exception, under the influence of one or other party of the aristocracy: which indeed, we believe to be the true reason of their careful exclusion from Schedule A of the Reform Bill.

The claims above advanced are stated and enforced in the National Petition which is about to be presented to the House

* Some of the places mentioned on this page are different from those referred to in the manuscript forwarded to Mr M. The facts embodied in the statement above given, are derived from various but unquestionable sources. They are corroborated by an analysis, made within these few days, by a supporter of the present administration, (Mr Joseph Parkes) in reference to the recent division on the Corn laws; who, amongst other things to the same purport, states that thirty-six boroughs, containing a population of less than 5000 each return fifty-nine members to the House of Commons. We are not aware that a list of these rotten boroughs has yet been published. It may be obtained, in manuscript, on application to the Secretary of our Association.

of Commons. You profess yourself to be friendly to the working-classes: permit us, Sir, respectfully to ask if you will evidence your friendship by affixing your name to our petition? If you answer in the negative, we shall not question your right to form your own opinion, and to act accordingly; nor will we impugn the sincerity of your friendship to the working-classes; but to their *claims* you will beyond dispute stand practically hostile: for, in this sacred warfare, 'he that is not with us is against us.'

Some have censured us because we have addressed the legislature in the language of *demand*. They ought, however, to have known that to demand is as constitutional as to petition: though the latter has doubtless been far more customary. But before the birth of the father's father of any one now living, our ancestors laid their demands before the legislature; and thereby ultimately succeeded, where mere petitions had altogether failed. The apprehension of a similar result rewarding our exertions, is far more likely to be the real ground of the objection, than aversion to the language we have used. They who gain what they petition for, may reasonably continue to adopt that mode of address, but with the *millions* the days of petitioning are, we believe, for the present nearly past. A guardian who refuses to admit the heir to the possession of his property, may with propriety be once, twice, or thrice petitioned for the surrender of his trust, but should such petitions be pertinaciously despised, we apprehend that the surrender would be *demanded*; — demanded too in terms which would show the heir to have acquired the knowledge of his rights, and to be determined to enforce them.

Others affect to despise our claims as frivolous or insignificant. If they are so, why do our rulers put the peace of the nation to hazard by refusing them? But whatever they may appear to others, they are, to us, neither insignificant nor frivolous. A peer who owes a few pounds to a labourer may consider the debt to be a trifling one; but to the poor man whose children are crying to him for bread which he is unable to provide for them, the non-payment of that debt is no trifle. Nor are any of our claims frivolous *in themselves*. There is not one of them which is not directly or indirectly connected with the efficient working of the oft-extolled principle of the British Constitution (but which to us has hitherto been nothing better than a mocking falsehood) 'that no man shall be taxed but by his own consent.'

In addition to the claims thus placed before you, there are others which are only so far of inferior importance as that when those already stated are obtained — in other words, when the People's Charter shall have become the law of the land — we shall be able without much difficulty to secure their legal recognition. For whatever advantage you may take of our honest avowal, we have no wish to conceal from you the fact that the foregoing rights arc claimed only as means to an end which lies beyond them. *That end,* whether you approve of it or otherwise, *is the establishment of such a mode of government as shall ensure the greatest possible happiness to all classes of the community.* This short sentence embodies the sum total of our radicalism. Perhaps you may, to your surprise, have discovered from it, that you too are, in principle, a radical. We hope you are so; for we cannot conceive how any christian, and least of all a christian minister, can consistently be otherwise: though it would be too much to expect you to go with us in what we believe to be the legitimate application of this fundamental axiom of our conduct. As, however, we think ourselves entitled to the same full liberty of thought and action which we cheerfully concede to others, we proceed to remind you that,

Seventhly; *We claim to be allowed to purchase food for ourselves and families wherever we can procure it cheapest.* On the continent of Europe, and elsewhere, bread is frequently sold at little more than half the price at which we are compelled to buy it here; and agents are offering themselves who are not only willing, but anxious, to bring this cheap bread to our own doors; but the government under which we live, influenced by the landowners of the country, persist in forbidding this: thereby compelling us to earn our bread by superadded toil; and at the same time hurrying those of us who are engaged in manufactures into increasing wretchedness by drying up the foreign demand for the products of our labour! From which you will perceive that though we, in common with the working-classes in many other places, have stood aloof from the recent agitation on the subject of the corn laws, our silence has not originated in ignorance of their injustice, their impolicy, or their cruelty; but in our belief that this agitation was, at least in part, an attempt to divert our attack from the stronghold of oppression; and especially in our assurance that when the six preceding claims are realized, it will require but little time to sweep away every vestige of a law which produces artificial scarcity in a world of plenty.

106

Eighthly; *We claim that the working-classes shall be exempted from all beyond their just proportion of the burdens of the State*. The exclusive, or partial legislation of which we have spoken, has in nothing shown itself more odiously than in the unfairness with which our legislators have shifted fiscal imposts from their own shoulders to those of the unrepresented, and therefore defenceless, part of the community. A member of parliament, a bishop, or a peer, though possessing an income of 200,000*l*. per annum, is allowed to have his letters, and even his small parcels,* transmitted to any part of the kingdom at the public cost; while for the postage of a letter from a distant child or parent, *we* are taxed to the amount earned by us in half-a-day of arduous toil! If any of *us* should have the good fortune to have fifty pounds bequeathed by a friend, the taxgatherer would demand five pounds of it under the name of 'legacy duty;' while the landowners of the kingdom have, for many generations, inherited property of the value of seven hundred millions sterling without the payment of a farthing of such duty! The property-tax, because it touched the pockets of the rich, was repealed more than twenty years ago; the taxes on tea, coffee, sugar, and soap — articles essential to the comfort of the poor — have been continued to the present time! These are but specimens of a course of conduct towards us, the relinquishment of which we feel ourselves entitled to demand.

Ninthly; *We claim that the Church shall be wholly separated from the State*. Although we have no doubt of the validity of this claim, it is yet with considerable hesitation that we advance it on the present occasion; since we are anxious, as far as possible, to avoid every thing which might be justly deemed offensive to you personally. But after mature deliberation we think that honesty on our part, and justice to yourself, require us to apprize you of the sentiments which no inconsiderable number of your parishioners† entertain respecting the church of which you are a minister.

We do indeed, Sir, consider it to be, as some of its dignitaries have termed it, 'the poor man's church,' for we believe that

---

* *A pair of gloves* was not long ago sent a considerable distance under cover of a frank: in the same month some members of our Association paid three shillings and fourpence for the postage of a pamphlet addressed to a deceased and highly valued friend.

† Including some members of Mr Madge's congregation. The motion that this Letter be printed was seconded by a Churchman.

every farthing of its enormous revenues is obtained from the working-classes: in proof of which we need only to remind you that *labour pays for every thing*.* Were all the great and wealthy of the land to expatriate themselves to some far distant shore, the emoluments of the church establishment would not thereby be necessarily diminished: but if all who cultivate the fields and gather in the harvest, with all who are engaged in trade and manufactures were to leave the country, we apprehend that the revenues of the bishops and clergy must altogether cease, until some other sons of labour could be found to occupy our place. From which it follows, that after having performed an amount of daily toil which ought to be sufficient to provide for ourselves and families, and added thereto that which is required to support the fiscal imposts of the government, we are every day compelled to toil yet longer for the maintenance of a church whose benefits are few and doubtful, but the evils of which are alas, too palpable: for though we willingly admit that there have been, and still are, within the Church of England, men, both clerical and lay, who would confer honour upon any sect, it is abundantly notorious that her dignitaries and clergy have, as a body, ever been amongst the foremost abettors of oppression, and the most determined enemies of social improvement.

We are well aware that some classes of non-producers are highly valuable parts of the community: and if it can be shown that a church establishment is either right or useful, we will cheerfully continue to toil for its support. But believing as we do that such an establishment is unjust in principle, inimical to the temporal interests of the nation, and unfavourable to the progress of religion, we claim that Christianity shall be liberated from the trammels with which the state has bound her, and seek support upon the only principle ever recognised in scripture — the voluntary contributions of the people.

We have no wish that the revenues of the church establishment should be appropriated to the benefit of any one class of the community; least of all that they should be transferred to the pockets of a rapacious aristocracy. The reformation three centuries ago, with many subsequent transactions even down to

* The annual labour of every nation is the fund which originally supplies it with all the necessaries of life which it annually consumes, and which consist always either in the immediate produce of that labour, or in what is purchased with that produce from other nations. — Smith's 'Wealth of Nations.' — p. 1.

the Irish Tithe Bill of last year, sufficiently attest that ecclesiastical revenues may be diminished without the people deriving their fair proportion of the benefit. Under the existing system this will always be likely to be the case: but a parliament elected on the principles of the People's Charter would be constrained (so far as such a safeguard was adequate to control the selfishness of men in power) to appropriate those revenues to the promotion of education, the payment of the national debt,* or to other objects conducive to the general advantage.

And we would further remind you, that until the attainment of this desirable consummation, we have not only the claim above advanced in reference to the church; but also a claim upon the church, or rather upon the holders of her benefices. Under the Mosaic law (to which the clergy so frequently refer for sanction to their system, but which to us appears to afford it no sanction whatsoever, inasmuch as the Israelitish tithes were voluntary offerings — not compulsory exactions) the tithes

---

* Were it deemed advisable to appropriate the whole of these revenues to the payment of the Debt, this might be done in one of three ways.

1. By a simultaneous confiscation of all the property of the establishment: which being estimated at a hundred millions sterling would at five per cent compound interest cancel the debt in forty-three years; or at four per cent in fifty-four years.

2. By appropriating the *reversionary* interest of ecclesiastical revenues to this purpose. Expediency might require that the parish churches, parsonages and glebe lands should be given to the episcopalians for ever; and that the existing interests of all incumbents should be protected; (an arrangement to which no churchman could reasonably object): then, taking the yearly income of the church as stated by Sir Richard Phillips ('Facts' col. 865) at about five millions, and deducting one million as the annual value of the parsonages and glebes, the reversion of the remaining four millions, at five per cent compound interest, would in fifty-five years effect the extinction of the debt.

3. A preferable plan would be to appropriate *one half* of this reversion to the reduction of the debt, and the other half to the diminution of taxation. This plan would of course require nearly twice as long a period as that above proposed: but the three great evils under which the nation groans, viz, a national church, a national debt, and its consequent crushing taxation, *would be every day diminishing* and in rather more than a century, without the shadow of injustice to any one, the whole would be extinguished: leaving only the current expenses of government to be provided for.

Many endowments of schools and dissenting meeting houses, together with not a few other charities in the application of which the will of the donors has been departed from, might be justly applied in aid of the working of this plan.

were commanded to be 'given to the Levite, the stranger, the fatherless, and the widow.' And you are doubtless aware that, proceeding on this principle, the tithes in England were anciently divided into four parts, one part being for the maintenance of the bishop, one for the repair of the parish church, one for the maintenance of the rector, and *one for the poor of the parish*. In after times, the bishop being provided for from other sources, the tithes were divided into only three parts. We therefore claim on our own behalf, and especially on behalf of the widows and fatherless around us, that one-third part, or at the least one-fourth part, of the proceeds of every benefice shall be given to the poor as their right.

Tenthly; *We claim the total repeal of the New Poor Law, and the enactment of a statute which while it shall secure the rights of property, shall also recognise and protect the rights of those who have it not*. We hold that all the land in the kingdom; naturally belongs to all the people in the kingdom; and that in the absence of more artificial arrangements, every man is entitled to his share of the whole;* but it having been deemed conducive to the general good that the land shall be held by some and not by others, and this arrangement being dovetailed into the very frame-work of society, we have neither the power nor the wish to interfere with it: except that we feel ourselves entitled to demand the repeal of *the law of primogeniture*, which we consider to be hostile to the dictates of natural affection, and in various ways injurious to the community. But in lieu of the landed rights which we thus surrender, we hold ourselves entitled to claim a full and sufficient maintenance out of the common stock whenever sickness, adversity, or age, renders us unable to earn it by our own exertions. For ourselves, for our widowed mothers, and for our aged and afflicted relatives and neighbours, we claim that neither we nor they shall find it difficult to obtain relief — that such relief shall be awarded to us as our *right*, not conferred upon us as a *boon* — that poverty shall not expose us to incarceration in a prison-workhouse — and especially that those whom God hath joined together, shall not be put assunder, while guiltless of all other crime save that of being poor.

These, Sir, are the claims we make; and which we are determined perseveringly to urge until they are either granted, or

* This in England and Wales would give about three acres each to every man woman and child; or, allowing more than half for roads, waste, and improvements, about *seven* acres for every family of five persons.

110

proved to be unjust.

Those who withhold from us the rights which we have thus demanded, are apprehensive that we are about forthwith to resort to physical power for the enforcement of our claims, — they are not the first criminals who on hearing the rustling of the leaves have alarmed each other by the cry 'The officers of justice are upon us!' — and profess to deprecate such a mode of conducting the dispute. With how much sincerity or consistency this profession is made by the abettors of a system which requires eighty thousand sabres and bayonets for its enforcement, we shall not take upon us to decide. But for ourselves we can truly affirm that 'our imaginations sicken at any prospect of civil discord, even if oppressors only were to be the victims; and that we therefore earnestly hope that the edifice we are seeking to rear may never be established upon a foundation of blood, to be cursed by widowed mothers, and undermined by the fatherless. We are, moreover, of opinion, that whatever is gained in England by force, by force must be sustained, but that whatever springs from knowledge and justice will sustain itself. Therefore it is that we seek to build up the sacred temple in peace — to raise up a social and political edifice, founded on national enlightenment and justice — a temple in which all classes may freely worship, without tax, tribute or reproach, in which all may unite to devise wisely and execute justly, and where the energies of all may be directed to the solving of that great political problem — how shall all the resources of our country, mental, moral and physical, be made to produce the greatest happiness for all its members?'

But though the employment of physical force is as remote as possible from our wishes, the time may come, and may perhaps be near, in which the defence of all that is dear to us will compel us to have recourse to it. If our rights as citizens and as men are threatened to be eternally withholden from us — if the burdens of the nation are always to be disproportionately thrown upon the working-classes, while property is suffered to remain untaxed — if we are evermore to be forbidden to purchase our bread at the cheapest market — if a knot of Poor Law Commissioners is always to treat poverty as a crime, and to cut in sunder the marriage-tie — if our addresses to the Legislature continue to be visited with contempt, and the hope of redress becomes extinguished in our bosoms — then, Sir, we honestly tell you that we do not mean to submit. On the heads of our oppressors be the guilt and its consequences.

111

We are not unaware of the interests which are combined against us; nor of the disguise with which wealth, influence, and long-continued custom invest injustice and oppression; but after carefully surveying the forces of our opponents we deem ourselves fully equal to the conflict, and are only anxious that it shall, if possible, be a purely moral one. If we are asked from whence we derive our claims, we point to *Heaven; there* is the hand which in forming us *men*, inscribed the charter of our rights, *there* the power which will secure to us their enjoyment. With a cause resting on the firm rock of eternal justice, — with the mighty millions rallying round its standard, — above all, with the arm of omnipotence for our strength and protection, we feel ourselves authorized to hope for success. Nor have any, save those who 'love the wages of unrighteousness,' reason to deprecate that success: for again we remind you that our object is the greatest attainable promotion of the general good.*

We are told that we ought not to interfere with politics — that it would be better for us to attend to the duties of our calling, — and so on. We reply that we reckon the rescue of ourselves and families from the jaws of oppression to be amongst the highest of the duties which devolve upon us. We hold, moreover, that every man ought to be a politician; because every man is bound, to the utmost of his power, to promote the good of the land in which he dwells. But in truth, we have adopted our present course less from choice than from compulsion. We have been long and laboriously gleaning in the fields of industry, and have often wondered that we were unable to collect sufficient to supply our wants. At length we have discovered that certain parties, who are either too ignorant, or too idle to gather for themselves, have stolen a great part of the produce of our toil. Hence the origin of the discontent we feel, and the cry which we are raising. So that, in reality, it is not so much we who interfere with politics, as politics which interfere with us.

We can truly assure you Sir, that towards yourself, personally, we entertain not a spark of animosity. We honour your office, we respect your character, and remember with gratitude the pecuniary aid which, partly through your kindness, some of us received in a time of scarcity of employment. But though we

* This will, of course, include the better treatment of soldiers and seamen. On this ground the principles of radicalism are silently but surely working their way amongst the military. Indeed Lord John Russell's letter to the Earl of Derby contains internal evidence that the Government is already afraid to place confidence in the army. So be it.

hope ever to be grateful for favours conferred upon us, you could only despise us if we were willing to sell our birthright for 'a mess of pottage.' We ask not *charity*, but *justice*. Give us our own, and we shall but little require the benevolence of others.

In conclusion, permit us to appeal to you on behalf of our unhappy country; and to implore you to assist us in attempting to save it from the rocks on which the fatuity of our rulers is running it. As a minister of christianity, we entreat you to pour the oil of peace upon the rising billows. Your knowledge of human nature, and of the unconquerable energies aroused by conviction of being in the right, — not to advert to higher considerations, — will we hope preserve you from falling into the egregious mistake of supposing that peace can ever be ensured, while *the millions are at once enlightened and oppressed*. So long as we were kept in ignorance, there was little difficulty in enslaving us: but now that we have acquired the knowledge of our rights, and begun to feel our strength, you must, we think, perceive that an attempt to perpetuate oppression, must endanger the national tranquillity.

Finally, we appeal to your sense of justice. Place yourself, so far as imagination will enable you, in the condition of not a few whose nature and immortal destiny are equal to your own. Imagine yourself doomed to endure the heat of the summer's sun, and the severity of the winter's cold, and then, as the reward of your toil, compelled to subsist on less than a sufficiency of the coarsest bread; or imagine yourself confined to your workshop from earliest morn to an hour not far from midnight, leaving scarcely time enough for necessary repose, none for the renovation of health or the improvement of the mind, and that after all you found yourself unable to provide an adequate supply of even the meanest fare for those dependent upon you; — imagine that all this time every stackyard exhibited unequivocal proofs of plenty, and the sons and daughters of indolence, as though in mockery of your woe, frequently rolled past you in all the gorgeousness of wealth; — imagine that your aged parents, or your widowed mother, after having contributed sixty years of toil to augment the general opulence, were starving on the pittance allowed them by a board of Guardians; — imagine that you saw the wife of your bosom, and the children of your love drooping beneath the poverty which you had ineffectually struggled to remove, and that you felt yourself hastening to increase the number of those whom oppression has consigned to an untimely grave; —

113

imagine that you could distinctly perceive a large proportion of these evils to spring from the gross imperfections of the institutions under which you lived; — and, as you trace the dark outlines of this appalling picture, remember that though to *you* it is an imaginary case, this, and worse than this, is a sad reality to tens of thousands of your brethern; suppose it to be so to yourself, and that you were surrounded by gentlemen who could render you valuable aid in seeking the redress of your wrongs, or, like the priest and Levite pass by on the other side, and then, Sir, *'as you would that men should do unto you, do even so unto them.'*

We are, Rev. Sir,
Yours respectfully,
(Signed on behalf of the Association)
G. T. GREEN, Brushmaker, *Chairman*
J. A. LEATHERLAND, Silkweaver, *Secretary*

12 Extract from 'The Rights of Woman' by R. J. Richardson

Pamphlet written in prison, 1840

> While Europe's eye is fix'd on mighty things,
> The fate of empires and the fall of kings;
> While quacks of state must each produce his plan,
> And even children lisp the Rights of Man;
> Amid the mighty fuss, just let me mention,
> The Rights of Woman merit some attention.
>
> BURNS

Edinburgh: printed by John Elder, High Street;
    published by John Duncan, 114 High Street.
London: John Cleave, Shoe Lane, Fleet Street.
Manchester: A. Heywood, Oldham Street.

MDCCCXL

... Having occupied some time in shewing you the natural degree of woman, also her scriptural qualifications and her physical inequality, I shall now proceed to the main feature of the question, or rather to the question itself — 'Ought Women to interfere in the political affairs of the country?' As I have before prepared you, by an abstract dissertation upon the natural rights of woman, I do most distinctly and unequivocally say — YES! And for the following reasons:

First, Because she has a natural right.

Second, Because she has a civil right.

Third, Because she has a political right.

Fourth, Because it is a duty imperative upon her.

Fifth, Because it is derogatory to the divine will to neglect so imperative a duty.

The first reason I hope I have sufficiently argued before and established its truth.

The second is, in a certain degree, answered by the establishment of the first reason; but in addition I may say, that it is nowhere written in the body of the civil law, that woman, by reason of her sex, is disqualified from the exercise of political

115

right except by her own voluntary act. Grotius, Puffendorf, Montesquieu, Vattel, and other famous civilians, have nowhere consented to such an unjust exclusion; the only instance on record where we find this right disputed, is in the famous controversy between Philip of Valois, and Edward III, concerning the Salic law, by which females and their descendants are excluded from the monarchy of France, and from the inheritance of the allodial lands of the nobility, the latter part of the law has long become obsolete, and the former is nowhere acted upon except in France, proving that the doctrine of the exclusion of females from political power is not consonant with the law of nature and nations.

Again, civilians teach us the doctrine of community of persons and community of rights, as the best mode of establishing a pure commonwealth, in strict accordance with the genuine principles of liberty. Surely then it cannot be argued, that any inequality should prevail, or that any distinction should exist in a community, where all things are held in common, or in trust for the good of the commonwealth; nor will it be said that the members of such communities, male and female, have not each an equal voice in the making of the laws necessary for the political government of that community. Of course I now speak of society in its purest state, but it is a legitimate argument in favour of my position; for as all political law is based upon the civil law, so are those political institutions best that proximate nearest to the original standard of civil liberty.

Civilians tell us also, that for all the uses of society woman stands upon an equal footing with man; for all the purposes of civil government, woman is equally admissable to office; for the due promotion of the welfare of the state, woman is essentially necessary in conjunction with man. These three positions I shall mention when I advance my arguments in favour of Reason Third.

I ask, upon what ground can this civil right be abridged diverted or abrogated? I ask those who tyrannically withhold from woman her political rights, on what assumption do they do so? I challenge them to sustain their opinions. I invite them to discussion, and will appear to maintain my proud position as the vindicator of the rights of woman against any one who may be so lost to a sense of shame as to oppose helpless woman in pursuit of her just rights.

The third reason I advance in justification of my emphatic

116

approval of the question at issue is, because I conceive Woman has a political right to interfere in all matters concerning the state of which she is a member, more especially as applied to Great Britain, for the following reasons:

1st — Because, by the ancient laws of the English constitution, she is admissable to every executive office in the kingdom, from the monarch upon the throne to the parish Overseer,* the village sexton,† or the responsible office of post mistress, which is still common in small towns.

2nd — Because, by the present law of tenures, of powers, of contracts, of bargains and sale, of inheritance, of wills, and every other matter or thing touching the rights of property and transfer, woman (except in *femme covert,*) is qualified to be, and therefore, is admissable, as a contracting party, save during her minority or a ward in chancery, then her affairs are managed by trust.

3rd — Because, woman is responsible in her own person for any breach of contract, for any offence against the peace and laws of the land. In the church, by the penalties of imprisonment, excommunication, and premunire; in the state, by fine, imprisonment, banishment, and death.

4th — Because she is taxed in the same degree with others for the maintainance of the state and its appendages under all circumstances.

5th — and lastly, because, she contributes directly and indirectly to the wealth and resources of the nation by her labour and skill.

On these five reasons I found my opinion upon the great question, 'Ought woman to interfere in the affairs of the state?' and to that question I again answer Yes! emphatically YES!

To the first of these reasons I will add, if a woman is qualified to be a queen over a great nation, armed with power of nullifying the powers of Parliament or the deliberate resolutions of the two estates of the realm, by parity of reason, a woman in a minor degree ought to have a voice in the election of the legislative authorities. If it be admissable that the queen, a woman, by the constitution of the country can command, can rule over a nation, (and I admit the justice of it,) then I say, woman in every instance ought not to be excluded from her share in the Executive and legislative power of the country.

To the second reason I will add further, if a woman can

* See Bott on the Poor Laws.
† Lucy Turner was many years parish clerk of Eccles, Lancashire.

exercise the powers of a contractor, or vendor, or become heiress, testatrix, executrix or administratix, and act in such important capacities over matters and things daily arising out of transactions with real and personal property, I say that it perfectly justifies my opinion that woman is not only qualified, but ought by virtue of such qualification, to have a voice in the making those laws under which the above transactions take place.

The third reason I will illustrate by saying, that, if woman be subject to pains and penalities, on account of the infringement of any law or laws, — even unto death, — in the name of common justice, she ought to have a voice in making the laws she is bound to obey.

The fourth reason is next in importance to the last, so long as the legislature claim and levy a portion of the worldly income of a woman for the support of the state, surely it is not presumption in woman to claim the right of electing that legislature who assume the right to tax her, and on refusal, punish her with pains and penalties; it is unjust to withhold from her her fair share of the elective power of the state, it is tyranny in the exreme, and ought to be properly resisted.

The fifth Reason is equal in importance to the last, and in support of which, I shall extend my arguments. It is a most incontrovertible fact, that women contribute to the wealth and resources of the kingdom. The population in Great Britian in 1831, consisted of 16, 255, 605, which may be classified under the head of agriculture, mining, and manufacturing; from these three sources the wealth of the country is raised. Now let us begin with agriculture, and see what share the women take of the labour necessary to produce the food of the people, the rent of the landlord, and the taxes of the state. In the first place, the dairy is managed almost exclusively by women and girls; the small live stock, such as poultry, &c., wholly so. Look to the cheese counties of Glocester and Chester, where the female population is almost wholly employed in the dairy. Look to the milk and butter counties around the large towns, and see the number of females who are employed in milking and making butter, and bringing them to market. In a farmyard the smallest child performs some labour or other, feeding poultry, driving cows, &c. In the fields, again, we find women performing every kind of labour except draining, hedging, ditching, fencing, ploughing, and mowing. We find them driving, sowing, setting, harrowing, drilling, manuring, weeding, hoeing, picking stones,

118

gathering potatoes, turnips, pulling carrots, mangel wurzel, shearing, binding, gathering, hay-making, &c. &c. The boys and girls too, are employed in picking stones, driving, scare-crowing, tending sheep, gathering roots, &c. In the barn, with the exception of thrashing and handicraft work, women perform every other occupation. There is no country in Europe where the women are such slaves upon the soil as they are in Scotland. I have many times counted twenty or thirty women in one field to about four or five men and boys. It is quite common to see women in the same unequal proportion to men labouring in the fields at every kind of predial labour; and many times I have been tempted to exclaim, Surely the curse of God is not upon the woman instead of the man! for in the language of holy writ, he declared to Adam, 'in the sweat of thy face shalt thou eat bread.' And many times I have in my heart blamed men for allowing their women to be such slaves, to perform such labour that nature never intended them to do, nor befitted them for the task. Inured to such toils and hardships, she becomes masculine; and the force of all those tender passions implanted by God in the breast of woman to temper the ruggedness of man, become weakened, her real virtues forgotten, and her proper usefulness destroyed. To the men of Scotland I say, Shame! To the women I say, endeavour to throw off the degradation of predial slavery, return to your domestic circles and cultivate your finer feelings for the benefit of your off-spring. How can you expect to be free, when you are willing slaves, and nourish in your lap a new race of hereditary bondsmen? How can you expect men, who seek only 'to command and overbear' others, to look to other than their own selfish interests? Rouse you, and let future historians record your zeal in the cause of human redemption, and you will confer a perpetual obligation on posterity. Debased is the man who would say women have no right to interfere in politics, when it is evident, that they have as much right as 'sordid man.' None but a tyrant, or some cringing, crawling, hireling scribe, succumbing to the footstool of power, would dare to say so.

Let us examine the mining population, (i.e.) those who produce, by their labour out of the bowels of the earth, all the iron, lead, copper, tin, and other metals, besides coal, salt, slate, stone, &c. There are fewer females employed in this department than in either of the others, because of the greater strength of body and mind required to undergo the fatigue and danger of mining; but I may fairly say, that one third of those employed in mines are women, more especially in the coal mines, which are the most numerous of any other. In the coal mines of Staffordshire, Lancashire, Durham, and Northumberland, women are constantly employed the same as the men, earning from four to twelve shillings per week. It is no uncommon thing to see them suspended by a rope in the act of being lowered several hundred feet below the face of the earth into the mine, where *they draw waggons laden with coal* to the bottom of the shaft ready to be raised up, and also where they squat down on their knees, and sometimes in a half reclining position, for the purpose of hewing with a small pick, 6 or 8 lb weight, the coal from the seam. In many instances the seam or stratum of coal, being only 14, 16, 18, 20, or 24 inches thick, and in this narrow space, women, the fairest and tenderest of God's creatures, are found with a solitary candle, or Davy-lamp, stretched at full length, hewing out the coal, and this too for little wages; as they are paid for by weight, of course, where it is so difficult to get, less will be got. To see them at meal times rising from the mouth of the shaft, more 'like demons from the lower deeps,' than those angelic creatures, our poets call women, is a sight that would 'harrow up the souls of men,' if they possessed the feelings of humanity, and create a feeling of disgust for the institutions that can allow 'woman, lovely woman,' to be forced by poverty and distress from her domestic duties down these hell holes of coal mines. And yet, such is the apathy, such the cold, selfish indifference of the women of these islands, that they will sit by their hearths, enjoy the comfort of that fire made from coals dug out of the bowels of the earth by their poor countrywomen, and yet breathe no sigh of pity, speak no word of sorrow, nor ask of their husbands and fathers why are these poor collier women thus abused, degraded, and enslaved by their country's laws?

Who will say the poor women who at the hazard of their lives contribute to our comfort when the icy bonds of winter, and the cold biting blast of December compels us to seek refuge from cold in the artificial heat arising from coal got by her hands, have no right to a vote in the legislative powers of the country? None! not even the savage; but, should one be found that will dare to deny or withhold that right, he is less than man, he is a ——— nothing.

We next come to the manufacturing population. Here will I fearlessly assert, that one half of the population employed in the manufactory of cotton, silk, and wool, are women and girls.

120

In cotton, which by the last census in 1831, 1,337,127 persons, male and female, were employed, I believe one half of them are women. In the blowing department, few or perhaps no women are employed; but in carding, drawing, and roving, I should say a majority of those employed are women. In throstle spinning, nearly all women; in mule spinning, partially so; in weaving by power, principally women; in winding and reeling, wholly so. In hand-loom weaving one half are women, either as winders or weavers. In those hideous dens called 'Factories,' tyranny is triumphant, and slavery wretched. The numerous acts of parliament passed to regulate the Factory system, are proofs of their being in want of legislative protection; and well they may be in want, while those who stand in need of protection are excluded from all share in the legislative power of the country.

Here, then, is a population principally employed in manufacturing cotton to the extent of L.200,000,000 annually, and principally females too. Now, what is the actual condition of this degraded class of our countrywomen? At an early age, even before their tender frames receive the nourishment and secretions necessary to befit them for the duties nature ordained they should perform in after life, many years before the age of puberty, are they taken to these *hell-holes* to earn their little pittance, in order to enable the parents to purchase the miserable sustenance which the rapacity of the capitalist deigns to allow them to support the cravings of Nature. Many have been sent in the factories at six, seven, eight, and nine years of age. Yes, from their sleep are they *now* taken, and carried sleeping upon the backs of their fathers, mothers, or brothers, and, for twelve hours a-day, compelled to toil and endure the heated atmosphere of these manufacturing hells; and many times, before the abolition of night-work, did these little girls and their brothers toil the long and dreary night, whilst those for whom they toiled were sleeping on their beds of down, regardless of these outrages upon humanity. Immured in these dens, oppressed by fatigue, fed with insufficient diet, their little minds abused, their bodies scourged, their frames wasted, the pith of womanhood dried up and withered, they grow up in years, in many instances deformed in body, or die prematurely with the first attack of disease; some are women and mothers years before their natural period; but are they taken from these accursed mills by their husbands? — No! once a Factory slave, seldom do they leave it but with death: fathers, mothers, sons, daughters, all are condemned to this horrible system of slavery.

121

The wife will rise from her marriage-bed at five o'clock in the morning, and with her husband proceed to her daily occupation in the mill, the wife in one department, and the husband in another — there is no honeymoon for them. Should she be 'as ladies wish to be who love their lords,' there is no ease, no time for nourishment and rest for her: — work, work, work, early and late, until the latest moment of her travail; there must be no time lost — no steam wasted, toil she must, until nature, bursting through the tyrant's laws, forces her to relinquish for two or three days her life of slavery to give birth to her burden, which, alas! is doomed to the same slavish life, or a lingering sickness and premature death. There is no month of ease and relaxation for her; in a few days she is hurried, regardless of her health and strength, leaving her innocent babe to the *care* of a nurse, who, with bottle-teat and Godfrey's cordial, keeps the little victim quiet until the mother returns from the mill to her meals. In this manner does she continue at her life of slavery for a paltry sum of 8s. to 12s. per week. It is the same in the power-loom-weaving department, but with this difference, that many are paid by the piece. In the silk department the business is cleaner and more healthy; the atmosphere purer and cooler; the labour less toilsome, and often paid by piece: the silk winding is wholly performed by women, and to a very great extent are they employed in other departments of this branch of manufacture.

I must not forget to notice the calico-printing department — I have seen much of it in England — where it is performed principally by men, and in a few instances, as mere assistants, by women. But what was my surprise when I visited the print-fields of Leven in Dumbartonshire, where I saw — O shame upon the men of Leven! — their wives and sweethearts performing the work of horses, carrying heavy burdens of wet calicoes after washing them in the cold and rapid streams, working at the tables, grasping in their delicate fingers the clumsy printing block and the heavy hammer, and printing the most difficult patterns of long cloths and shawls. 'This is the work of men,' said I to the lasses, 'and you ought not to perform it: your places are in your homes: your labours are your domestic duties: your interests in the welfare of your families, and not in slaving thus for the accumulation of the wealth of others, whose slaves you seem willing to be; for shame of you! go seek husbands those of you who have them not, and make them toil for you; and those of you who have husbands and families, go home and minister to their domestic comforts.' Such were my opinions, and such are my opinions. The only palliative in their favour was, that they were conscious that they were not in their proper places; but that, as they had no voice in making the laws, they could not help their degraded position, but they would strive to obtain that power to the best of their abilities — I believe the lasses of Leven are truly patriotic, and worthy of good laws, happy homes, cheerful hearths, loving husbands, and prattling children.

In Woollen Manufacture, women are very extensively employed in about a ratio of two-fifths to men; the labour is heavy too, but not so oppressive as in the Cotton department.

In the finishing processes of cotton, women are very extensively employed. In hand-loom-weaving, it is no uncommon thing to see in a weaver's cottage under the window on the ground floor, a loom, at which the weaver's wife is employed at the same time she is surveying her domestic affairs; for instance, she will leave her loom, peel potatoes for dinner, put them upon the fire, then return to her loom: should her child cry in its cradle, she will stop, leave her loom, give it the breast, or a plaything, or get it to sleep, and return to her loom again, and so on alternately the day through; perhaps in another corner of the house a daughter will be employed upon another loom, and another daughter winding — by this kind of domestic labour she will earn 3s. 4s. or 5s. per week. A stout active young lass for weaving twenty-eight yards of calico will earn 6d., and if constant through a long day will earn 10d., which will be 5s. per week; but from this must be deducted lost time in going for warps, and taking home the cuts or pieces, besides the usual deductions, abatements, &c. This class of workers suffer much from abatements, more especially if they be workers in silk, where the worker is frequently obliged to put up with abatements of one-half their earnings, or be driven to an arbitration, with almost the certainty of losing employment. In the Lace business, two-thirds of those employed are women and girls, and for a miserable pittance. In the hosiery business of Leicestershire and Nottinghamshire, women are very extensively employed, and most grievously oppressed. In Loughborough, Sheepshead, and the surrounding villages, tradespeople are in an awful state of wretchedness — ill fed, ill clothed, ill housed, miserably paid, and infamously abated. In the manufacture of Gloves, women are almost exclusively employed, and very ill paid. In the Pottery district, vast numbers of women and girls

123

are employed in the printing, painting, and other departments, the labour, apparently pleasing, is nevertheless irksome and unhealthy, in consequence of the heated atmosphere of their painting rooms, and the great quantities of turpentine used by them, which evaporating, fills the heated atmosphere, and being inhaled by them, produces very unpleasant effects.

In the Hardware districts of Birmingham and Sheffield, I am almost inclined to think there are as many women employed as men. I visited many establishments, and I invariably found great numbers of women employed in stamping, filing, polishing, sorting, painting, japanning, pin and needle making, steel pen-making, toy-making, and many other branches of hardware manufacture. Many times have I seen handsome young girls up to the elbows in nasty oil, and their faces besmeared with the same unctuous matter; surely, thought I, this is not the legitimate labour of 'those tender creatures we call ours.' No; I have concluded it is the labour of man, which tyrants have imposed upon women in order to increase their profits; for in few instances have women been called from their domestic duties to the manufactories, except for the purpose of reducing the wages of the man. Women have *lent themselves* to these avaricious money-grubbers, and poverty has driven them to the deed, which is the only reproach I cast upon them; but it has many palliatives, and one, the greatest of all, they have not the protection of the law, nor the benefits of society.

I have now shown you that woman bears her share in the burdens of the state, and contributes more than her fair proportion to the wealth of the country. I ask you, is there a man, knowing these things, who can lay his hand upon his heart, and say, Woman ought not to interfere in political affairs? No: I hope there is none for the honour of my sex — I do sincerely hope there is none.

I must now draw to a conclusion, by alluding to the fourth principal reason; viz; 'That it is a duty imperative on woman to interfere in political affairs.' I think, nay I believe, that God ordained woman 'to temper man.' I believe, from this reason, that she ought to partake of his councils, public and private, that she ought to share in the making of laws for the government of the commonwealth, in the same manner as she would join with her husband in the councils of his household. It is a duty she owes to herself, to her husband, to her children, to posterity, and to her common country. When we consider that it is to woman we owe our existence, that we receive from her

124

our earliest thoughts and the bias of our minds — that we are indebted to her for all that makes life a blessing — would it not be unwise, ungrateful, and inhuman in man to deny them every advantage they can possess in society; and would it not be wrong and criminal, in the highest degree, in woman herself to neglect the most important part of her duty, namely, the making of good laws for the guidance of those whom she is instrumental in bringing into the world, and for the good government of the society of which she is an ornament and a member? Every bad law injures society in some way or other; an accumulation of bad laws weakens the bond of peace; and the continuance of bad laws destroys the freedom and happiness of mankind. If woman be silent in the passing of bad laws, she neglects her duty; if she is unconcerned about the accumulation of bad laws, she is criminally apathetic; and if she remains unmoved at the continuance of bad laws, she connives at her own ruin; is a party to her own disgrace; links the fetters to her own limbs; rivets the yoke of slavery to her children's necks, and deserves to be ruled over with a rod of iron. My last principal reason, viz. That is it derogatory to the Divine will to neglect so important a duty. I hope I have given sufficient proof in the foregoing pages of the rights and duties of women. I consider that she who neglects her country's good neglects her God. The Creator gave man the earth for his heritage, and bade him go forth, multiply, and replenish, and subdue it — not literally man, but mankind. How, then, can the earth be subdued but by government? and who are the governors and the governed? — Mankind; they are endowed with reason for that purpose, and by the force of such endowment, laws are made congenial with man's nature, for man's government, which constitutes society. There is no distinction made betwixt man and woman, therefore it is a duty imperative upon her to deliberate with man in all affairs of government, for with man she has a concurrent jurisdiction over the things of the earth. If she neglects her duty in the affairs of government, she does that which is derogatory to the Divine will; and, according to the true doctrine of rewards and punishments, brings the penalty of such derogation upon herself. If she fails to exercise a concurrent jurisdiction over the things of the earth, then does she again bring pains and penalties upon her own head, and her punishment is manifested in the passive obedience and slavish subjugation of which we have so many harrowing proofs.

My dear Miss, I must conclude with an earnest appeal to you

125

in defence of our countrywomen. I know you have a brave and noble spirit worthy of your sex; therefore to you do I appeal in their behalf. Go on fearlessly advocating the right of woman to interfere in the affairs of state. I will be with you in your labours, and encourage you in your zeal, to promote the welfare of your country. Tell your countrywomen that it is a duty they owe to God, their country, themselves, and their posterity, to reform all the laws and institutions of the country which do not tend to promote the happiness of the people: to remove, by their combined efforts, the barriers that stand between them and their God, between His laws and the happiness of His people; to throw down the bulwarks of curruption that hem society within the pale of despotism, and shield them from the light of truth; to strike off the fetters that manacle the limbs of the British slaves, that they may march onwards to the goal of freedom, and establish society upon the basis of liberty; that henceforward, now, and evermore, they may adore that God who gave to man the earth for his heritage, and implanted in his breast the glowing principles of liberty, seasoned with the bounteous gift of reason. Tell them, too, they live in a land rich in its natural resources, as the allegorical land of milk and honey, but that bad laws and wicked legislators withhold from them those luxuriant resources which God gave to all men in common; tell them that but for these bad laws and wicked legislators the people would have plenty to eat, plenty to drink, plenty to wear, with good store of all that would render mankind happy and comfortable; tell them that these bad laws will never cease to be, nor wicked legislators cease to rule, until every man of twenty-one years of age, and every woman of twenty,* obtain, by their strenuous exertions, a voice in the election of those whom reason and honesty qualify for law-makers and administrators. Tell them this will never come to pass until the women of Scotland, England, Wales, and unfortunate Ireland, stand by and encourage their husbands, fathers, brothers, and sons, forward in the cause of freedom; and that they band *themselves* together to oppose the progress of despotism, wherever, and whenever, it shall appear — combat it inch by inch, foot to foot meet it — and by their united voices scare it from their threshold, and defeat its purposes.

Trusting to your noble spirit for the dissemination of these my humble opinions, and to your untiring energy for the constant and unremitting exertions in the cause of liberty, I

* Spinsters and Widows.

take my leave for the present; but fear not I shall be ever ready to vindicate the *Rights of Woman* against the oppressor's calumny, and the despot's scourge.

R. RICHARDSON

State Prison, Lancaster Castle

13 Address of the Female Political Union of Newcastle upon Tyne to their Fellow Countrywomen

From the 'Northern Star', 2 February 1839

Well ye know
What woman is, for none of woman born
Can chose but drain the bitter dregs of woe
Which ever to the oppressed from the oppressors flow.
                                                    SHELLEY

FELLOW-COUNTRYWOMEN, — We call upon you to join us and help our fathers, husbands, and brothers, to free themselves and us from political, physical, and mental bondage, and urge the following reasons as an answer to our enemies and an inducement to our friends.

We have been told that the province of woman is her home, and that the field of politics should be left to men; this we deny; the nature of things renders it impossible, and the conduct of those who give the advice is at variance with the principles they assert. Is it not true that the interests of our fathers, husbands, and brothers, ought to be ours? If they are oppressed and impoverished, do we not share those evils with them? If so, ought we not to resent the infliction of those wrongs upon them? We have read the records of the past, and our hearts have responded to the historian's praise of those women, who struggled against tyranny and urged their country-men to be free or die.

Acting from those feelings when told of the oppression exercised upon the enslaved negroes in our colonies, we raised our voices in denunciation of their tyrants, and never rested until the dealers in human blood were compelled to abandon their hell-born traffic; but we have learned by bitter experience that slavery is not confined to colour or clime, and that even in England cruel oppression reigns — and we are compelled by our love of God and hatred of wrong to join our countrywomen in their demand for liberty and justice.

We have seen that because the husband's earnings could not

128

support his family, the wife has been compelled to leave her home neglected and, with her infant children, work at a soul and body degrading toil. We have seen the father dragged from his home by a ruffian press-gang, compelled to fight against those that never injured him, paid only 34/- per month, while he ought to have had £6; his wife and children left to starve or subsist on the scanty fare doled out by hired charity. We have seen the poor robbed of their inheritance and a law enacted to treat poverty as a crime, to deny misery consolation, to take from the unfortunate their freedom, to drive the poor from their homes and their fatherland, to separate those whom God has joined together, and tear the children from their parents care, — this law was passed by men and supported by men, who avow the doctrine that the poor have no right to live, and that an all wise and beneficent Creator has left the wants of his children unprovided for.

For years we have struggled to maintain our homes in comfort, such as our hearts told us should greet our husbands after their fatiguing labours. Year after year has passed away, and even now our wishes have no prospect of being realised, our husbands are over wrought, our houses half furnished, our families ill-fed, and our children uneducated — the fear of want hangs over our heads; the scorn of the rich is pointed towards us; the brand of slavery is on our kindred, and we feel the degradation. We are a despised caste; our oppressers are not content with despising our feelings, but demand the control of our thoughts and wants! — want's bitter bondage binds us to their feet, we are oppressed because we are poor — the joys of life, the gladness of plenty, and the sympathies of nature, are not for us; the solace of our homes, the endearments of our children, and the sympathies of our kindred are denied us — and even in the grave our ashes are laid with disrespect.

We have searched and found that the cause of these evils is the Government of the country being in the hands of a few of the upper and middle classes, while the working men who form the millions, the strength and wealth of the country, are left without the pale of the Constitution, their wishes never consulted, and their interests sacrificed by the ruling factions, who have created useless officers and enormous salaries for their own aggrandisement — burthened the country with a debt of eighteen hundred millions sterling, and an enormous taxation of fifty-four millions sterling annually, which ought not to be more than eight millions; for these evils there is no remedy but

129

the just measure of allowing every citizen of the United Kingdom, the right of voting in the election of the members of Parliaments, who have to make the laws that he has to be governed by, and grant the taxes he has to pay; or, in other words, to pass the people's Charter into a law and emancipate the white slaves of England. This is what the working men of England, Ireland, and Scotland, are struggling for, and we have banded ourselves together in union to assist them; and we call on all our fellow country-women to join us.

We tell the wealthy, the high and mighty ones of the land, our kindred shall be free. We tell their lordly dames we love our husbands as well as they love theirs, that our homes shall be no longer destitute of comfort, that in sickness, want, and old age, we will not be separated from them, that our children are near and dear to us and shall not be torn from us.

We harbour no evil wishes against any one, and ask for nought but justice; therefore, we call on all persons to assist us in this good work, but especially those shopkeepers which the Reform Bill enfranchised. We call on them to remember it was the unrepresented working men that procured them their rights, and that they ought now to fulfil the pledge they gave to assist them to get theirs — they ought to remember that our pennies make their pounds, and that we cannot in justice spend the hard earnings of our husbands with those that are opposed to their rights and interests.

Fellow-Countrywomen, in conclusion, we entreat you to join us to help the cause of freedom, justice, honesty, and truth, to drive proverty and ignorance from our land, and establish happy homes, true religion, righteous government, and good laws.

14 To the Middle Classes of the North of England

Placard issued in July 1839, copy in H.O. 40/43; printed in the 'Northern Liberator', 21 July 1839

Gentlemen: — We address you in the language of brotherhood, probably for the last time. Up to the very last moment you have shut your senses to reason: but now that the last moment for moral appeal has arrived, perhaps you will listen to this last appeal of the people.

With a folly that will be the wonder of future ages, you have placed a blind confidence in the Whig Aristocracy: you have surrendered into their hands your 'right of thought', and any decree they please to send forth you look upon as if it were a decree from On High.

And now let us ask you a few questions touching the claims which this Aristocracy has upon your respect and confidence. Reflect upon these questions and answer them like rational men.

Are you and your posterity mortgaged to pay the borough-mongers' debt? Are you not compelled to pay on an average three times the value for bread, meat, wine, spirits, teas and everything you consume, in order to support the Jew swindlers and a perfumed, insolent Aristocracy?

Are you not shut out from the manly sports and recreations which once were the health and pride of Englishmen? If, after your six months' confinement in the ware or counting house, you wish for a day's sport over the lake or mountain, are you not told that the fish, the fowl and the wild animal all must be preserved for my lord's use and amusement, and if you persist to assert your natural rights over them, are you not punished with fine and imprisonment?

Will the Aristocracy associate with you — will they endure an alliance by marriage with what they impudently denominate your base blood?

Do they not, in one word, despise and oppress you as much as they do the working men, the only difference being that you are able, and would appear *willing*, to bear the yoke, whilst we

131

are unable, and thank God neither are we willing to bear it?

Is not the money plundered from the people and spent in the debauch of the Court or the profligacy of the Continent; is the money, we ask, not virtually abstracted from your trade and profits? Would we carry our money away to squander it on the dancers, gamesters and prostitutes of the continental cities, or would we lay it out at home in food, clothing, and other necessary articles, to the great benefit of domestic trade and manufactures?

We entreat you, not for our sakes, but for *your own*, not for the sakes of our families, but for *your own wives and children*, to take up these questions like men, and calmly and rationally discuss their truth or falsehood.

Discussed they now must be physically or morally — one way or the other — even if you are content to remain quiescent slaves, you will be permitted to remain so no longer.

But then comes your bugbear, 'If you, the working men had power in your hands there would be no security for life and property.'

One fact, you will yourselves admit, is worth ten thousand arguments; if these facts do not convince you, to talk of reasoning any longer is altogether out of the question.

Look to America; in the mercantile states of that republic all power is in the hands of the people, their will is law; and is the manufacturer less safe in his business, the trader less secure in his property, than in England? Why the very fault of American society is the over encouragement and importance that is given to its trade.

Look, too, to Switzerland, whose laws must receive the sanction of the whole male population, assembled in arms, from sixteen years of age upward. Where is the country on the face of the earth can boast more security for life and property, more absence of crime, more positive virtues than are to be found in the mountains, vales and cities of Switzerland? Look at the soothing tranquility of these Democratic countries, and contrast them with the murderous anarchy that even at this moment desolates Aristocratic Spain.

Dear are our families to us, dear our humble homes; our feelings are as human as your own, and if compelled to take the field in vindication of our sacred rights, we shall do so with our hearts yearning for our helpless families, whom many of us must never see again; to this alternative we are driven by a dire and uncontrollable necessity; we are not 'men of blood'.

132

But blood is on the land; it falls without a record; hecatombs, — upwards of 100,000 souls are yearly sacrificed to famine and a broken heart; the old, the helpless, the unresisting die, and no man writes their epitaph.

If you be not as blind, as hardened of heart as ever Pharoah was of old, you must perceive that a mighty, a thorough, a radical change must now very speedily take place in the constitution of society in these islands, a change which it is not in your power to avert, though it is in your power to give it a peaceful character.

Do you call the courage of the people in question? Why even the Tory 'Times' acknowledges that contempt of death is natural to every errand-boy in England.

But it is not a question of courage we are discussing now, it is a question of *necessity*; watch your own child, as with tears it implores for a morsel; see the eye of your own wife and sister grow dim with famine; feel hunger tearing your own vitals; then hear the shot-peal calling you to death or freedom; opening to you a chance of escape from the hell you endure, and you will rush into the shock of battle with a joy bordering on madness.

And what will be the result of that strife of blood, which you alone can avert? If successful, the people will look on their fallen brothers and apostrophize their mangled remains thus: 'Well, you were sacrificed by the middle classes; they could have saved you but they would not; they assisted and encouraged the aristocracy to murder you! Let desolation dwell in the homes that made your homes desolate!' Middle classes: vengeance swift and terrible will then overtake you.

On the other hand, should the people of England be put down — supposing for a moment the impossibility — what then? Why, to use the word of more than one Whig journal, they will 'DISPERSE IN A MILLION OF INCENDIARIES' your warehouses, your homes, will be given to the flames and one black ruin overwhelm England!

Are you prepared for this? If you are contented to be trampled and spat upon by the Aristocracy; if you have no pity for your brothers and sisters in the humbler walks of life; if you feel not for the myriads who actually perish of cold and hunger; still ask yourselves, are you prepared to see your own homes in a blaze; your property given to flames and no insurance to redeem it; yourselves perhaps your wives and children shrieking to midnight outlaws for that mercy which in the day of your power you denied to them?

133

Praying that God, who endowed you with common sense and human feelings will free your mind from the prejudice and dispose you to do your duty in this terrible crisis,

We remain (if not, your own faults) your sincere friends,

THE COUNCIL OF THE NORTHERN POLITICAL UNION

15 Constitutional Arming

From the 'Northern Liberator', July 1839; reprinted in Thomas Ainge Devyr, 'The Odd Book of the Nineteenth Century' (1880)

The Whig and Tory newspapers, especially the 'Standard' are giving flaming accounts of a meeting held near Newport, in support, they say, of the Queen and the Constitution. It was attended by Sir Charles Salisbury, Thomas Protheroe Esq, William Brewer Esq, the Revs Isaacson and R. A. Roberts, Messrs Phillips, Jones and Hall, and a large body of *farmers*. Sir Digby Mackworth Bart, wrote to express his sorrow at being absent, and offered the aid of his *military experience* in case of a corps being formed. Addresses were moved and carried to the queen and the Lieutenant of the county, *the last offering their services as an armed body to defend the constitution*! A great number of signatures were appended to both addresses.

Now this is gratifying; this is right; this is well-timed; this is as it should be; this smacks really of the 'Constitution' of which these gentlemen appear to be so fond. That constitution lays it emphatically down, both as a *right* and a *duty*, for *all* Englishmen to be armed for self-defence, and for the defence of their rights and liberties as guaranteed to them both by statute and prescription. These gentlemen have set an excellent example. We trust the Lord Lieutenant of the County, whoever he may be, will accept of their services so properly and spiritedly tendered, and that Her Majesty will at his suggestion, reward their loyalty by commanding them to enroll themselves and sending them a handsome pair of colours for the occasion.

The Rev. R. A. Roberts seems to have made a highly Constitutional speech on this occasion. He said they had come forward to oppose those who were endeavouring to poison the minds of the people, and to subvert the laws and constitution of the country! He said they were resolved that these laws, the result of ages of wisdom, should remain inviolate! They were met to declare that England should not be revolutionised and brought down to the level of 'miserable Ireland'! Bravo! It

135

really warms the cockles of our heart to hear language like this; energetic, English, truly constitutional, from the lips of a beneficed divine of the Established Church! The Rev. Mr Stevens never made use of more nervous, more decided, more truly English terms! This is precisely what we say here in the North of England.

We will have no Malthusian 'Marcus' to poison the minds of the people with incitements to child-murder! We will have no Broughams and Martineaus to stigmatize marriage as a crime and charity as a folly! No; we are for the ancient laws of England. We join the Rev. R. A. Roberts, we insist upon the old *forty-third of Elizabeth*, that charter of the poor of England. We, (like the Rev. Gentleman) will not have English labourers reduced to the Irish potato and seaweed level! We stand firm for universal suffrage and annual Parliaments, as they existed up to the unfortunate times of Henry the Sixth! We have made up our minds, as Mr Roberts has, to stand by the trial by jury as constituted by Alfred the Great! We eschew all standing armies, and love the people to be universally armed, and rely upon the *Posse Comitatus* or levy the county under the command of the *sheriff*, whose *duty* it is to see that all the queen's male subjects able to bear arms *have arms to bear*! We hate 'innovations' as much as the meeting at Newport, and will never submit to a *Bourbon Police*, whilst the old English name of constable is remembered! In all Mr Roberts' detestation of these Whig innovations we heartily concur; nor can he hate the '*Prig of the Globe*' more than we do for calling these time-honoured customs and usages 'the prejudice of the rudest periods!' Well, as soon as the Newport corps is enrolled, we hope the example will be followed. We trust the men on the Tyne and Wear *will not be backward in offering themselves to defend the Queen and the Constitution*. We know they will not. We can venture to assure the Rev. Mr Roberts that if he wants thirty thousand determined fellows, well found with muskets, pikes and pistols, he has only to send northwards and they will be forthcoming. Arms! Arms! (we say) The Queen and the Constitution for ever! and no revolutionary innovations!

PART III

Chartist Activity

The decision to petition Parliament and to elect delegates to a National Convention both involved the organisation of mass meetings. Although written material of all kinds was of more importance in Chartism than in any earlier working-class movement, the typical way in which the rank and file associated themselves with the movement was still by attending demonstrations and meetings. The orator was still of greater influence than the journalist, and the orator is the figure whom it is most difficult to re-create. This section contains some examples of speeches as reported in the press, and starts with the description of a monster rally. The description, which goes into considerable detail, shows the enormous amount of preparation which went into these events, the formality with which they were conducted, and gives at least some idea of the impact which such events must have had in the localities in which they occurred. Peter Murray McDouall and John Collins had both been imprisoned in the period immediately after the Convention, and had been prominent members of the Convention. McDouall was a young surgeon from Lancashire, who had been drawn into radical politics as the result of his work amongst the handloom weavers and factory operatives. He was associated in the early days with Matthew Fletcher, but after the latter's withdrawal from Chartist politics, McDouall remained, starting his own journal in 1841 in Ashton-under-Lyne, and remaining one of the leaders most committed to a policy in which violence was not ruled out. John Collins was a Birmingham working man, a member of the Political Union, who continued to attend the Convention after the leading members of the Union had withdrawn in February 1839. He was always, however, strongly committed to a non-violent moral force position, and to the greatest possible co-operation with sympathetic members of the middle class.

The National Convention at the beginning represented a broad section of extraparliamentary radicalism. By the time it finally disbanded in September 1839, the most moderate

137

section, represented here by the report of a speech of J. P. Cobbett, had already withdrawn, whilst it is fairly clear that those who were actively preparing for insurrection were active in different parts of the country, and no longer had much time to spare for the Convention. The group of documents relating to the Convention illustrates the type of rhetoric of four tendencies. The first, the conventional radicalism of Cobbett, which was close to that of the parliamentary Radicals; the second, the 'English Jacobinism' of Frost — very much in a tradition which went back to the Reform Bill period and before; thirdly, the voice of Marsden, handloom weaver from the north, whose radicalism related constantly to the actual living and working conditions of his family and fellow workers, and which was pressingly concerned with issues of employment and poor relief, and fourthly, the 'continental' type of revolutionary rhetoric of George Julian Harney. Had these samples been taken over a wider period of time, the differences between the tendencies would certainly have been more marked. In 1839 they were as close together as they were ever to be, and it is not always easy to detect the essential differences of tone.

After presenting the Petition, the Convention had the task of deciding what action it should ask of its constituents. The placard calling for 'ulterior measures' represents something of a minimum programme, but even here there was no complete agreement. Three types of activity are illustrated — exclusive dealing, arming and drilling. The documents relating to the idea of a general strike, or 'sacred month', are the arguments against it published by Feargus O'Connor and William Hill in the 'Northern Star'.

The last item in this section is an example of the way in which the Chartists often used the existing institutions of the community for their own purposes. In towns and villages they would often 'invade' the church on a Sunday — i.e. turn up en masse and take their seats in a church whose incumbent was unused to seeing more than a handful of working men seated respectfully on the back benches. It was difficult for the vicar to complain about such attendance, although there were those who did, especially when the Chartists insisted on his preaching on a text of their own choice. In this case the prayer for the imprisoned Chartists contains a strong attack on the government and its policies, but it was nevertheless delivered in solemn tones, in front of policemen with their heads bared.

138

16 Account of Chartist Rally in Manchester to welcome Peter McDouall and John Collins on their Release from Gaol

From the 'Northern Star', 22 August 1840

For some time past the Radicals of Manchester had contemplated giving a dinner and public entry to Dr McDouall, on his liberation from Chester Castle, where he was suffering imprisonment at the instance of a tyrannical government. The noble and patriotic defence made by the Doctor on his trial had won him the respect and admiration of every lover of his country; and an invitation to visit Manchester on his liberation was therefore, some weeks back, transmitted to him on behalf of the Radicals there by the Whittle-street branch, and which invitation the worthy Doctor accepted.

Subsequently to this, on the liberation of Lovett and Collins from Warwick gaol, Mr James Leech was appointed a delegate from Manchester to meet those noble-minded patriots at Birmingham, on which occasion Mr Leech invited Mr Collins (Mr Lovett having gone on to London) to be present at the demonstration to McDouall, which invitation was accepted by Mr Collins.

The knowledge that both these men of the people would be present on the occasion created a great sensation, not only in Manchester and Salford, but also in the surrounding towns; and every one looked forward to such a display of the power of the people as should convince the tyrants and their jackalls that Chartism was not dead — but had only slept awhile. In the meantime the Whittle-street branch, upon whom the management of the demonstration had principally devolved, were indefatigable in their exertions to render it effective. Procession and dinner committees were formed, and their activity left nothing to be desired. In order that there should be no pretence on the part of the authorities for interfering with their contemplated legal and constitutional proceedings, Messrs Maddocks and Melville were appointed a deputation to wait on Sir Charles Shaw, the head of the police, and inform him of their intentions. Sir Charles was absent in Scotland; but at a subsequent period Messrs Sleigh and Irvine, who are next in command of

139

the force, had an interview with Mr Wheeler, printer, who had been particularly active in getting up the demonstration. They assured him that there would be no interference on the part of the police. That if any policeman did interfere, they should not resist, but take his number, and he should be punished; and if any one else obstructed them, they should hand him over to the first policeman they met. The town was also placarded with flaming posters, announcing the procession would start from Stevenson's-square, at five o'clock on Saturday, the 15th, and proceed to Cross-lane, Salford, a distance of two miles, where Dr McDouall and Mr Collins would meet them, and all would return to Carpenter's Hall, where those patriotic leaders of the people would address them. The placards also announced a dinner to these gentlemen on Monday the 17th, at the Hall of Science. Tickets 2s.

There was a considerable fall of rain on Saturday morning, and fears were entertained that it would render the procession less effective, but those fears were groundless. After noon the weather cleared up, and continued fine (one or two slight sprinklings excepted) to the close of the day. The crowd began to assemble in the square about five o'clock. Among the first persons on the ground were the two marshals of the procession (Messrs William Grestley, and Joshua Ward) on horseback. These gentlemen wore splendid green scarfs, trimmed with white, and green and white favours. A deputation from Wigan, with a splendid banner, next arrived. They were followed by the committee of the boiler-makers, who also appeared with a handsome banner. Body after body continued to arrive, and banner after banner, including visitors from Stockport, Ashton, Leigh, &c. &c., till past six, at which time the procession was marshalled in the following order, with the exception of the dyers, who did not take up their position till it had arrived at Bridge-street:

ORDER OF THE PROCESSION

Two marshals on horseback, with green scarfs, and
green and white favours.
Portrait of Dr McDouall, surmounted by the
inscription — 'The Tyrant's Foe.'
Twenty committee-men, with staves, scarfs, and
favours.

140

THREE NATIONAL FLAGS: —

White flag.   Green flag.   White flag.
ROSE.   HARP.   THISTLE.
Splendid Banner of the Brown-street
Branch (No. 1.)
On one side a portrait of Dr McDouall, with the
Inscription — 'P. M. McDouall is our Friend.'
On the reverse the motto — 'God and our Rights!'
Eight young women, dressed in white, wearing
green and white favours, and carrying
four splendid garlands.
The Manchester Female Radical Assocation.
New Forester's Band.
Council of the Dressers and Dyers of Manchester
and Salford, with wands.
MAGNIFICENT BANNER;
On one side, the Dyers Arms, surmounted by the
Inscription: — 'The Operative Dressers and
Dyers of Manchester and Salford.'
On the reverse, the inscription: — 'The Prosperity of
the Working Classes is the Foundation of the
National Greatness.'
Band.
Operative Dressers and Dyers, six a-breast.
Grand Banner;
On one side the Dyers Arms, with the inscription,
'Branch Good Intent.'
On the reverse, the Royal Arms, with
'V. R.' on the top.
Various Trades, six a-breast.
Splendid Green Flag;
Inscription, 'Liberty and Equality,'
Surmounting the Rose, Shamrock, and Thistle.
On the reverse the same device, surmounted by the
Motto, 'Labour, the Source of all Wealth.'
The Members of the Whittle-street Branch,
Six abreast.
Tricoloured Flag.
Inscription, 'The Rights of Man.'
Operatives, six abreast.
LARGE BANNER;
On one side a Painting, representing the

Massacre of Peterloo.
On the reverse, on a black ground, the inscription,
'Murder demands Justice.'
Operatives, six abreast.
SPLENDID BANNER OF THE WIGAN ASSOCIATION.
On one side, a full-length figure, larger than life, of
FEARGUS O'CONNOR, Esq.,
Holding in his hand a scroll, with 'The People's
Charter; Wigan District!' inscribed thereon.
In the distance is seen
Hunt's Monument, surmounted with the
Cap of Liberty,
With the Tri-coloured Flag flying, and on its base the
Inscription, 'To the Memory of H. Hunt, Esq.'
The whole surmounted by the words:—
'O'Connor; Hunt's Successor!'
On the reverse, the British Lion, rampant, is trampling
Under foot 'Starvation Bastiles, Debts, Funds,
Jew Jobbers, Aristocracy, Shopocracy, White
Slavery, and State Paupers.'
A Mitre is seen falling. The Lion holds in his left
Paw a Flaming Dagger, from which is suspended
A Black Scarf, with the inscription,
'Down, Down, to hell; and say I sent you there!'
On a scroll, over all, the words:—
'Tremble! Tyrants, Tremble!'
Operatives, six abreast.
BANNER OF THE MANCHESTER BOILER-MAKERS.
On one side the Boiler-maker's Arms, motto,
'Humani Nihil Alienum.'
Surmounted by the inscription:—
'Friendly Boiler-makers.'
On the reverse, a beautiful allegorical representation
of Unity, Benevolence, and Concord, with the
Inscription, 'Success to Trade!'
Boiler-makers, six abreast.
Carriage, with Members of the Procession Committee.
Carriage, with Members of Dinner Committee.
Carriages, with various friends.
Old Foresters Band.
Black Banner.
On one side, 'Repeal of the New Poor Law Bill.'
On the reverse, 'Universal Suffrage, Short

142

Parliaments, Equitable Adjustment.'
Operatives, six abreast.
GRAND BANNER OF THE MANCHESTER POLITICAL
UNION.
On one side, a beautiful figure of Justice, leaning on
the British Lion.
On the reverse, the inscription, 'Universal Suffrage,
Vote by Ballot, Annual Parliaments.'
Carriages, with various friends.

In this order the procession moved from Stevenson-square
along Oldham-street, Mosley-street, York-street, King-street,
Bridge-street, Bailey-street, and Chapel-street, to the Crescent,
near Cross-lane. On arriving at this point it wheeled round, and
having formed in order for returning, halted, anxiously awaiting
the appearance of Dr McDouall and Mr Collins. It was known
that Collins had arrived the preceding night, and had prodeeded
to Cross-lane to meet the Doctor, who was expected there that
afternoon from Liverpool, by railway, where he had on
Thursday evening addressed an overwhelming audience at the
Queen's theatre. They had not waited long before a tremendous
shout was heard at the top of the Crescent. All eyes were turned
that way; and a moment afterwards an open carriage and four,
the postillions in green and white liveries, with favours of the
same colour, was observed approaching at a sharp trot, preceded
by one of the marshals who had gone to meet it. It contained
Dr McDouall and Mr Collins, as well as Messrs Leech and
Melville, who had been deputed to precede the procession to
receive the distinguished visitors. Mr Collins appeared to be in
good health; but the Doctor bore evident marks of the shameful
treatment he had received from the merciless Whigs while in his
dungeon. The carriage advanced to join the procession amidst
the shouts and clapping of hands of the assembled thousands,
the band of the Old Foresters advancing to meet it, playing 'See
the conquering hero comes!' When it had reached the latter part
of the procession, which was now the nearest to the point it
came from, the carriage halted, and an interesting ceremony
ensued. Another carriage, containing a deputation from the
Hulme Female Radical Association, was driven alongside that
containing the distinguished patriots. One of the ladies then
stepped into the Doctor's carriage, holding in her hand a
splendid green scarf, lined with white satin, and decorated with
a white satin rosette, which she was commissioned to present to

143

the Doctor from the ladies of the Hulme Association. The Doctor rose, and took off a splendid white beaver hat, presented him by the men of Andershaw on his liberation from a Whig dungeon, while the lady proceeded to fasten the scarf over his shoulder, amidst the heartiest cheers we ever remember to have heard, the Doctor all the while bowing his acknowledgements. This ceremony over, the carriage, followed by others, proceeded at a slow rate along the side of the procession, amidst the most deafening cheers, till it almost reached the head, where all the carriages took up their position to return (the carriage containing the Doctor being first) immediately after the young women who carried the garlands.

This return was the most triumphant demonstration in favour of the principles of the Charter it was ever our lot to witness. The Crescent, which is a magnificent street, presented, as far as the eye could reach, a dense mass of human beings; while, as the procession went down Chapel-street, the windows, the roofs, the lamp-posts, every point from which a view could be obtained, were seized upon with the greatest avidity. The street was so thronged that it was with the greatest difficulty the procession could move on at all; and from the situation we occupied, we could see persons carried off their legs for fifty yards together, by the rush of the crowd. Every one, too, seemed desirous of shaking hands with the Doctor, who appeared nothing loth; and we should think his right arm will be stiff for the next fortnight in consequence of the continual shaking of hands. The procession crossed Victoria Bridge, and soon arrived opposite the Exchange, where the shouts of triumph on the part of the people were unbounded. The 'nobs' came running out to witness the sight; and they will not easily forget the impression which it must have made upon their minds.

Unfortunately it was now almost dark; and it was quite so before the procession reached Carpenters' Hall; but we are satisfied that there never was a demonstration took place in Market-street equal to the present for numbers and enthusiasm. On passing the 'Guardian' Office, there was considerable groaning, and loud cheers were given opposite the office of the 'Advertiser'. In front of the Mosley Arms Hotel, three cheers were given for Feargus O'Connor, that being the house where he stops on his visits to Manchester.

On the procession approaching Carpenters' Hall, a rush took place to obtain seats. This was productive of an unfortunate result. The influx into the hall was so great, and the rush so

144

terrific, that those who had the management inside thought it would be prudent to shut the door till Dr McDouall and Mr Collins, with their friends, should make their appearance, there being only one entrance to this immense building, which will hold 3,000 persons comfortably. This they accordingly did; but, unfortunately, the distinguished visitors, who were greatly fatigued, stopped at a house near the Hall to obtain some slight refreshment; and, when they presented themselves at the doors, hundreds, and, perhaps, thousands, finding the doors shut, and naturally concluding the place was crammed, had gone away. The consequence was, that, though the gallery and orchestra were crammed, the body of the hall was not above three-fourths full. Several policemen presented themselves at the doors, and they were admitted on payment of the usual charge.

On the entrance of the distinguished patriots, the applause was absolutely deafening. On their appearance in the orchestra, the whole company rose; and they were received with the most overwhelming marks of enthusiasm. The orchestra presented an animating appearance; the garlands were tastefully arranged in front; and the young ladies who carried them were seated on either side of the chair.

When silence was obtained, Mr JAMES LEECH, on the motion of Mr DAVIS, was called to the chair by acclamation.

The CHAIRMAN, having taken his seat, congratulated those present on their having done their duty that night in being present on this occasion. He was sorry that the arrangements had been such as to preclude vast numbers from entering the room, and who would have otherwise been present. (Cries of 'True, true!' and 'Thousands!') It was, however, too late to remedy the evil now, and therefore he would say no more about it. There was one thing he particularly wished to impress upon their minds. It was this: not to show any marks of ill-feeling or disapprobation towards any individual who might be present, whether he wore a blue, or whether he wore a red livery. (Cheers.) He trusted they would do their duty by the sacred cause in which they were engaged; and show towards their enemies those feelings of kindness which their enemies would not show towards them. (Hear, hear.) An address had been prepared, to be presented to their dungeon-proved friend, Dr McDouall; and he would now call upon their friend, Mr Wheeler, to read that address.

Mr WHEELER then came forward, and read the following address. It was received with loud cheers, and at its conclusion

145

it was handed to the worthy doctor by Mr Wheeler:—

TO PETER MURRAY McDOUALL

We, the inhabitants of Manchester, in public meeting assembled, beg to congratulate you upon your liberation from your late confinement; and, by making you thus welcome, we would show our tyrants our love of patriotism and hatred of oppression. We feel proud to meet so brave a champion of our glorious cause. You bearded corruption to its very teeth — you told its advocates truths which made them tremble, and shook the citadel of tyranny to its very centre. Did they think that, by imprisoning our advocates, they would crush our principles, and achieve the savage work of their destruction? It was but a temporary triumph; and we hail it as a glorious ordeal through which our principles had to pass, that they might come forth in their purity, and, like the morning sun, clear away the dark mists of ignorance and error, and illumine the glad world with its refulgent beams. Our oppressors cannot fetter the human mind, which laughs to scorn their puny efforts to arrest its onward progress. While we view with indignation the despotic and tyrannical conduct of a corrupt government, we cannot too highly express our esteem for and attachment to you for your bold and unflinching conduct in the hour of trial. You then nobly did your duty in arousing the just indignation of the people against a Government which had broken every vow and violated every pledge made to the people! Though confined in a dungeon your spirit was still abroad, encouraging the people to persevere in their holy struggle for freedom; and we feel assured the time is not far distant when the principles for which you are contending will triumph, and a full measure of justice will be dealt out to those noble-minded men who have so disinterestedly sacrificed their fortunes and their liberties for the regeneration of their country.

Go on, then, brave and noble patriot! Yours is no party struggle, it is a struggle to rescue our common country from a worse than Egyptian bondage; it is the cause of the millions which groan beneath the tyrants' rod. Continue, then, in the glorious career you have marked out for yourself; and when liberty shall once more shed her invigorating influence over this nation, and peace and happiness shall beam in every countenance, then shall your name be enrolled amongst those of the great and good men who in all ages have pleaded the cause of the oppressed against the oppressor; and then shall it be daily remembered in the prayers of a contented and a happy people.

That Heaven may long bless you with health and happiness, and guard you against the secret machinations of your enemies, and give you strength to persevere in this mighty cause till the brand of slavery be erased from each man's forehead, and till each son of Britain shall stand erect in the dignity of manhood, knowing his rights, and knowing, daring to maintain them — that a consummation so devoutly to be wished may speedily take place, is the sincere prayer of the inhabitants of Manchester.

The CHAIRMAN said he did not doubt that most of those present had read with delight the noble, the undaunted, the unflinching defence which had been made upon his trial by the friend who was here present to-night. (Cheers.) He shuddered when he reflected on the number of victims which had been lately made to political expediency, not to political justice. But the reign of tyranny was becoming short; and if the people would only keep on as they had begun, their tyrants might in their turn be banished from their native soil. (Cheers.) He would now introduce to them one who had earned the esteem of every lover of freedom in England, their worthy and dungeon-proof friend, Dr McDouall (Loud cheering.)

Dr McDOUALL presented himself amidst a perfect storm of applause. When it had subsided, he said, Mr Chairman, friends and fellow-countrymen, and fellow Chartists, I rejoice to meet you once more; and I rejoice still more, now that I meet you again, to come forward the same Chartist that I was before I went into prison. If there has been any addition to me and my principles, it has been an addition of firmness, energy, and determination to persevere in the same course — (cheers) — and to advance, by every possible means, the sacred cause, to advance which we have met here to-night, and for which, if necessary, I am ready to suffer again and again. (Loud cheering.) I fear not their dungeons — I value not their sentences — I care not for their Juries (Tremendous cheers.) No, my friends; I value justice more — I value equality more — I value your rights more. (Cheers.) My friends, I fear them not; and I told them on my trial I did not fear them. They have tried to break down my spirit by heaping injury after injury upon me; but, like a well-built arch, it became the firmer and the stronger the greater the weight cast upon it. ('Bravo, McDouall,' and cheering.) If there was anything (he continued) which could add to the enjoyment he felt that night, it would be that the Charter should be made the law of the Land. He was rejoiced, on his arrival among them, to find Manchester occupying the proud position that she ought to do; and nothing would be capable of adding to his satisfaction except the proclaiming the Charter as the law of England. He had had time to study when in his dungeon; and he trusted he had studied to stick by their cause, and suffer again, if it were necessary, for his principles. (Loud cheers.) By a reference to the 'Star' of that week they would see, that a meeting which he was about to hold in Chester, on his release from his dungeon, had been interrupted. He had there been compelled to dissolve a highly peaceable and legal meeting, by order of the police, and under the threat that if he did not do so by peaceable means, they would disperse them by force. (Shame, shame!) That attempt to disperse a legal, constitutional, and peaceable meeting by the police, was attended with a greater amount of good than the delivery of twenty lectures on Chartism, because it showed the shopkeepers of Chester, many of whom were favourable to the meeting, that they were under the lash of the magistrates and the police as much as the working men. And they felt it, for they cursed them both. But there was another description of feeling shown at that meeting — and he mentioned this not that they should place any reliance on the army — but it was a feeling on the part of the artillery quartered there, which, if he had not put an end to the meeting, would have ended in a bloody conflict between them and the police. (Cheers.) He did not mean to say that the soldiers would have taken their part — (hear, hear) — they did not want it — (cheers) — all they wanted was a legal and peaceable change which should give them their rights; but still it was gratifying that such a feeling should exist in the army, and he was proud to record it — he was proud to state that there were men in the army who, if they heard a Chartist tried, did not forget their rights, although they wore the red coat of a soldier. What did they say on the occasion? They said, 'although we are soldiers, we have the feelings of working men. We heard your defence, and we will not let the bloody police disperse your meeting.' (Great cheering.) Thus they (the Chartists) had gained two things by this dispersion. First, the shopkeepers had cursed the magistrates, and several had offered to be chairman. Secondly, the opinion of the soldiers had been pronounced in their favour, and their principles had been disseminated among

148

them. (Cheers.) The Secretary of State had, in this instance, no occasion to depend upon the police and the soldiers; and he (Dr McDouall) could assure him that if he had spies among the police, he (the Doctor) had spies among them also; and it was owing to this circumstance that he had prevented a perhaps fatal collision between the soldiers and the police. He had, when on his trial, said he would begin agitating the moment he quitted the gates of his prison; and he had done so. From Chester he had proceeded to Liverpool, and at the Queen's Theatre there he had, on Thursday night, held one of the largest meetings which had ever taken place in that town; and a vote of thanks had been proposed to him on the occasion by an officer of her Majesty's customs. (Cheers.) From Liverpool he had come to meet them; and if anything were wanted to convince him of the spread of Chartism, it would have been in the splendid procession of that day. He firmly believed their glorious principles were more widely spread and more generally adopted now than they were on the day he entered his dungeon. (Cheers.) If there was one man in the world who was more willing than another to assist in spreading still more widely those principles, that man was himself; and he was willing to place himself entirely at the command of the working classes till Chartism should become the law of England. (Loud cheering.) No doubt some mistakes had been made during the past agitation; but he sincerely believed they were more owing to want of judgment than to any thing else. A bad turn had been given to their efforts with regard to physical-force demonstrations; and another error was the denouncing the middle classes. The physical-force demonstrations had entirely failed; and he thought nothing had been gained by attacking the middle classes. It was not that he placed much reliance on the middle classes; but still, if their services could be rendered available, they should be accepted. They might be narrowly watched, and allowed rather to assist than to lead the movement. Since he had left his dungeon, he had seen no argument which, in his mind, went to overturn the principles of Chartism. One argument, indeed, had been advanced; and that was, that the working classes were not prepared to exercise the Suffrage with advantage to the country. When this argument had been alluded to, he had put the question, why should not like causes produce like effects? And he had looked to America, and found the same principles carried out there; and when he looked to both sides of the St Lawrence, and saw on the American side a great and civilised people, with an abundance of wealth, busy towns, magnificent buildings, docks, shipping, and the hum of a busy and industrious population; and on the other side, where the people were told they were not fit to be entrusted with the Suffrage, when he saw a thin population earned a scanty subsistence amidst uncultivated heaths and gloomy forests, residing in a few scattered hamlets, which covered the heads of rebels — rebels against a Government who would turn bayonets against their breasts, and fire the roof over their heads, if they sought for those rights possessed by America — when he saw all this, he was compelled to conclude that, if Englishmen possessed the same rights as Americans, the same effect would be produced in the one country as in the other. (Cheers.) The great abundance of wealth possessed by the American people was the result of labour, which was second only to nature itself. If the people of this country would only reflect, that from their labour sprung all its wealth and magnificence, they would ask themselves why, when every thing else was going on improving, their rights alone had made no progress whatever? It was because they did not possess the Suffrage. Many agitations had been got up in the country; but there was none to equal that for the Charter. The masses, then, must be moved again — (cheers) — they must be set on foot once more, and the tide of opinion must again move along the land — that flood which was powerful enough to overturn everything but labour itself, and to establish their rights upon an unalterable basis. If any individual would point out any other agitation more important than this, he for one would give way; but when he saw what they had already achieved against the power of a corrupt press, and of a more corrupt Government, and in defiance of any power whatever but that of the millions — (cheers) — who supported them, he was more convinced than ever, that if they were only united to effect one purpose, they would be powerful enough to effect any purpose they pleased. There was no time like the present time. (Great cheering.) He had deeply and attentively studied the present state of affairs while in his dungeon, and there was one thing which promised either a peaceful change or a bloody one. He alluded to the money affairs of the country. After twenty-five years of peace, new taxes were being placed on the shoulders of the people of this country by a reforming Government. (Shame, shame!) When he turned to France, he saw that the revolution — not the late revolution, which merely deposed a Bourbon and substituted a baboon — (great laughter) — but the great revolution, which began in equality, but ended in aggrandisement — he saw that that revolution took its rise in money affairs, and in the imposition of taxes in the time of peace. The French people began to feel these taxes, as the English people do now. First one begins to complain, and then another, and then two or three together in the streets, and at last the impetuous stream rushes along, sweeping all before it. Could there be a better one than that they had seen that day? (Great cheering.) Besides the money affairs, there was another cause of the revolution for which a parallel could be found in this country. Voltaire and others overturned the bigotry of the people and the grandeur of the Church, and in pulling down the mitre he brought the throne along with it. (Cheers.) Looking at the doctrines of Voltaire, and reasoning from analogy, was there not a striking similarity in this country at the present moment? They had Socialism spreading throughout the nation; and if Socialism was not calculated to bring down the church, he did not know what was; and if it did that, and did no more harm than that, he for one, did not care how soon it took place. (Laughter.) They had also the Total Abstinence and Temperance movement — (loud cheering) — this was calculated greatly to advance their cause. When men left drinking they commenced thinking. The first thing a thinking man thought of was his dinner — (laughter) — and if he could not get any he complained till he was satisfied on that score. He then began to look out for clothing, and his other physical wants; and when these were satisfied he looked to the cultivation of the minds of his children. When they had got all this the people of this country would still complain; and why should they not? They would do right always to complain till they received the full wages due for their labour. (Cheers.) Let them look at the situation of the agricultural and factory populations of this country. See the peasantry in rags, and misery, and distress — and then look at the broad and fertile valleys covered with waving corn and luxuriant pastures, and the palace of the tyrant rising among the trees. (Loud cheering.) Then let them turn to the town, and let them point out one trade that was not over-stocked and over-peopled. (Cries of 'Not one.') Let them look to the factory people, where death presented itself under a hundred different forms, and where thousands were sinking with disease and misery into a premature grave, the victims of tyranny and murder combined. (Cheers.) Let them look to the food and clothing of the labourers even when in full employment, and let them ask which was their refuge in time of want? They might enter the army — they might enter the ranks of the rural police — they might emigrate, and carry their intelligence and their skill to other nations, and they might become criminals. They might become criminal, not because they had an innate disposition to do so, but because of their poverty and distress. But who was the cause of that poverty? The Government — the oppressors who robbed them. (Tremendous cheering.) There was no refuge for working men, then, except those which were of the worst and most fatal description. What rights did they possess to enable them to protect even the small wages they now received? They had the right to meet, and the Government had a right to disperse them. They had also the right to petition; and they might just as well petition for a hogshead of gin. (Laughter.) They had the right of Trial by Jury, and where their conviction was certain if the offence of which they were accused was a political one. (Great laughter.) It was now high time for this nation to set about obtaining their rights in earnest; and while he would recommend that the Charter should be established, he would not recommend them to take one step beyond the law. From small beginnings great endings ensued; they would gather strength as they went on, and if they were determined they would raise a tide of feeling in their favour that would flow to the foot of the throne itself. The tide of opinion ebbed and flowed; and they had lately seen it ebb, and leave the leaders of the people high and dry on the shore. That was because they were not united among themselves for one purpose. When they were not united they would necessarily be weak, and Government would take the advantage of them. Many noble patriots had come forward in the cause of liberty. They had had a Frost — (great cheering) — and his noble and patriotic friends, who had come forward and cast all upon one reckless die; and now these noble-minded men, while they wept for the fate of their distant country, sent their voices across the wide expanse of waters that separated them from it, and implored their country-men again to unite for the great cause for which they suffered. (Loud cheers, and cries of 'We will, we will.') Although he witnessed the fate of these patriots, and although the country was stained with the blood of the best and bravest of its inhabitants, that should not hinder him from advocating the great and glorious cause for which they suffered wherever he could raise his voice or thrust his head. (Cheers.) He had but just left a dungeon, and they saw he came before them neither silent nor dispirited. He would carry the Chartist flag round the whole country; and he would look for their respect and confidence no longer than while he did his duty. (Cheers.) He would go round the land and show the people that the men of Manchester were not dead — and he could wave his green scarf (the Doctor still wore the scarf presented by the women of Hulme) to show that the women of Manchester were alive to the importance of the cause. (Long continued cheering.) And now he would conclude, for they must be all tired with the fatigues of the day. (Go on, go on.) As he had told the Judges on his trial — and those present that night were far better judges of the matter than them, — (laughter,) — as he had told the Judges, he would see the Charter the law of the land yet; and he would yet meet constitutional John and plain Jack on the floor of the House of Commons — though if he did not meet them there before that time, he did not think there would be much chance of his doing so afterwards, — (great laughter,) — and have a talk with John about the constitution and with Jack about the law. (Renewed laughter.) He would tell them both that he had greatly improved by his imprisonment, and that he hoped to give them the same retirement they had given him. (Cheers and laughter.) Let the Charter be the polar star of the people, and let them not trouble themselves about corn laws or foreign politics. Let them steer for one haven, and let that haven be the Charter. Let them touch the helm with firmness and decision, peacefully, but energetically. For himself, his mind was made up upon the subject. He might meet with difficulties, but he had a mind wherewith to encounter them. His pulse had not quickened when he went into prison, nor when he came out of it. He knew no fear, and he feared no difficulty. (Cheers.) He would go on as he had done before; for the prospect of liberty would cheer him on, as the light in the cottage window cheered on the benighted traveller. He need not ask them to stand by him; and, possessed of their confidence, he should feel himself strong and ennobled — secure, though within the clutches of tyranny, and free, though under the yoke of the oppressor. The Doctor then sat down amidst a volley of cheers and clapping of hands.

The CHAIRMAN said it would now be his duty to introduce to them a man whom he had known and esteemed for some time; and who, he felt, had still greater claims on his respect since he had witnessed the manner in which he had been

153

received by his fellow-townsmen at Birmingham after he came out of Warwick Gaol. He alluded to his friend, John Collins, who would now address them.

Mr COLLINS was received with the same lively marks of interest and favour which had greeted the appearance of Dr McDouall. He addressed the meeting as fellow-slaves, and said he felt particularly proud of that opportunity of addressing the working men of Manchester. He had that morning been reading in one of the Manchester papers an article which was written with a very bitter feeling; so bitter as to be manifest in every line. In that article the writer, in reference to those whom he called the 'poor Chartists,' stated that last week he witnessed the extension of mercy by Lord Normanby to the Glasgow cotton-spinners; that this week McDouall had been set at liberty; that favours had been extended to various political prisoners; and that Collins was again blowing the dying embers of Birmingham Chartism to a blaze. (Laughter.) He thought the display of feeling they had that day made would at all events convince the writer of this article that it did not require much blowing on his part to blow Chartism in Manchester to a blaze. (Cheers.) He had long been convinced that no converts were ever made to an opinion by fine, or imprisonment, or banishment; and if he had wanted any additional argument that this was the case, it would have been afforded by the magnificent display that day made in the streets of Manchester in favour of men who had been imprisoned for their cause. (Great cheering.) He felt sure that the plans which had been adopted by the enemies of labour were the very best calculated to spread the Charter far and wide, and to impress upon the breast of every man the necessity of making any sacrifice, however great, for the attainment of that most desirable object; he felt certain that the advocacy of Chartist principles in courts of justice, and the refusal of Parliament to inquire into the treatment of Chartist prisoners, must impress on the mind of every thinking man the importance of the principles they advocated. The very excellent remarks which had fallen from Dr McDouall had given him a great deal of pleasure; and he would avail himself of that opportunity of conveying to the worthy doctor, in the name and on the behalf of the committee and the great body of the Chartists in Birmingham, the expression of their congratulations on his leaving his dungeon, and of their sympathies with his sufferings while immured in it. He would also assure him that on Monday the men of Birmingham had redeemed their pledge at a great meeting on foreign politics at Holloway Head — that pledge which had not only been made there, but at Peep Green, Kersal Moor, and all the large meetings throughout the country — the pledge that they would never agitate for any other subject — never turn to the right hand or to the left never cease their exertions till the principles of the Charter became the law of the land. (Great cheering.) His friend, McDouall, had said that since he came out of prison (where he had been himself), the only argument he had heard against the Charter was, that the working classes were not prepared to exercise the Suffrage. Now, he thought this was a mistake on the Doctor's part. He thought this was no argument at all, but merely assertion. He thought proof was necessary to constitute an argument. To be sure he did not profess to be very learned in these matters, because, from the time he was very young, he had worked for his bread; but he never thought assertions were arguments. Now, he believed that the working men as a class (for, of course, there were exceptions) were — he was going to say *as* fit, but he would say *more* fit, than any other to exercise the franchise. (Cheers.) And when their opponents said the Chartists wished to give every dishonest man a vote, he would reply that the statement was a foul calumny. The Charter made an express provision to the contrary, while, at present, if a man possessed the requisite amount of property, he voted, whether honest or dishonest; so that, even if it were true the Charter made no provision to the contrary, the Radicals might reply that they did not see why a poor rogue should not have a vote as well as a rich one. (Cheers, and laughter.) If he were disposed to look on the assertion as an argument, he would say, by giving them a vote you would raise them in their own opinion. A man who was treated badly became reckless of consequences; but if, on the contrary, he knew he had the confidence of his neighbours, he would endeavour to show that confidence was not misplaced. It might be illustrated by 10,000 instances from every day life. When a man stepped out in the morning with his shoes well blacked, he took care to pick his way through the streets lest he should soil them; but when they had become thoroughly dirty, he came splashing through every gutter home. (Laughter.) It was the same thing in morality. If a man were treated as not fit to be depended upon he would act accordingly. Neither was it the way to raise a man to imprison him for advocating the rights of liberty; and he was sure the treatment of the advocates of the people's cause would only increase the indignation of the

155

people, and deepen more and more the impression of the justice of their principles and the injustice of their oppressors. (Loud cheers.) Look at their situation. A population ill-fed and ill-clothed, toiling incessantly from morning to night. He held in his hand a copy of correspondence which took place respecting himself and his friend Lovett — (cheers) — and it contained the testimony of Sir Eardley Wilmot, a magistrate and M.P., that ninety-nine out of a hundred labourers were worse fed and clothed than felons in the prison. (Cries of 'Shame, shame!') They had experience of its truth. They heard of times of adversity and times of prosperity. Why, what was the difference to the working man? If times were a little better they only served him to get out of debt, and to take away his things from the pawnbrokers — (hear, hear,) — and then came the panic again, and he got into debt once more, and his goods were again pledged. The talk of prosperity and adversity was all stuff and nonsense — it was all adversity to the working man. ('Well done, Collins,' and cheers.) With the people breaking stones upon the roads, and their wives and little ones starving at home, was it to be wondered at that some should have talked of physical force. He could speak freely on this head, as he had never advocated physical force — he had been called an old Brummagem ginger-bread woman for not doing so — (laughter) — yet he did not wonder that some men, goaded to madness should have resorted to threats of violence, especially when he considered the sort of education they had received. (Hear, hear.) Some had none at all; and others were taught words instead of ideas. They had been taught to look up with veneration to generals who had sacked towns, depopulated villages, and made thousands of widows and orphans, and consider them the greatest men the world ever saw; and was it to be wondered at that they acted as they had done. He trusted they would soon be able to wield the far superior power of moral force, and which would enable them to establish themselves in that position which they ought to occupy. Much as had been said on the subject of physical force, it had all along been the great argument of their enemies, who had turned this country into one great arsenal to put down the demand for the Charter. (Cheers.) They might continue to spread their blue-coated gentry throughout the land, but they would never be able to change the eternal truth contained in their principles — they might go on extending their military force as much as they pleased, but they would never reconcile the people of this country to poverty, misery, and degradation.

156

(Great cheering.) God had decreed that they should eat their bread by the sweat of their brow; but man had ordained that their brows should sweat, but that the bread should be eaten by others. This they were not content to do. (Cheers.) But he would now conclude. They were tired, and he was tired. ('No, no!') He was tired, at least, and he felt it was not in good taste to keep them there any longer after the fatigues of the procession, especially as he should again have an opportunity of addressing them on Monday. He hoped, indeed, that he should meet them often — for it was only by the interchange of converse between man and man that they could hope to improve their condition. It was not by groaning, or shouting, or hissing, that they would gain their object, but by meeting and instructing each other. Again thanking them for the glorious display which they had made that day — and again congratulating them on the presence of McDouall once more amongst them, he begged to express, in Mr Lovett's name, his regret at not being able to visit them. Nothing but weakness of frame prevented him from coming; his heart had never quailed — his spirit had never shrunk from the cause — (cheers) — though his body had been bent down, and, he was sorry to say, his constitution was so weakened and impaired, that it was doubtful whether he would ever be the man again he formerly was. (Loud cries of 'Shame, shame!' 'The bloody Whigs!') Still the heart and the spirit of the noble patriot never failed him; and he (Mr Collins) was the bearer of the expression of his attachment to the cause of liberty, and of his determination still to advocate it with all the strength that tyrants had left him, and with all the ability that God had given him. Mr Collins then sat down amidst prolonged cheering.

Mr WHEELER announced that, owing to the premature shutting of the doors, the committee had got into difficulties, and a collection in aid of the expenses would be made at the doors. He also exhorted those present to subscribe to the relief fund, and announced that all the dinner tickets for Monday were sold, and that persons would be admitted to the gallery on the payment of sixpence each.

A vote of thanks was then proposed to the Chairman, when a person in the room proposed 'Three cheers for Feargus O'Connor.' On the suggestion of Mr Collins, three cheers were given for all the political martyrs, and the vote of thanks to the Chairman having been passed, the meeting broke up.

THE DINNER.

The dinner took place at the Hall of Science, in Camp Field, on Monday evening. This building is the largest available for public meetings in Manchester, and is capable of containing 3,000 persons. On the present occasion it was laid out for dining 500, the greatest number the room would conveniently hold for the purpose. There were eight tables extending the whole length of the room, besides the cross-table for the distinguished guests. The hall was hung round with the banners which figured in the procession, and decorated with garlands. A portrait of McDouall was hung on the right of the Chairman, and a capital likeness of Richardson was placed on the left. The portrait of O'Connor was at the lower end of the room, facing the Chairman.

About seven o'clock the guests began to arrive; and at half-past seven the Old Foresters' band entered the Hall, and enlivened the company with a few sprightly airs. Some of the wives of the Manchester political martyrs were also present. At a few minutes to eight the Chairman (the Rev. Mr Schofield, of Every-street Chapel), accompanied by the distinguished guests (Dr McDouall and Mr Collins), Messrs James Leech, Deegan, Heywood, Dr Fox, and delegates from Ashton and Derby, entered the room, and took their seats at the cross-table, Dr McDouall being on the right hand of the Chairman, and Mr Collins on the left. They were received with the most enthusiastic applause, the band striking up, 'See the conquering hero comes!'

The CHAIRMAN having asked a blessing, the company fell on the eatables, the band playing, 'Oh, the roast beef of Old England.' The dinner, which was plain and substantial, was provided by the dinner committee themselves, they not being able to get any one to undertake it, because they would not allow any intoxicating liquor to be drunk. It was cooked at the Hall, which possesses every facility for the purpose, and was served up hot, and, as far as we were able to learn, gave satisfaction to every one present. A bit of a scramble took place for the plum-puddings, but it was more the result of the eagerness of the guests than of any want of arrangements on the part of the committee.

On the cloth being removed, at about twenty minutes to ten, The CHAIRMAN said it now devolved upon him to propose the first toast; it was 'The Sovereignty of the people.'

Mr COLLINS — I beg leave to move that we drink that toast

158

upstanding, at all events, and with three times three.

The toast was drunk with three times three, all the company standing.

Air — 'The Marseilles Hymn.'

Mr JAMES LEECH responded to the toast. He said the 'Sovereignty of the people!' had been so often dinged into their ears, on all public occasions, for the last ten years, that the toast appeared almost a matter of course, and a mere form. No meeting of the Whigs had taken place without their bawling it out lustily, they all the while having the firm determination to trample under foot the last remnant of the liberties of the people, under the idea of serving their own party interests. So far as the well-being and happiness of the working classes of this country was concerned, the sentiment of the 'Sovereignty of the people' had been reduced by the Whigs to an insulting and bitter mockery. (Cheers.) But the working men were at length beginning to form a proper estimate of their own importance in society; and when they properly understood their own rights, all the effects of bad legislation would speedily vanish before them. Who, let him ask, were the people? The Queen was called by some one of the people; and her husband was, he supposed, another of the people. Then there were Right Rev. Prelates, and the Hon. Members of the House of Commons, the drones who fattened upon the pension-list, and all the tools and satellites of power, they also were estimated as the people. But they, the working classes of the country, who by their labour, their ingenuity, their skill, and their industry produced all the wealth and luxuries enjoyed by the others; they were not considered by these men as belonging to the people, and therefore the toast was a bitter and insulting mockery on their part. (Cheers.) He hoped it would shortly be a reality, and not a mockery, and that they would show the world the 'sovereignty of the people' was a reality and not a theory. In a land flowing with milk and honey, the people were starving, while a set of idlers usurped all the wealth, and then denied that those who produced it were the people. Why, the idle rascals! if it were not for the care the working classes took of them, they would run through the streets in a state of nakedness. (Laughter.) They had passed a law to send every man to the treadmill who was found naked in the streets; and the very law they had passed would apply to themselves, if a common measure of justice was dealt out to them.

159

(Cheers.)

The CHAIRMAN said the next toast on the list was, 'The Charter, and nothing less, though dungeons await its advocates.' (The toast was drunk with three times three.)

Mr CHAPPELL, of Stockport, responded to the toast, and, in the course of his remarks said, he represented a town where twelve men had been thrown into a dungeon for advocating the principles of the Charter. Should their time be spent in prison in vain? Should they now turn their backs on it, and say they would have nothing to do with it? Would any man or woman there consent to take anything less than the Charter? He hoped the time was not far distant when the men of England, Scotland, and Ireland would arise as one man for the Charter, and base the throne on equality and justice. (Cheers.)

The CHAIRMAN said they had now arrived at that particular stage of the proceedings, when it would be necessary to advert to the more immediate business of the evening. The toast he was now about to propose was the health of their worthy guest, Dr McDouall.

No sooner were the words out of the Chairman's lips than the whole company rose and gave nine cheers, and the band struck up 'Scots wha hae.' as though the toast had been formally announced, though it was quite evident that the Rev. Chairman's address had been cut short by the enthuiasm of the meeting. The Chairman having at length announced the toast in due form.

Dr McDOUALL rose, and was again greeted with every demonstration of cordial esteem. He said he felt, as it were, quite overpowered in rising to address them. The change from a prison to such a scene as that which now met his eye was very great. When he compared the damp walls and solitary hours of his dungeon with the gay company and faces around him, the great change struck upon his heart, and prevented a free expression of his feelings. It would not be necessary for him to enter into a detail of the feelings of pleasure with which he witnessed so large an assembly as the present brought together, not to do honour to one individual in particular, or any number of individuals, but to do honour to the principles for which he had suffered, and who were resolved to have the Charter, and nothing but the Charter. Nothing could give him greater delight than to go on with them to agitate for the Charter, led by that tune which goes at once to the heart of every Scotsman. (Cheers.) He was not going to allude to the dungeon into which

160

he had been thrown by the Whigs. He despised them and their dungeons too. (Great cheering.) They had laboured hard and long to destroy him; but, though a small person, his body had the strength of iron, and his spirit had been unbroken by all their machinations. (Cheers.) He had gone through their dungeons, and had felt their force; but he had forgot their prosecutions and he remembered only them. (Long and tremendous cheering.) From the moment he left his dungeon gates he swore in his heart he would have revenge. (Tremendous cheering.) He should not have that species of revenge which was implied by the general acceptation of the term — his revenge would be to see the Charter the law of the land — to contend, peaceably, if he must — yes, peaceably if he must — (laughter) — for the great principles to carry out which they were united, and for which he hoped all present were prepared to suffer, and, if necessary, to die. (Cheers.) He was young in years, and he should yet live to see the Charter established; and nothing could add more to his resolution to support the cause than the imprisonment the Whigs had given him; and if he had been altered at all by that imprisonment, it was that he would now go a little further than the Charter. While in his dungeon, he had studied the subject attentively; and he looked at the Charter but as the stepping-stone to social improvement — as an arch, a door-way, through which the people must press to obtain their rights, and cover the nation with real and substantial benefits. He thought persecution was the surest way to establish those principles. He ardently and sincerely wished the Whigs would go further with their persecutions; and if they produced the same effect upon others as upon him, they would regret they had ever sent one Chartist to prison to study more intensely how they might carry out its principles. The Whigs had learnt nothing from the experience of the past; and he was afraid that neither judges, nor jury, nor sentences, nor agitation had produced any effect on them. The people might lash them as they like, but if they got any thing else from them but villainy, fraud and oppression, he was much mistaken. The effect of these persecutions was to bind more strongly together the people and their leaders, and to plant the standard of Chartism a little further in advance. Both leaders and people had been opposed by a corrupt press; but let them but once firmly unite, keeping one point, and one only, in view, and then there would be found no barrier strong enough to resist them — no government powerful enough to put them down. (Cheers.) The present government had already tried to do

161

so, but had they succeeded? No. They had not destroyed the Chartists, but the Chartists had destroyed them, or were in the course of doing so. They had risen in public esteem, and brought thousands over to their side in the teeth of their oppressors, and that in defiance of the paid press. The working men of this country had shewn they knew how to distinguish their enemies from their friends; they had now got a press of their own — (loud and long-continued cheering) — long might it advocate the rights of labour. There were many now in prision connected with the people's press; but they must come out as he had done — their tyrants could not deprive them of a week or rob them of a day; and, however slow the progress of time, their dungeon doors must at length be thrown open, and they must be set at liberty. Yes! the time was fast approaching when they would meet their friend, and his friend also, Feargus O'Connor — (rapturous cheering) — and he cared not how soon that time arrived. But that time would come; and when O'Connor was free, there would be another true, good, and honest man at liberty. (Loud cheers.) The gaols in almost every part of the country were filled with victims. Indeed, there was no occasion for him to point it out; there were evidence there present to prove the assertion. If they looked at home they would find where Whig tyranny had passed, and where Whig tyranny might yet meet with its reward. But the Chartists had not only established a press of their own; there was scarcely a court of justice in the country which had not been converted into a Chartist meeting, and where its advocates had not written up the name of Chartism over the wigs of the Judges. (Laughter.) They had converted the courts into rostrums; they had surmounted the impediments thrown in their way by both judges and juries; and his worthy colleague, Collins — (cheers) — and himself were there that night to celebrate their triumphs, in spite of every obstacle. From what he had heard of late events in Birmingham, and from what he had witnessed in Manchester on Saturday, and again that night, he came to the conclusion that the Whig persecution had utterly failed, and that, instead of putting down Chartism, they had only arrested a few Chartists. (Cheers, and laughter.) They had lately heard great talk of the clemency of the Whigs, but he did not know where to look for it. If ever there were a time for the exercise of clemency it was when the Queen married, and thus cast a new burden upon the shoulders of the people; this was the time to cast off the burden of honesty and liberty which weighed upon

162

the gaols, and thus make amends for the burden they had placed upon the pension list. (Hear, hear.) They now heard of the Queen's gracious intention on their behalf when a certain event should take place. On that occasion it was said there was to be a gaol delivery — (roars of laughter) — and of the two deliveries he knew which would give the greatest satisfaction to the country. (Cheers.) At the same time he should have no objection — and he thought they would have no objection either — that the 'little Doctor' (alluding to himself) should officiate at both. (Great laughter and cheering.) If it would not be trespassing too much upon their time, allow him briefly to allude to what had taken place previous to his friend Collins and himself being thrust into prison. They all knew that the late Convention, which had been elected by the people, surpassed in ability and honesty the House of Commons; and, as a body, exhibited talent and prudence, and left documents and deeds behind them, which would have conferred honour upon any legislative assembly. (Cheers.) No doubt, errors had been committed; but they were that description of errors which experience would have quickly rectified; and he mentioned them, not to cast blame upon the members of that Convention, or upon the people who elected them, but simply to prevent their renewal.

The first great error was the physical force idea. A wrong course was taken in this respect; and much deception took place with respect to the real strength of the people, who had been gathered together without art, and kept together without science. (Hear, hear.) Thousands upon thousands joined their associations, but no real union or organization was ever effected; for, if they had been, the Convention would have continued sitting in defiance of Government, and no one would have dared to resist them. It appeared to him that these associations might be aptly compared to a bundle of sticks, which might easily be broken separately, but, united, would set the strongest and the most powerful at defiance — if they had been united, they would not have turned out to be a broken reed in the hour of danger. At the same time, he did not wish to remove the sentiments he had formerly expressed or entertained. His heart was in the right place, still; but he was bound to look, in the first place, to the welfare of the cause itself, and secondly, to the security of his bail. (Hear, hear.) He thought, then, that the best plan would be to forget physical force, and in the beginning and in the ending of their proceedings to adopt

163

peace as their motto. He would not tell them, as the Whigs had been in the habit of telling them, that what he said to them as a body did not apply to them as individuals; nor would he imitate Daniel O'Connell, who recommended blarneying a man before he was knocked down, but he would counsel peace in reality. He did not do this out of any consideration for himself, but he considered it politic at present to be cautious. The storm must come, unless their enemies gave them their natural privileges, but while they saw it approaching, he would counsel them all to say nothing about physical force. He had never advised that which he was not himself willing to adopt, and he would ask the people to follow only where he led the way himself. (Cheers.) However much good might have arisen from the imprisonment of some of the labourers in the cause, the people must for the time being have been injured. If a man was a good speaker or a sage general, his loss would be severely felt during his imprisonment, while a benefit would be felt on his arrest, his trial, and his liberation, while the Court of Justice would be transformed into a Chartist meeting; but still it would be better to do without this, if possible. There was another error which had been committed. The middle-class, as a body, had been denounced, and this, he thought, was decidedly wrong. As a body, he, himself, entertained contempt for the middle-classes, and pity for their ignorance; but still he thought such denunciations useless. There were two courses open to the people with respect to the middle-classes. If they were determined on carrying on their plans alone, then the sword must be brought into action. But this would be highly dangerous to their cause — all would be thrown upon the hazard of the die, and there would be many chances against them. If, on the contrary, a junction took place between the two parties, a benefit might be derived from it. He should be the last man to ask the working classes to go over to the middle class men, or even to invite them to join with them; but he should go against his conscience if he counselled them to refuse their assistance if they were willing to join the people in their movement. (Hear, hear.) Still he would not allow them to possess any controul over the movement; — (hear) — and if they consulted their own interests they would join it, for they were interested in ͟ining cheap Government, and consequently in the carrying ͟arter. The speaker then alluded to the various agitations ͟d been set on foot, and advised the people to have ͟o with any of them, but to stick to the Charter. He would adopt no agitation, he said, that had not the Charter for its basis. With regard to this subject he wished to notice a special delusion now abroad — the most deceptive trick which had been brought forward since the Reform Bill; he meant the agitation now getting up through the country on the subject of our foreign policy. It had attracted his attention immediately on his leaving his prison; and when, on inquiry, he found there was a talk of the impeachment of Lord Palmerston, and heard that some of the leaders of the Chartists were engaged in it, he began to suspect that all was not right, and although he had not heard much of it, he had good reason for considering it the most special delusion ever thrown out as a bone of contention. Their friend Collins, who knew more of the matter than he did, would no doubt explain all about it. Their first object, it appeared, was to excite in the minds of the people of this country a fear of invasion. (Hear, hear.) They wished to excite those prejudices which existed in all nations, the most barbarous as well as the most civilised, against foreign invaders — and they talked about Russia invading this country, and driving away our flocks and herds. Why, suppose she did. Perhaps, in that case, some of our starving population might be enabled to get a taste of mutton — (laughter) — while those who had no *stake* in the country might happily become possessed of a mutton *steak*. (Great laughter.) Who would believe the people of this country would submit to the Russians, who were the most contemptible people in the world. One English line-of-battle ship would sink ten of their cockle-shells, and 1,000 English working men would beat 10,000 of their army. And suppose they did come, would it be any worse for them, the people? ('No, no!') It appears that the evils of foreign invasion would at least fall upon the rich as well as upon the poor; but the evils of Whig Government fell upon the poor alone. (Loud cheering.) No, working men of this country had nothing to fear from an invasion — (cheers) — to them an invasion would be welcome — (loud and continued cheering) — and especially if it were an invasion of their brother Americans. (Continued cheering.) Would the people do anything else, under those circumstances, than put their hands into their pockets? No; and no system could be worse than the present system of legislation. What did the people of this country care about Lord Palmerston, or Constitutional Jack, or Plain John? (Laughter.) What was it to them if these men conspired still further against the nation? It would only be another crime the more; and as soon

165

as the Charter became the law of the land, they would all be swept off together. This agitation about our foreign policy came very ill from Birmingham, and especially from an Attwood. In case of a war with Russia, which was evidently the end the leaders of this agitation proposed to themselves, Birmingham would be perhaps the only town which would profit by it. He understood, that at a meeting they lately held in Birmingham, they had the Circassian flag flying over the hustings. (Hear, hear, hear.) Though he would willingly serve the Circassians, he would scorn to fight under their flag — or even under the flag of Britain. (Hear, and cheers.) The only banner he would ever fight under, was that of the rights of labour, and for the People's Charter. (Loud cheering.) But these agitators had got a double object in view. It was not only to excite the country to war with Russia, but also to destroy the present movement for the Charter. They had taken away — he would not say the best of their leaders, for they were unworthy of the title, and paid them for advocating what they called the rights of citizenship. In his opinion the suffrage was the best right of citizenship, and he wanted no other. (Cheers.) The men of Birmingham had done right to reject them, and he understood not one hand had been held up for their resolutions. He had thought proper to make these remarks, as many arguments had been advanced by this party calculated to mislead the people; and the effect of them would only be to divide their ranks, and ruin the sole object for which working men ought alone to contend. The great principles of the Charter ought not to be narrowed down to an impeachment of a Secretary of State; and all minor differences ought to be avoided for the purpose of advocating its principles, which would give equal rights and liberties to all. He had intended to have said something that evening with respect to the power of the masters; but, as he had occupied so much of their time, he would bring his remarks to a conclusion, by observing, that, as the men of Manchester had now so strikingly shown their attachment to the Charter, he should now offer himself to them as an advocate of its principles. To no other movement would he lend himself; and when any other was brought forward he would oppose it. Many ˹crifices had been made in this cause — and many had fallen by ˹ way. They had seen Frost narrowly escape. Frost, the just ˹ he worthy father, the equitable magistrate, — (cheers,) — ˹ banished his native soil because he dared to advocate ˹ labour. He, for one, and John Collins for another, were determined to advocate the Charter, which was the best guarantee for those rights; and when it was established, the commerce and trade of the nation would be enlarged, her ports filled with shipping, her cottages happy, and peace and happiness be the lot of the working man. God grant that that soon might be the case; and now that he was liberated — now that he was once more free, he would put his shoulder to the wheel as long as he had a spirit above the shackles of a slave — as long as he had a spirit to contend with the oppresors of his fellow men. The Doctor sat down amidst tremendous cheering.

The CHAIRMAN said the next toast on the list was 'Frost, Williams, and Jones; and may they be speedily restored to the bosom of their families.'

The toast was drank in solemn silence, the band playing a solemn dirge.

Mr TILLMAN addressed the company as assertors of their rights. He would not call them slaves, for they alone were slaves who submitted willingly to tyranny. The toast to which he had to respond was one of a most delicate subject. He advised them to make every exertion for their return; and argued, from the case of the Glasgow Spinners, that if they were unanimous they would be successful in those exertions.

The CHAIRMAN then proposed the next toast — 'Messrs Collins and Lovett, and all our liberated friends.'

Mr COLLINS was received with immense cheering. He assured them that it was with very peculiar feelings he rose to acknowledge the high honour they had done him by the manner in which they had drunk his health, as well as that of Mr Lovett, and the other liberated Chartists. If anything could recompense him for his sufferings, it would be the knowledge that through them he had obtained the esteem and respect of his fellow-men. And even this recompense, great as it was, formed but a small part of his consolation. The sufferings and imprisonment of the Chartist leaders had not been without their effect, in respect that they had called the attention of the people of that country to the principles of that Charter for which they suffered; and the consequence had been, that the enemies of the liberties of the country rued the day when they throught they would put down Universal Suffrage by the tyrannical statutes of Whig and Tory legislation. (Cheers.) There was a certain adage, the truth of which was admitted on all hands — 'The blood of the martyr is the seed of the Church;' and he felt sure that, by the sufferings of the advocates of the Charter, its glorious principles

167

would be advanced at a railway speed. (Applause.) Allow him, then, in his own name, to return them his thanks — allow him, also, to return them thanks in the name of his friend, Lovett — (tremendous cheering) — than whom, he was sure, a better man existed not in the country, nor a more devoted friend to the people's cause. ('I wish he was here,' was remarked by some individual.) Some one had said, 'I wish he was here;' he (Mr Collins) wished so too. It was not a false pretext which prevented his being there. He had seen him in the dungeon's gloom, and he had heard his aspirations for his wife and children — he had heard his devotions for the success of the people's cause; and had observed that it was not in the power of persecution to make him swerve from advocating the rights of liberty, the privileges of the people, and the happiness of the whole human race. (Great cheering.) What was it that brought this patriotic individual into prison? It was no threatening language held on the spur of the moment — it was no vain and empty boast, but it was the effect of a calm, deliberate resolution. The Convention had decided that it was of the greatest importance to publish a certain address from them to the people, and which was to be signed by every member. Lovett, who foresaw the danger, immediately said, 'No; it is sure to bring down a persecution on all who sign it. One victim will be enough! I'll sign it!' and he did sign it, as secretary to the Convention. (Rapturous applause.) And why was Lovett thus willing deliberately to run into danger? Because the rights of the people had been invaded — because a peaceable meeting of the men of Birmingham had been dispersed by an unconstitutional force. Therefore it was that Lovett had raised his voice, and protested against this tyranny; and rather than that the working classes should quietly submit to have their rights and privileges trampled under foot, either by blue or red-coated slaves of power, he (Mr Collins) would say, as Lovett had said, 'Welcome once more the imprisonment of Warwick gaol.' (Tremendous cheers.) And he would now again say, it was a brutal — it was an unconstitutional act, on the part of those who committed it. (Applause.) And now, having disposed of this question, he would allude to another. He saw women before him whose husbands were now suffering for their cause, and for his own. No doubt those present sincerely sympathised with them and their husbands; but he could assure those persons that it was but a small part of those sufferings of which they were capable of forming an adequate idea. They might be able to imagine the

168

scanty fire, and the stone walls, and the long gloomy nights of the cheerless dungeons. But these formed but a small part of their sufferings. When the minds of the poor prisoners reverted to their once cheerful firesides, and when they pictured to themselves that now their wives were comfortless, and, perhaps, destitute, and mingling their tears with those of their children — and, when a train of ideas like these was broken in upon, by the shutting of ponderous doors, the drawing of massive bolts, and the clanking of heavy chains, then it was that they felt that they were indeed sufferers, though in the cause of freedom. To be sure, when they again reflected on the principles for which they suffered, they were enabled in the midst of their dejection to say — 'The principles of truth and justice require that I should be thus treated, rather than that those principles should be allowed to die.' He himself had been actively engaged in agitation since him emancipation, and had, therefore, been much separated from his wife; but he could not stop one quarter of an hour in her society without a reference being made to some event which occurred during his imprisonment, and each of which had been the cause of much suffering. But why did he allude to this? Not certainly to raise any painful feelings in their minds, but to press upon them to take care that the temporary widow should not suffer from want, while their husbands were imprisoned in the cause. He was sure they would take care of them; and it was unnecessary for him to say any thing more on the subject. (Hear, hear.) And here he would observe, that those who opposed the working classes, asserted that the greater part of the criminals of the country were working men, and that almost all the vice in the land was to be laid at their doors. These calumnious assertions were actively bandied about by those who kept them in subjection. Why were not the working men properly treated in this respect? Because they had never stepped forward to do themselves justice. Who had been the authors and writers for the press of this country? Almost always the middle and the higher classes; these men were notoriously ignorant of the opinions and feelings and habits of the working classes. Who knew anything of the history of the working classes? Some books had been published with some pretensions of the kind; but they really contained nothing at all to the purpose; and he should not be surprised if a good history of the working classes should one day be published by one of themselves, and which would really deserve its title. Then, again, if there was any good thing done by any of the middle classes, it appeared in all the newspapers. If any of them gave a few pounds for a charitable purpose, every body was sure to hear of it; but nobody heard of the kindly sympathies of the working man, for his unfortunate brother, when he sat whole nights by his sick bed, or when he clothed his ragged children, and shared his hard crust with his family. (Hear, hear.) All this was done privately, and no noise was made about it, and therefore there was no idea on the part of the middle classes, that working men possessed any feeling or humanity. Thus all the good was attributed to the middle classes, and all the bad to the working classes. They formed their ideas of working men from reports of courts of justice and police-offices; but who were the persons, the thieves and bad characters, who usually figure there? Were they working men? (Cheers.) No! They were men who did no work, but who lived upon plunder, and it was as unjust to class them with the working men, as it would be to class them among the middle class. (Hear, hear, and cheers.) He was quite certain that, during the time he was in Warwick gaol, there were quite as many of the middle classes who took their trials there for crime as there were of the working classes. He had alluded to this subject because he was a working man himself; and he would never submit to hear his class slandered without elevating his voice in their defence. (Cheers.) Their friend, Dr McDouall, in addressing them the other evening, had told them that if they desired a proof of what working men were capable of effecting, they would find it in the magnificent buildings which they had erected throughout the land. He thought the minds of the working men were another proof. While the pyramids of Egypt and Pompey's pillar were crumbling into dust, the spirit of the institutions of Greece and Rome shone forth in the popular mind at the present day; and yet they were told that they were not fit to be entrusted with the franchise. Let them look at any country, at any period of the world's history, where democratic institutions prevailed, and they would find they had uniformly proved beneficial. He had already alluded to Greece and Rome; he would now give them a modern instance — the Democratic Cantons of Switzerland. In that country at present prosperity blessed all classes. The laws were few and simple, readily understood, and promptly obeyed. Custom-houses, excise-laws, and prohibitory duties of all descriptions were banished from among them. Justice was promptly and cheaply administered; and on any attempt being made to attack their rights, the spirit of liberty

170

animated every heart and nerved every arm to defend them. (Loud cheers.) Again, let them look at Norway. She had not half the natural resources of her neighbour Sweden; but owing to the institutions of Norway being democratical, and those of Sweden aristocratical, the former country flourished and prospered, while the latter bore evident marks of decay and misery. Then there was America. (Cheers.) Certainly America had one stain upon her star-bespangled banner: the slave trade; but that, like its damning brother we had in this country — the infant slave trade — (tremendous cheering) — did not proceed from the democratic institutions America now possessed. No. It was the last remnant of Aristocratical Government — a plague-spot that resulted from Kingly dominion. (Cheers.) He was perfectly sure he possessed the sympathies of his audience, who were most of them working men. He trusted that they would not much longer be contented to bear the brand of slavery that had been affixed upon them. He trusted they would proclaim aloud, 'We never will be contented slaves — we never will be contented to toil like beasts of burden, and be deprived of the power to support the wives of our bosoms, and the children of our loins.' (Great cheering.) Let them never mind the talk of physical force — let them say nothing about it, and the force of truth should stalk through the land, and cover their oppressors with eternal shame, and tyranny should be ashamed to show itself. Their enemies dreaded the power of truth more than any thing else. Let them proclaim their wrongs, and never mind what was said of them for doing so. Let them not be afraid even of suffering imprisonment. Let their conduct be determined, let their exertions be increased, and the day of their success would not be far distant. From the manner in which they had responded to the sentiment proposed by the Chair, he did not think they came there so much to express their attachment to him as to the great principles of liberty for which he had suffered. Those principles were mighty, and must prevail. Though there were difficulties in the way, there were none that might not be overcome with prudence and determination; and men who understood those principles would be able to carry them out. Mr Collins addressed the meeting for some time longer, and then sat down amidst great and reiterated cheering.

The CHAIRMAN proposed the next toast, 'Feargus O'Connor, and the speedy liberation of all Chartists.'

The toast was drunk with three times three, the company all standing, and the band playing the air of 'Rory O'More.'

Mr LITTLER, of Salford, came forward to respond to the toast. He said Feargus O'Connor was one of the greatest patriots the world ever saw; and he had been presented to this country by one of the greatest traitors to his own country that ever existed — he meant Daniel O'Connell, — (cheers,) — a man who fattened upon the spoils of his betrayed and misled countrymen. The people of England had received Feargus O'Connor with open arms; for advocating their claims he had been thrown into a dungeon; and he felt certain that when he came out of his dungeon he would come out as the gold seven times purified, and that he would be the same Feargus O'Connor still, — (loud cheers,) — and that he would never cease agitating till the principles he had so ably advocated had become the law of the land. Though Feargus O'Connor was as the caged lion, he was not asleep — he was still studying their interests, though he had been snatched from them. He (Mr Littler) had lately communicated with him; and he could assure them he stuck more firmly than ever to his motto, 'Universal Suffrage, and no surrender!' and he trusted that henceforward it would also be adopted as the motto of them all. — (Cheers.)

The CHAIRMAN then said that, in connection with the previous toast, he had to propose 'Arthur O'Connor, the exile of Erin.' (Cheers.) Mr Deegan would respond to it.

The toast was drunk with great enthusiasm, and the band played 'The Exile of Erin.'

Mr DEEGAN, in responding to it, said he was glad it was now twelve o'clock, as it would save him the trouble of making a speech. He did not know why he was called upon to respond to this toast, unless, indeed, it was because he was in Irishman. (Laughter.) He felt himself incompetent to do justice to this toast. He thought that every one, English, Irish, or Scotch, must deserve the thanks of all the Reformers in the country, who abandoned rank, fortune, and connections, rather than be the tool of a corrupt Administration. He thought the conduct of Arthur O'Connor ought to endear him to every man who had the cause of liberty at heart, for he had sacrificed a peerage and £20,000 a-year, rather than make a sacrifice of his conscience. He should not make a long speech, but he trusted that what they had heard that night would awake them up. They had heard it often said, that all the working men wanted was a fair day's wages for a fair day's work; but he thought they ought to get all they earned, and he would not give a bunch of radishes for any reform which would not give something like what was

172

represented on that canvass. (Here Mr Deegan pointed to a representation of a Social Community, which adorns the hall.) He meant he would not value any reform which did not give them a comfortable home. (Cheers.) Let them not spend their time in denouncing Whig or Tory; but endeavour to convince every person opposed to them that the happiness and prosperity of the whole country depended upon an equitable distribution of wealth. The working classes must be determined to enjoy all the wealth they themselves produced, or otherwise they would always be in a state of strife and dissatisfaction. He thanked them for the manner in which they had drank the health of Arthur O'Connor; and, although it might never reach him, yet it might be a source of satisfaction to his friends in prison, that the labouring class and the people of Manchester had done themselves the honour of drinking the health of a man who had shown magnanimity and disinterestedness in the cause of an oppressed people. (Loud cheering.)

The Chairman said the next toast on the list was, 'The 'Northern Star,' and the whole Radical Press.'

Drank with three times three. Air — 'Marseilles Hymn.'

Mr ABEL HEYWOOD said there was only one addition he should like to make to the toast he had the honour to respond to, and that was, the 'Northern Star,' and its worthy editor, the Rev. W. Hill. (Loud Cheers.) The name of the proprietor of the 'Star' was entirely beyond it with respect to anything which might be said in reference to the merits of the 'Star' itself; but still it would be impossible to descant on its merits without giving an equal tribute of praise to the individual who first established it. (Cheers.) To the men of Lancashire and Yorkshire who assisted the proprietor in establishing the 'Star,' the people of the United Kingdom were also largely indebted. The noble and dauntless proprietor of the 'Star' was the first to agitate the kingdom for the establishment of the Charter — the result of this was the establishment of the 'Star,' and the establishing of the 'Star' was the groundwork upon which the McDoualls, and Lovetts, and Collins were established. Would to God they had a 'Northern Star' in every town throughout the kingdom! Would to God that every town could write upon the pillars of their churches, 'A 'Northern Star' to be obtained here.' The very existence of such papers would be a guarantee that the Charter would be obtained. Only three weeks since he saw the lion in his den — (enthusiastic cheering) — bearded by the vile Whiglings who misgoverned them — he saw the noble

173

and fearless lion crushing the contemptible — what should he call them? — the contemptible beetles. (Laughter.) The spirit of the man was not crushed — (loud cheers) — he was as firmly as every attached to his principles — as determined as ever to carry the Charter. But should the tyrants keep him where he was — should they send him to his grave — the people of this country would not let the 'Star' die — it would still shine. (Loud cheering.) To those other papers which advocated the people's rights they also owed their thanks; and to the editor of the 'Northern Liberator' especially their cordial thanks were due. To the 'Statesman' also the people of this country were a little indebted, and to other papers published in various parts of the country their mite of praise would be freely given; but to the 'Star' which alone was the people's paper, they would freely give their tribute of heartfelt admiration. (Cheers.)

The CHAIRMAN then gave the last toast on the list — 'The ladies.'

Drunk with all the honours, the band playing 'The bonny breast-knots.'

Mr WHEELER responded to the toast in a humorous speech, which excited much laughter and applause.

It was now half-past twelve, and the chairman and the distinguished guests having quitted the Hall, the company broke up.

Thus concluded the reception of McDouall and Collins by the men of Manchester; and whether we consider the great interest excited among the people; or the intense feeling displayed towards those liberated patriots; or the harmony and cordiality subsisting among the Chartist on the occasion, it must be allowed on all hands that a more important and heart-cheering demonstration never took place in Manchester, distinguished, as it has always been, for its attachment to the political rights and privileges of the working classes. A new era in Chartism may be confidently dated from these most gratifying proceedings, which reflect honour on all connected with them.

17 Newcastle Placards, July 1839

From Thomas Ainge Devyr, 'The Odd Book of the Nineteenth Century' (1880) p. 180

CHARTIST PLACARD

Julian Harney was arrested last night in Bedlington.
MEN OF DURHAM AND NORTHUMBERLAND. — Your oppressors have set the majesty of the people at utter defiance. They have determined that you shall live a life of toil, and die a death of hunger when you can toil no more. If you do not submit to this, they will consign you to a bloody grave by the grand old argument, 'the bayonet, the bullet, the halter.'

CORPORATION PLACARD

Whereas. Certain ill-disposed persons are in the habit of meeting within the limits of this borough and using inflammatory and seditious language, calculated to make Her Majesty's subjects discontented with their condition and to produce terror in the minds of the population.

This, therefore, is to give notice that these tumultuous assemblages will not be longer suffered to take place within the precincts of this borough.

JOHN FIFE, Mayor
In the name of the Corporation
God Save the Queen

CHARTIST COUNTER-PLACARD

Whereas. Certain men calling themselves the Corporation of Newcastle-on-Tyne, have presumed to call in question the inalienable right of Englishmen to meet, discuss and petition the Queen and Parliament for a redress of their grievances; and

Whereas. These men have presumed to forbid the exercise of

175

a right founded in the Constitution, and have assumed the power which does not belong even to the Queen and the Parliament;

Now, therefore, we the council of the Northern Political Union, proclaim to the people of this Borough and the surrounding neighbourhood, that it is their duty to meet for the exercise of this Constitutional right, and show to the Corporation of Newcastle-on-Tyne that this assumed power of theirs is held in utter contempt by all good Englishmen.

God Save the People

POSTSCRIPT. — A meeting will be held in the Forth every evening at half past six.

18 The General Convention of the Industrious Classes

(a) Report of a speech given by James Paul Cobbett, delegate for the West Riding of Yorkshire, at a dinner for the delegates

From the 'Northern Star', 9 February 1839

He returned thanks for having been elected a Delegate for the West Riding of Yorkshire. He would not belong to a Convention that included any of that patriotic treachery which distinguished Daniel O'Connell. (awful groans and yells) He (Mr C.) would support the Charter generally speaking; but he did not think so much about the Ballot, although Mr O'Connell had often protested that he blubbered and wept when he went to bed because he could not persuade Lord John Russell to adopt it. (Loud laughter) He adduced an instance of a poor man being most cruelly treated by a great merchant in New York, for having voted for a Democrat instead of a Federal candidate, although it was under the screen of the Ballot. This helped to show that the Ballot was a fallacy. He desired the Republican Constitution as it had been within two hundred years recognised in England. But if the people were fairly and fully represented, then he would agree to a Legislature of King, Lords and Commons. He was not much attached, however, to any form of Government, being of opinion with one of the greatest of our poets that the best Government was that which was best administered. (Cheers).

(b) Letter from John Frost to William Lovett, Secretary of the Convention

From the 'Northern Star', 6 April 1839

Newport Monmouthshire
April 2nd, 1839

My Dear Lovett, — I left London on Thursday morning, and I arrived at Gloucester in the evening. On Friday I started for Stroud, to fulfil the promise I made to the Convention, to have a little serious conversation with 'Little Finality's' electors. The

177

morning was very fine. When I got to Stroud, I saw the walls placarded announcing a meeting of the inhabitants, 'to take into consideration the National Petition'. When I arrived at the inn where the committee was sitting, I was received with three hearty cheers. The people were assembling in thousands, and at two, the procession started for Redborough Hill where it was intended to hold the meeting. The procession was preceded by an excellent band of music and some of the most beautiful colours I ever saw. There were, in the procession deputations from Gloucester, Cheltenham, Cirencester and a great many other places. It was one of the most pleasing sights I ever witnessed. The hill appeared teeming with animated beings; there could not have been less than ten thousand persons. From this hill is one of the most pleasing prospects I ever saw. Before you you see the beautiful valley of Stroud, and in the distance you see the rich meadows skirting the Severn. Beyond these, the hills of Monmouthshire; and I could almost see my happy home. What pleasing ideas are, and ought to be, associated with that word! To the right were several manufactories, and before the platform were vast numbers of weavers and labourers, most of them in a state of great poverty. I could not help for a moment turning philosopher: here, thought I, are the works of nature and art; a most fertile country; an abundance of everything calculated to make life easy; food and raiment; and there sits Lord John Russell, the patron of a religious education, exerting all his powers as a law-giver to render those beings miserable who raise the food and produce the raiment. The average wages are, as I understand, from 6/- to 7/- a week; let it be 8/-: out of this about four shillings goes in taxes. The learned and pious secretary of state recieves about £6,000 a-year, besides perquisites, for filling, no not filling, Mr Lovett, for doing the work, and dirty work it is, of the office. His Lordship quarters himself on six hundred of these poor weavers; here are six hundred of these poor men paying half their wages in taxes; deprived of the common necessaries of life to enable his lordship to live in luxury! Oh beautiful system, the envy and admiration of the world! It would be a good plan, Mr Lovett, were his lordship and his colleagues to collect their own salaries, and to collect them as tithes were formerly collected, in kind. How pleasing it would be to see 'this scion of the noble house of Bedford', accompanied by Cupid, going round the houses in Stroud, with sacks on their shoulders, taking the breakfast from one poor weaver and the dinner from another; going into the shops and helping themselves to tea, and sugar, and soap &c. &c., and coming out with their sacks and pockets filled with these good things. This would place 'the envy and admiration' in a most striking point of view; we should then see the thing in its true colours. Finality and Cupid fixed on 1200 weavers, swallowing them alive. My God! Is this system to continue much longer? A working man was called to the chair. He opened the business in a short and sensible speech. The first resolution was in favour of the National Petition and the People's Charter. This was carried with great enthusiasm. The second, 'That Mr John Frost be appointed the representative of the industrious classes of people of Stroud to the General Convention.' If his lordship could have heard the shout with which this proposition was recieved, he would almost be inclined to say 'Othello's occupation gone.' In speaking to this resolution I told the people of Stroud, that on my return to London I would send his lordship a copy of the resolution; that I would call on his lordship to meet me before the people of Stroud, and let them decide who should be their representative; and that, should his lordship refuse to comply with a request so reasonable, I would consider myself the real representative, and his lordship the nominee of four large manufacturers. After a few observations on the state of the country, the lowness of wages, the great distress which prevailed *and the remedy*, I gave the electors, and others, a short history of the political opinions of his lordship when out of place, and his practices when fixed on the public purse. The special commissions to Hampshire and Wiltshire; the Irish Coercion Bill; the loan to Russia, and its effects on freedom abroad and at home; the Dorchester labourers; the Calthorpe-street concern; the Rural Police; and last, though not least, the 'Poor Law Amendment'. I gave them a short history of the origin of the poor laws. The history of Henry VIII; his character, his despoiling the religious houses of their estates; and the use to which the proceeds of these estates were applied before the Reformation; the services of Mr Russell to his kind and benevolent master, not forgetting the German troops; why he was made a nobleman; how he got hold of Woburn Abbey, Tavistock Priory, Convent-garden, and many other valuable properties; his deeds during the reign of Edward VI. I showed the people of Stroud how the members of parliament of those periods violated the trust reposed in them, by exercising the power of the law-giver to their own advantage, and to the injury, the lasting injury, of the people of England. I

179

showed them how acts of parliament had been repealed, and I talked to them of the possibility, THE BARE POSSIBILITY, of repealing acts now on the statute book. I gave them a short history of the poor law ammendment act; the causes assigned by members of both houses for passing that act; its effects on society, immediate and remote; the the treatment of the poor in many of their bastiles. I spoke to a most attentive audience, and I am persuaded that his lordship will have some difficulty in rubbing out the impressions. I talked to them about striking me off the commission; I informed them what the opinion is of the inhabitants of Newport as to my services as a magistrate. I showed them the sort of magistrates who were high in favour with the present government, and the sort of conduct which raised magistrates in the estimation of the authorities. I was about closing several times when I thought of the 'striking off'; I would then select some fresh topic, and I hammered at the little fellow until, I suppose, there cannot be a whole bone in his body. Be good enough, Mr Lovett, to ask one of our medical friends to visit his lordship, and for him to prescribe; he must certainly, after all that pummelling, be in a bad way. I told them that if this beautiful system should weather out another election, I would meet his lordship at Stroud and tell him to his face what I told the electors on Good Friday. A number of the electors told me they would vote for me; and I believe there is not a member now sitting in the House of Commons more despised by the electors than is the member for Stroud. After I ceased speaking, Mr Vincent proposed the following resolution:— 'That this meeting feels called upon to denounce the public conduct of Lord John Russell, the miscalled representative of the people of the borough, together with the administration of which he is an individual member; and to declare that his lordship and his colleagues are guilty of high treason to the principles which they formerly professed.' Mr Vincent, in a very powerful address, finished the business, and I am thoroughly convinced that at the close of his address there was not a single elector on the hill who was not ashamed of the poor haughty little aristocrat. The people in that part of Gloucestershire are all alive. It would be of immense advantage to have a missionary there for a month. Deputations were at Stroud from different places, requesting some one to attend and to hold public meetings. We are getting on well, very well, in Monmouthshire; the cause is progressing rapidly and steadily. I have this moment seen the 'Sun' of Monday: ah! ah! the Birmingham delegates

180

have resigned, and the 'Sun' says that the Convention is about dissolving. Oh! no, no; dissolve, aye? — there are too many firm men in the Convention to dissolve because three of its members seceded. We'll nail our colours to the mast and go down with the whole ship rather than surrender. Dissolve indeed! give up so noble a cause because we have a few men who have not nerve to meet the coming struggle! 'These are the times that try men's souls;' and those who have not the courage to meet the storm, let them resign. The Birmingham delegates assign as a reason for their seceding the language uttered at the Crown and Anchor on the 11th. I was chairman of that meeting, and when I return to London, I will, in an address to the men of Birmingham, answer the letter. I am exceedingly anxious to see the 'Sun' of Tuesday; I expect to see in it an account of the meeting at Birmingham on Monday. We have the men of Brimingham with us, if we have lost the delegates; and I hope that other delegates have been appointed to supply the place of the seceders from the Convention. I long to be at my seat in the Convention; Monday morning I shall be found at my post. Give up the cause aye! My kind regards to the Convention. I am, dear sir, truly yours,

John Frost

(c) *Speech of Richard Marsden, delegate for Preston, in the Convention*
From the 'Northern Star', 2 March 1839

Mr Marsden, delegate for Preston, then brought forward his motion, relative to the distress of the country. I do not (said he) rise for the purpose of pressing my motion to any conventional decision, but I do think it is of such importance that the country should know and so be aware of the evils which press upon the industrious classes, and that we are ready to grapple with the details, surmount the difficulties, and defy the dangers of removing them, that I bring my motion, and I have two separate objects in view in so doing. I wish to let the nation see that we are not frightened from a consideration of what affects the interests of the poor. I wish them to see that the subject is not new to us (Hear hear). I wish them to understand that we have both witnessed and felt the evils — (hear hear) — and above all I wish them to know that we will no longer submit to them. (Loud cheers). I wish them to know this, and in return, I wish them to let us know what they expect us to do, in case of the rejection of the petition. (Hear hear) He (Mr Marsden) belonged to a class of man perhaps worse paid than any other, and whose labour had been sadly depreciated in value, while their numbers and their privations had increased in proportion — (hear) — till their sufferings were no longer to be endured; and only this choice seemed to be left to them, to seize their food where they could find it, or lie down and die. (Hear hear). I am a handloom weaver, and can well recollect, when I could earn thirty shillings per week — such was the case of the handloom weaver in 1814 — and now the same ammount of labour performed would not produce seven shillings. In some fabrics the loss was less than in others, but in none was the reduction of value less than seven shillings in the pound. (Hear). However careful the weaver might be, however fair his prospects, there were mischances to which he, in common with all mankind, was subject; but, unlike almost every other class who had an opportunity of providing for them, they came upon him with crushing power, because naked and defenceless, his wage had never been such as to allow him to lay anything by with which to meet such casualties as sickness, or unwilling idleness, a bad warp, or the thousand chances of a fluctuating trade. When the weaver then gets his cut and goes with it to the warehouse, all that he gets for this, which has cost him a week's labour, is not more than five shillings, and for this he has to pay away more than half for fire, rent, light etc., leaving such a miserable pittance, that unsupported nature sinks under accumulated suffering; lassitude is mistaken for idleness, his neighbours begin to mistrust him, and thus with credit ruined and poverty around him, what but misery can be his lot? The very sources of pity on which he relied, are in some measure dried up; and despised abroad and wretched at home — with a starving yet beloved family calling aloud for bread — what but desperation can be his? or who shall blame him for the consequences? Let me give you a few instances of what has fallen under my own observation, in cases which cannot be construed or denied: — First. James Calbert, residing in the same street with myself, in Bamber Bridge, near Preston; within the first six months had a child born to him under such circumstances, that, to my knowledge, there was not in the house one mouthful of food, for he sought relief from the shopkeeper with whom he dealt, he sought in vain; he went to his employer — he asked for bread and he recieved a stone; in despair he turned to the poor and oppressed — his neighbours — but one degree removed from the position he himself was in, and in them he found the good Samaritans, from them he got relief. – Second. John Waring, with a wife and family of three children failed in getting his piece out on a Saturday night (a case that very frequently occurs, owing to weakness consequent upon lack of food). On the next day (Sunday), one scanty meal of oatmeal porridge was all they got. On Monday they were destitute, even of this, and it was because I knew them to have gone to bed in the vain hope of avoiding cold and hunger, that, unable of myself to aid them, I immediately set off and by representing their case, succeeded in obtaining for them a few shillings. Third. Thomas Varty got his piece in on Saturday night, yielding him five shillings. He had nothing in his house at the time. He had two shillings to pay one person, tenpence to another, twopence to another, and sixpence to remain at the warehouse, leaving eighteenpence upon which he and his family lived over Sunday. On Monday they had nothing – on Tuesday the husband came to my house, and asked my wife to assist in getting my neighbour up, as she was too weak to rise, having been quite exhausted by a child tugging at her breast all night. (Hear hear and 'how disgraceful') But this is not all. In my street alone I have known five families begging from their fellow-sufferers to keep alive for a day or two. (Hear) I have hitherto been speaking of others whom I have known. Let me now speak of myself; not with any view of securing a more marked attention of your part, but to prove that I speak not from hearsay but from having suffered, and, therefore, to be pardoned for any seeming warmth of expression which may have appeared bordering on violence. (Hear hear) My father-in-law who then lived with me, had been unsuccessful one Tuesday night in getting out a piece; our house was left destitute of all means of subsistence. On Wednesday morning breakfast time came and passed without food – dinner-time came but no dinner with it – supper-time and we were yet in starvation; while such was the destitution of my house that not one article remained to pawn (Great sensation). All this time my wife had a strong healthy child tugging at her breast, like a leech draining her of her life's blood. When in bed I addressed some question to my wife, she did not answer. I became alarmed, and 'twas horrible to find that she had fainted from exhaustion (increased sensation) I rose, turned the meal bag inside out, shook the fragments on the table, collected them in a bowl, and made a little oatmeal porridge – and to this I unhesitatingly attribute her life being saved.

Mr Marsden contrasted this state of suffering with the money

183

idly wasted by the aristocracy at balls and parties; and then passed on to a review of the evils of the factory system, both moral and physical, and showed that in every case they entailed only suffering; that the most disgraceful tyranny prevailed, for not in one mill out of twenty would a man be received who was known to be a Radical; he instanced a number of cases of tyranny, and one of revenge. What, continued the speaker, what must be the fate of our country, when its trade has left it, as it must shortly do? Every piecer will then have become a weaver; every rover a piecer; new generations shall have sprung up; and as there is no longer the same demand for labour, the masters will grind down the wages of those who are now well-paid to the level of the weaver, and the most dreadful consequences must be the result. As he said at the commencement his object was to give others an opportunity of expressing their opinions, and being unwilling to cause any disunion, he would withdraw an allusion to physical or moral forces, and leave the matter to the good sense of the country. He concluded by moving a resolution to the following effect: — 'That it was expedient to lay before the country through the Convention, the amount of suffering in the kingdom, with a view of obtaining the opinions of the constituencies as to the best means of obtaining a speedy and beneficial change.' Mr Marsden sat down amid continued cheering.

(d) Speech of George Julian Harney, at Derby on 28 January 1839, to the meeting which adopted him as delegate to the Convention

From 'The Operative', 10 February 1839

The motion to adopt the National Petition was proposed, and Mr Harney of London was called on to support the motion.

Mr Harney then mounted the platform and was received with loud cheers. He spoke as follows:

Fair women of Derby, brave men of Derby! I am proud and happy once more to meet you. To many of you I am not unknown. Three years ago on a winter's evening, I was dragged from my home without the least notice and consigned to a dungeon by the magistrates of Derby, because I had committed the heinous offence of selling an unstamped newspaper — because I had strove to set the press of England free. (Cries of

184

'shame'.) Yes my friends, I was for six months confined in a bastile because I dared, in defiance of wicked and infamous laws, to give the working classes that untaxed knowledge which they have the right to enjoy. The Tyrants bound me, but could not subdue me. They destroyed my business – they took from me my means of subsistence, and sent me forth a poor friendless boy to find on the road what subsistence I might. They sent me away friendless and forlorn; but I return to Derby not as I departed. I come back to look tyrants in the teeth, in the proud character of a leader of the people – as one of the chosen chieftains of the brave men of the north. My friends, on last Christmas Day, the day on which, according to sacred records, the Redeemer of mankind was born – on that day I met in the streets of Newcastle-upon-Tyne, one hundred thousand of the brave Northerners, and on that day, as we this day are doing, we raised our voices to heaven, upon God's green earth, and under the canopy of God's own skies, we swore by our homes and our altars – we swore by our wives and our children – we swore by the God of our fathers the oath of men determined to be no longer enslaved – we swore to live free or die. (Great cheering) We have met here to-day to demand our rights; we have assembled here to tell our tyrants that they shall tyrannise no longer. We demand Universal Suffrage, because we believe that universal suffrage will bring universal happiness – for universal happiness there shall be – or our tyrants shall find to their cost that *we will have universal misery*. (Cheers) We will have happy homes and altars free, or by the God of our sires, our oppressors shall share that misery we have too long endured (Cheers). My friends, we demand universal suffrage because it is our right, and not only because it is our right, but because we believe it will bring freedom to our country and happiness to our homesteads; we believe it will give us bread and beef and beer. What is it that we want? Not to destroy property and take life, but to preserve our own lives, and to protect our own property – viz, our labour. We are for Peace, Law, Order; but if our oppressors shall break the peace – if our tyrants shall violate the law, – if our despots shall trample upon order – then we will fall back upon the Constitution, and defend the few remaining of the blood bought rights left us by our fathers. The Whigs shall never violate the Constitution of this country as they have done in Canada. They charge us with being Physical Force men; I fling the charge back in the teeth of these canting Liberals. Let them call to mind their own words and deeds

185

during the humbug reform agitation; let them remember Derby in a state of anarchy, Nottingham and Bristol in flames; above all, let them look to Canada — have they not sent forth the women and the children to perish in the snow? have they not fired the cottages and desolated the hearths of the Canadians? have they not burnt the temples of the living God and the bodies of the dead? Again I say, we are for peace, but we must have justice — we must have our rights speedily; peaceably if we can, *forcibly if we must*. (Loud cheers) The want of Universal Suffrage has enabled our oppressors so long to ride rough-shod over us. They say we are too many — that population increases faster than the means of subsistence, if so, let those leave the land who do not love labour — let those who work not leave the country, and when the Aristocracy betake themselves to Van Dieman's land, and the money mongers to the devil, take my word for it, there will be enough left for you and me. But we will not leave the land of our sires — we will not quit the soil that gave us birth.

> If bugs molest me as in bed I lie,
> Shall I desert my bed for them? Not I,
> I will arise and every bug destroy,
> Now make my bed, and all its sweets enjoy.

(Loud laughter and cheers.) My friends, our country may be compared to a bed full of nasty, filthy, crawling, Aristocratic and Shopocratic bugs. Now in answer to our calumniators who say that we wish to destroy property, I answer, we will not destroy the bedstead, but we will annihilate the bugs. (Cheering and laughter) We will put down our oppressors, but our country we will save. (Cheers) Time was when every Englishman had a musket in his cottage, and along with it hung a flitch of bacon; now there was no flitch of bacon for there was no musket; let the musket be restored and the flitch of bacon would soon follow. (Loud cheering.) I will not further detain you this cold day, but thanking you for your patient attention and kind reception, I will retire, repeating to you that you will get nothing from your tyrants but what you can take, and you can take nothing unless you are properly prepared to do so. In the words of a good man, then, I say 'Arm for peace, arm for liberty, arm for justice, arm for the rights of all, and the tyrants will no longer laugh at your petitions.' Remember that —

186

Our green flag glitters o'er us
The friends we've tried
Are by our side
And the foes we hate before us.

Mr Harney retired amidst enthusiastic and long-continued cheering.

(e) Magistrates' reports from Cornwall on the Chartist Missionaries

Ludgvan, Penzance and Gwennap: H.O. 40/41

The Rectory, Ludgvan in Penzance
March 16th

My Lord

A meeting is to be held in the town of Penzance on Wednesday next of certain miscreants calling themselves deputies from the national Convention — I fully expect that if disturbed they will attempt the neighbourhood. As a magistrate I wish for your Lordship's advice and instruction how to act — this campaign is so treasonable and the principles they would inculate so destructive of life and property, that had they met within my district, I should have felt no hesitation in apprehending them on my own responsibility.

Your Lordship, in giving the advice, will be pleased to bear in mind the peculiar circumstances of this division of the County: swarming with miners, who are at the present moment happy and Contented, but easily excited. The numbers in which they can on the shortest notice collect, renders it absolutely necessary, that the power of the Law should be exercised and that vigorously. Much fear has been felt by the quiet part of our Community. On the one hand, these delegates recommend the deluded People to buy a Musket, telling them how well it looks on the Chimney Piece if kept clean and ready for use — and on the other urging them to resist the Poor Law — knowing the feeling against that Act, I fear more from that doctrine than any other — I feel particularly anxious about this matter, and if your Lordship would favour me with an answer by return of Post as the Meeting takes place on Wednesday, I should feel deeply obliged — and on that day will go to the Posts and be prepared to act in conformity with any advice or suggestion I

187

may be favoured with from your Lordship.
        I remain,
            My Lord,
                Your most obedient subject,
                    H. S. Graham

                                    Penzance, March 1839
My Lord
    I write to your Lordship from a part of Her Majesty's
dominions in which there is no clashing of interests between the
agriculturist and the manufacturer — in which the labouring
classes are in constant employment — where absolute poverty is
not known — where loyalty is proverbial and contentment
almost universal. — But all this desirable order of things is
threatened to be overturn'd and society disjointed by a party of
itinerant politicians — who style themselves *'Chartists'* — who
profess to be 'missionary Delegates from the National Convention' and who held their first meeting in this town last
evening — at which the most *seditious* and inflammatory
language was fearlessly made use of — Her Majesty was insulted
— the ministers were grossly abused, all the established
institutions ridiculed, and the working classes were called on to
arm themselves and to obtain by force some redress from some
alleged grievances = and to sign a 'national Petition' to be
presented to Parliament insisting on many unconstitutional
arrangements.
    The sensation which this meeting has occasioned in this
tranquil part of the world is quite extraordinary — the upper
classes of Society are in a state of alarm and men have called on
me urging me to do my utmost to suppress any such meetings in
future — but I do not know how to act and appeal to your
Lordship for instructions that may enable me to effect such a
desirable object = I think it right to state that the meeting was
held in a room hired for the occasion — I am quite ready to
follow any suggestions which your Lordship may recommend.

            I have the honour to be
                My Lord,
                    Your Lordship's
                        humble servant
                            Richard Moyl
                            Mayor of Penzance

188

Lord John Russell

My Lord

I have taken much pains to obtain accurate information of the language used by the Chartists at their recent meeting in this Parish, but I have been unable to satisfy myself that any of the proceedings were of a sufficiently important character to report to your Lordship. The whole affair appears to have been a complete failure — a large crowd was certainly collected, but I have the satisfaction to believe, that from this large Parish no new converts have been made, and that any temptation their language might have caused has entirely died away. — I have the honour now to extract for your Lordship's consideration, a few passages from the report of an intelligent constable who was placed by me to watch the proceedings.

After inveighing in a strong and not very connected strain against the New Poor Law, Lowry, one of the Delegates said 'I have a pike at home — I have two pikes — all our people have pikes and arms — all should have pikes — all should have arms — and they cannot stop them from having them. Why all this noise about the people having arms? All should have guns, for the man that could shoot a Pheasant would shoot a Tyrant — we will have our rights — no one can hinder us from meeting — you must form yourselves into Societies — we have now 60,000 ready to do their duty. The Queen shall sit down and make laws for us, we will not obey them — Our rights we will have — There will be a drawing for the Militia shortly, and I would recommend no man to get a substitute, but every man to go for himself — I will go — then every man that goes will have an opportunity of getting a gun without buying it'. —

The above extracts are the only ones to which I think it at all necessary to direct your Lordship's attention — Indeed I should hardly have troubled you with this but for the purpose of assuring your Lordship that a more complete mistake never was committed by the Chartists, and in supposing that they could make converts here. I cannot close without adding my very sincere approbation of the conduct of the Wesleyans of the Parish on the occasion — the leaders consulted with me and cooperated with me in the most effectual manner to prevent any outbreak and also to discourage the intruders, your

189

Lordship may be quite sure that the sole effect of the meeting has been to prove the weakness of the Chartists, and the absence of any sympathy with them on the part of our miners.

I have the honour to be
   your Lordship's very obedient servant,
      J. Philpotts

(f) Placard calling for ulterior measures — broadside posted in Manchester, July 1839

Copy in H.O. 40/43

Brethren, you require not to be told of the social and political evils which have resulted from the abusive indulgence of intoxicating luxuries; the social evils are seen in the miserable homes, emaciated frames, and diseased countenances of your wives and families. The political evils are found in the misery which pervades the land, the consequences of exclusive and class legislation by a set of men who only retain their power by the amount of money which you pay to them, and which, if you withold from them for a very short period, will at once dislodge them. Upwards of twenty-six millions are raised annually from these articles, the far greater part are supplied by the industrious classes, while to them the actual outlay is more than double. It is unnecessary to say anything to you of the other measures, they speak for themselves, their tendency is well known to you, their necessity is evident to you. We urge you, therefore, by all your hopes of freedom, and by all you hold most dear, to agree to the request, the urgent, the unanimous request of the Convention, as promulgated in the following terms:

1st. That you individually and collectively Withdraw your Moneys from Savings Banks as well as from all other banks and persons hostile to your just rights.
2nd. That you convert all your Paper Money into gold.
3rd. That you abstain from all excisable articles of luxury.
4th. That you commence at once an exclusive system of dealing, and deal only with those who are the advocates and supporters of your cause.
5th. That you exercise your ancient and constitutional right, and provide yourselves with the Arms of Freemen.

These means may not alone effect our object, but immediately after the 12th inst., when we expect a division in the House of Commons on the National Petition, we shall proceed to name the day when the SACRED MONTH shall commence, unless the measures of justice we are contending for have been previously conceded.

WE REMAIN, BRETHREN, YOUR FAITHFUL SERVANTS,
   The Members of the General Convention

W. G. Burns, counties of Forfar and Aberdeen.
T. R. Smart, Leicester, Loughborough, Shilton and Hinkley.
William Cardo, Mary-le-Bone, London.
John Warden, Bolton-le-Moors.
Christopher Dean, Manchester.
John Deegan, Hyde, Staley Bridge etc.
John Stowe, Colne District etc.
Peter Bussey, West Riding of Yorkshire.
P. M. McDouall, Ashton-under-Lyne.
John Taylor, Renfrewshire and Northumberland.
James Taylor, Rochdale and Middleton.
W. Lovett, for London and its districts (except Mary-le-Bone).
Feargus O'Connor, for the West Riding of Yorkshire.
John Frost, for Monmouthshire.
Matthew Fletcher, for Bury and surrounding districts.
L. Pitkeithly, West Riding of the County of York.
John Skevington, Loughborough, Derby and Belper.
John Collins, for Birmingham.
John Richards, North Staffordshire and South Cheshire.
James Woodhouse, for Nottingham.
Charles H. Neesom, for Bristol.
Robert Tilley, for Lambeth.
Robert Hartwell, for the Tower Hamlets, London.
James Moir, for Glasgow and the County of Lanark.
Richard Marsden, for Preston.
James Fenney, for Wigan, Hindley and West Houghton.
Joseph Hickin, for Walsall etc. etc., etc. etc, etc.

The Convention earnestly calls upon every Workingman's and Radical Association throughout the Kingdom to reprint, circulate, and by all and every means give publicity to the decrees of the Convention, to placard every House in every Town and Village with their recommendations as their local

191

circumstances demand.

To the *Radical Reformers of Manchester and its Vicinity*
NOTICE is hereby given, that a
PUBLIC MEETING,
will be held on Saturday Evening, July 13th, 1839, in Stevenson
Square, at six o'Clock, to take into consideration the Present
State of the Country, to support the PEOPLES PARLIAMENT,
and to reccomend her MAJESTY, to dismiss her Present Base,
Brutal, and Bloody, Advisers. Let EVERY MAN be at his POST.
by permission of the Boroughreeve and Constables

19 Exclusive Dealing

(a) Address of the Radical Association of Colne

Handbill reprinted in the 'Yorkshire Gazette', 22 December 1838

Friends Neighbours and Fellow Countrymen

Seeing the low condition which this country is brought to through the misgovernment of our Rulers, and their backwardness to redress our grievances, we have Resolved, to use every *lawful means* to raise this, our fallen country, to a state of happiness and independence; and to give to each of its members that Political Right, (the Right to Vote for the man that is to Represent him in the Commons House of Parliament,) which have been so long withheld from them.

We wish not to hurt the feelings of any man, whatever may be his Political Creed or Profession. But, seeing the thousands that are brought to poverty, and death, and in a land that abounds in every thing that man can require, we call upon you whatever be your station in Society, or profession amongst men — if you love your wife, your children, your country, or your God, to come forward, and unite to save your country from anarchy and confusion.

Knowing that 'Union is strength', and in the same proportion that we are united in the same proportion will our cause triumph. Will you allow it to be said, that, because you have not come forward to assist in this glorious warfare, that England, the glory of the world, and the envy of surrounding nations has become annihilated from amongst the nations of the earth, only to have her name handed down to posterity that she once was but is now no more?

If the object which we have in view be worth having, it is worth striving for. And, knowing that 'He that would be free, himself must strike the blow', we once more call upon you to come and join with those that are willing to sacrifice even life itself for their Country's Freedom.

In connection with the above we require your kind attention to the National Rent, which is to support the delegates which the Nation have appointed to meet in the convention in London, to require at the hands of the Government JUSTICE FOR THE MILLIONS! Therefore we humbly call upon the friends of suffering humanity to aid us not only with their voice, but also with their contributions to this important crisis, to help us to carry the great Radical Reform, in spite of all our enemies, and place Government upon a proper system.

P.S. — If you approve of our object, please to certify the same when this Bill is call'd for, and the person that calls for it will thankfully receive from your liberal hand what your kind and affectionate heart may think proper to give.

By order of the Committee
November 26 1838

Please to keep this Bill clean 'till call'd for.

(b) Deposition of James Marsden of Bradford and copy of handbill he had received, 26 July 1839

From the Harewood Papers, Leeds Public Library

West Riding	The Examination of James Marsden of Bradford in the said Riding Grocer taken on oath before us
of	William Rookes Crompton Stansfield, Matthew Thompson and Henry Wickham Hird Esquires,
Yorkshire	three of Her Majesty's Justices of the peace in and for the said Riding the twenty sixth day of July 1839.

Who says, on Thursday week a printed paper of which the annexed marked with the Letter A is a Copy was left at my Shop in Bradford, and on the Saturday following two persons who appeared to be of the Labouring Class called upon me at my Shop and said 'We call upon you to Solicit your Subscription for the defence Fund' I said I did not approve of their System and that I should not give them anything. They went out and looked up at the name over the door of my Shop, and appeared to be taking it down in a Book. On Tuesday last in returning from my Residence in Brick Lane in Bradford, I was accosted by a Man who appeared to be a woolcomber and who stated that I was an Enemy to the working classes and addressing some Women who were standing by, said that he wished that if they purchased anything from me it might never

194

pass through them and that such persons as me had obtained all we had by robbing the working people and that they were now determined to have it back and that before a fortnight from the present day I should see my shop entered and my goods dragged into the street.

James Marsden

Sworn before us
MattW Thompson
H. W. Hird

Address of the Working Men to the Shopkeepers, Butchers, etc. of the Town and neighbourhood of Bradford.

We the industrious classes having become aroused to a sense of our degradation and misery, conscious that exclusive Legislation is the great cause to which the many woes we endure are to be principally attributed, have resolved that this state of things, both cause and effect shall speedily come to an end.

We claim representative Government for all the people as a primary means of our Social Regeneration. The Suffrage is our inalienable right; and cannot be justly and shall not much longer be withheld. It is as manifestly unjust to withhold the Suffrage as it would be to withhold our weekly earnings the one being as much our natural right as the other. The object of this address is to submit to you our earnest request for your immediate and cordial co-operation in the glorious struggle of right against might. In this request we submit that we are not asking you to seek our Interests to the prejudice of your own. If we are to remain destitute and miserable it is not possible that you can be truly and permanently prosperous.

In all cases of refusal to this reasonable request we shall know how to discriminate between our Friends and Enemies. This course we shall adopt not as a matter of choice but as matter of necessity for the time has now come when every man must decide.

The General Convention have submitted the following question to the Radicals of Great Britain. 'Whether they will resolve to deal exclusively with Chartists; and in all case of persecution rally around and protect all those who may suffer in their righteous cause.'

Please to keep this Bill clean till called for.
J. S. Shackleton, printer, 51 Westgate Bradford.

20 The Sacred Month: Two Articles against the Strike

(a) Feargus O'Connor's letter

From the 'Northern Star', 3 August 1839

MY DEAR FRIENDS, — Often as I have addressed you, yet never before have I done so upon matter so serious, or business so important. I may stand well in your estimation, generally, but upon this point it is necessary that I should lay particular claim, and prove peculiar title, to your confidences. I am about to speak to you of and concerning the Sacred Holiday; and to do so with the best effect, I prefer giving you my opinions upon the subject, as they were delivered at times when they will stand discharged from motives which maybe attributed to some who have changed their opinions, and that very hastily, upon the subject.

This Sacred Week was of Mr ATTWOOD'S suggestion. In the autumn of 1837, Mr SALT made a tour to Manchester and other places, with a view to test public opinion with reference to the plan. When at Manchester he was told by the leaders that, before they ventured upon an answer, they should like to consult with FEARGUS O'CONNOR. I repaired thither, and to WHEELER, HEYWOOD, CURRAN, and others, I exposed the fallacy of the project; and, subsequently, at a public meeting, I expressed my opinion in the following terms; — 'This is a wild and visionary scheme of ATTWOOD'S, to starve the people into paper money. However, I have no objection to try the experiment, providing the rich who have suggested it, will deposit in the hands of committees, either money or food to stand the strike; that Mr ATTWOOD, and all bankers refuse for the time to discount; that merchants refuse their consignments; that masters refuse to sell, if men refuse to work. I do this to equalize suffering in the endurance of a crisis of which the result is to be generally beneficial; but I have no notion of allowing Mr ATTWOOD to prosecute his trade while a starving garrison bears all the brunt of battle, and to whom success would merely be increased suffering.' These sentiments were highly approved of, and banished from Mr SALT'S mind all

196

thought of success.

The next period at which the question was broached was in Committee of the Convention. I was one of that Committee; and the unanimous feeling was, that the Holiday was a reserve in case any assault should be made by Government upon the people in the prosecution of the other measures, and the time, and the necessity for which, the people themselves should be the best judges of. The question was next brought before the Convention by PETER BUSSEY, on the 3rd of July, in the shape of an amendment to a resolution of Dr TAYLOR, for the recommendation of the first class of ulterior measures. I there opposed the amendment. Dr TAYLOR over and over again stated, that of the numerous meetings that he attended, not one of them was prepared for the Sacred Month. Upon that occasion, Dr TAYLOR congratulated the Convention upon the temper of the debates, and the almost unanimous adoption of his resolution; on the following day the Magistrates commenced the rebellion in Birmingham, when TAYLOR was arrested for saving the lives of two policemen. One week intervened when matter, which would have justified a general strike took place, and the people did not strike except partially; this was no evidence that in their wisdom the people thought it prudent to adopt the alternative. Upon the following week the question was again brought before the Convention, without a particle more evidence than TAYLOR had adduced at Birmingham for negativing the appointment of the day, and, upon a majority of one, the fate of the nation and the cause was decided; and here, although I admit that, upon questions of principle, all are equal in the Convention, I must lay before you the constituencies, who, by their representatives, declared against the plan.

BUSSEY, PITKETHLY, and O'CONNOR, the only representatives of Yorkshire, opposed to it.

FROST, representing the Welch people, opposed to it.

DUNCAN and BURNS, the only Scotch Delegates then in the Convention, opposed to it.

SMART and WOODHOUSE, representing the great and impoverished Counties of Nottingham, and Leicester, opposed to it.

JAMES TAYLOR, of Rochdale, and RICHARDSON, though then not of the Convention, opposed to it.

CARPENTER, dividing Bolton with WARDEN, opposed to it.

Dr FLETCHER, the cleverest man in the Convention, and

one of the most unflinching patriots in the world, declared against its practicability, except all were ready at once.

O'BRIEN, the schoolmaster of public opinion for eight long years of undeviated practice, opposed to it.

Mr KNOX, representing the county of Durham, opposed to it.

Of its supporters the delegates for Marylebone, Lambeth, Southwark, Bristol, Brighton, Bath, and Hyde in Cheshire were seven of the thirteen who voted for it; thus you have seven, a majority of the thirteen, who carried the vote, representing constituencies of which I may venture to assert, with the exception of Bristol and Hyde, not five hundred men would stop work. And are we thus to allow the votes of constituencies, by no means organised, to destroy the whole of the North, the Midland Counties, and Scotland? Birmingham was not represented, and having decided the question at Birmingham, I contend for it, that even if fresh evidence had been adducible, the whole of the Convention should have been summoned upon a matter so grave and important, in order that the question might be wisely and not capriciously discussed; and now I appeal to you, whether or not the most important measure ever discussed by the Convention, should have been submitted to the very thinnest meeting of the body, and during the unavoidable absence of many of its members?

I now come to treat of the means of carrying out the project. Heretofore, in carrying out the first recommendations, you have had a complete co-operation of all the working classes, without reference to the amount of earnings. The men who earn 15s 20s 25s and 30s a-week were, in the instance of exclusive dealing, more efficient supporters of the measure than those who received a smaller amount of wages. But, I ask, will those men be likely, in a body, to keep the Sacred Holiday? I say not; and, if not, who will be sacrificed? The answer is easy. The most determined, resolute, and oppressed, will strike. Indeed the tyranny of the masters has long since compelled many to remain idle; and what guarantee have those for a general cessation from labour? The evidence which we have received has gone to say, that, 'if this place will strike, and that place will strike, we will strike,' but not otherwise. Behold then, the position in which the bravest and most oppressed would be placed; firstly, wholly at the mercy of their more fortunate comrades, and secondly, in the event of failure, at the mercy of masters, who, nine out of ten, look upon the project as a

198

God-send. Read, and read attentively the speeches, the able speeches of the several speakers at the Stockport meeting reported in the last 'Star', and from them you will learn, that exclusive dealing is not only recommended, but being carried into execution, while they declare the absolute necessity of a union with Ireland, to insure the success of the cause. This Union is now formed, the result of which, before the 12th of August, will be to re-ship the 5000 troops, which MR O'CONNELL boasted of having spared for the suppression of Chartism, together with the new levy of 5000 more.

If the people did generally keep the holiday 3 days would suffice while, if it is but partial, as many years would be a boon to the anti-population masters. If it was general no means at the disposal of our physical-force government, could suppress the moral demonstration of the people; if partial, they would 'let slip the dogs of war' upon an unarmed and defenceless people, and cut them off in sections.

The men of Lancashire, and the men of Yorkshire have been the heart and soul of this movement. By the London Delegates they have been declared the prime movers, while the same delegates have declared the preparedness of their own districts. Let us see, then: the test is easy. Let the men of Marylebone, of Southwark, of Lambeth, and of Tower Hamlets, prove the theory of their Delegates by their practice. Let them commence the strike, and the post which carries the tidings, will operate with a magic influence upon every working man through out the length and breadth of the land. You will bear in mind that the Convention has left to you the fulfilment of the work, and to you the right to say whether and when the work shall commence.

The first step should have been (instead of receiving *ex-parte* evidence from those who volunteer to give it) to form a committee in each district, for the purpose of consulting with the best informed of the several trades and labour communities. That was not done; do it now; for all that I am saying is but as advice to guard the people from disappointment and defeat, and the cause from damage. Show me the practicability of the plan, and where in the whole world is there another who will so rejoice at the prospects of success; but being mainly instrumental in creating the movement, where is the man more interested in its speedy and successful termination? I am, as it were, a hostage in the hands of the working classes, to prove my sincerity, when over and over again, I have told the people that I would have

199

Universal Suffrage or die in the attempt to attain it. My whole life from the origin of the agitation has been a burden, and might be cheaply had, was it not for the value which I believe the people attach to it. From the 6th of August, since we formed an alliance with the Birmingham and other traitors, every word spoken by every popularity hunter has been attributed to me, and when charged, have I not defended them at the expense of my own life? Our new associates have one and all deserted us; upon me, and me alone, they have left the burden of answering for their every violent word and foolish act. If Birmingham is fired, the press gives me the credit. If outbreaks take place, upon my shoulders is placed all the responsibility; this and more I am ready to bear, rather than weaken the cause by prophesying ill of the leaders. My very life depends upon the success of this cause. If I desert it, or shuffle in it, no murderer ever suffered death more deservedly: no man would be more sure to meet it instantly. Have I not, then, (though the vote had been even an unanimous one), a right to advise and commune with those in whose service I have spent the prime of life, and in whose work I have laboured as man never laboured before? Aye, and mistake me not now; for if the people persevere, I will be with them where the danger is thickest; but I am not going to stand tamely by, while the most glorious of all causes — the cause of liberty — is perilled by a false step. I have given you seven of the thirteen who voted for the measure, while four of the remaining six declared that they had not hope of their districts carrying out the recommendation; and Mr SKEVINGTON, one of the four, assigned as his reason for voting for the measure, that his colleague, Mr SMART, voted against it, and it was right that they should sometimes differ. Mr LOWRY and Dr FLETCHER, the other two who voted for it, are now decidedly opposed to it, from a belief that it would be a failure. Many men have threatened to abandon the Convention, or the cause, in the event of this or that measure not being carried. I never have, but I do now most emphatically warn you, that the attempt to stop work for a month would either have the effect of subjugating the working men more than ever to the will of their masters, or of terminating in a short and sanguinary sectional struggle, the result of which would be a licence for every rich man to shoot as many poor men as he thought proper.

I am aware that agitation is more the province of the poor, than the more comfortable labourer. I am aware that many who

200

are starving say, 'we cannot wait, we will not wait,' — show me that the result would not lead to a longer 'wait,' and it shall have my most hearty concurrence. I do but advise; you are to decide. I do it with the perfect knowledge of the fate of HUNT and others before my eyes, and yet I am not deterred. You must bear in mind that I now speak upon the evidence of the people, as communicated by their Delegates, and from large masses of evidence received from the people themselves.

If I thought that you could test the value of labour by a month's holiday, I would say have it. If I thought you could live in peace any way, and not subject yourselves and your families to greater privations, I would say have it. But you know — you all know — that the baker will not bake; the butcher will not kill, and the brewer will not brew; and then, what becomes of the millions of starving human beings? If a holiday of three days, or four days, had been proclaimed for the purpose of exhibiting the numbers determined to have Universal Suffrage, every trade in England would have joined us. We should have been all equally in the lion's den, and no reserve could have supplied the place of those who, upon a partial strike, may be easily replaced. Make your necessary arrangements; have a three days' holiday, instead of a month's strike, and what you fail to effect by it, would have been equally lost by the month. For three days you can live in peace, while you exhibit your strength, and for three days the more fortunate would contribute to the sustenance and support of those who have been impoverished by the system; but, I never will, with a certainty of my own dinner, recommend a project which may cause millions to starve. No; I would rather go to battle. I would rather brave all than hear the cry of your hungry selves and your hungry children, and know that my folly had been the cause. In this strike, Ireland would not be with you, because she is not prepared; while the result of the mission now about to be dispatched to that country, will, before the 12th of August, prove the necessity of delay. Merciful Providence! did ever cause progress as ours has done? And why now mar it, by one unprepared step? I see Universal Suffrage near at hand, and I dread the injury which folly may expose it to. *Working men, before you enter upon the project, equalise the danger, as the benefit is to be universal. Do not enter partially upon the undertaking, for if you do, the brave will fall, while the coward will fill his place at the anvil, the loom or the bench.*

If this prepare you, if you be determined, or stop you, if you

be unprepared, I am more than paid.
                 Again, I subscribe myself,
                      Your faithful friend and servant,
                      FEARGUS O'CONNOR
Council Room, Arundel Coffee House,
London, July 31, 1839

(b) *Editorial: 'The Sacred Month' — THE CRISIS —*

THE WARNING

We beg that all our readers will peruse most carefully the
excellent address of Mr O'CONNOR on this, the most
important subject that is now before the public mind.

We had purposed to make some strong remarks on this subject
last week, but waited, that we might do nothing without serious
enquiry and consideration. All reflection and observation con-
vinces us that we were right in the conclusion to which we had
then come, and which we shall no longer hesitate to express.

We have never, till now, seen reason to censure as rash or
ill-judged any public act of the Convention; but we cannot, on
this vital point, concede our settled conviction that the naming
of the 12th of August, was a most ill-judged and suicidal act.

To fix the general holiday to begin on the 12th of August,
would be to involve the whole cause in ruin and confusion — a
ruin which would probably be irretrievable — which would, at
all events, place us in circumstances of difficulty, from which
we should emerge only through blood and fire, or chains and
slavery more dire than any we have yet known.

The country is not fit for it; there is no state of adequate
preparation; there is no proper organization amongst the people;
they are not able to act in concert with each other; they are not a
tenth part of them in possession of the means of self-defence; they
are not agreed in their opinions, either as to the practicability or
the necessity of the measure: and we predict, most confidently
that if the suggestion of a month's general holiday be now
persisted in and attempted to be acted on, the consequence will
be, the splitting of the people into sections, and their falling, one
section after another, like the divided bundle of sticks, an easy
prey to the power of their oppressors.

We are quite ready to acknowledge that a general cessation
from labour would be a most irresistible form in which to
attack the locusts, and we say at once that —

202

> If, when done, 'twere well done,
> Then 'twere well it were done quickly;

but we know that it will not be well done — because we know that nothing can be well done for which due and fitting preparation has not been made, and we know that no due and fitting preparation has been made for this.

Any one of the suggestions of the Convention is enough to carry any object the people wish, if universally acted on. Is any one of them universally acted on now? Not one. What madness, then, to push this — the climax — the completion of them all — into full enforcement — not one of the others having been attended to! And why have these not been attended to? Is it because the people are disaffected to the Convention? Certainly not: the subscription in all parts of the country answer that; but the people require time to understand — time to organize, and time to bring into operation, any popular and general movement. Things done in a hurry are seldom well done, and had often better have been let alone. The people are now bestirring themselves — they are acting nobly: let them not be overtasked. Give them but a little time to organize and bring into effective operation a general system of exclusive dealing, and no power on earth can hinder them from carrying anything they please, without the aid of any other engine than that alone.

We do trust, therefore that whatever the Convention may decide on, the people will for themselves decide on letting the Sacred Month alone till that has been fairly tried.

We think the people know us well enough to trust our honesty — we think our experience and observation entitles us to claim some capability of judgement; and we repeat most deliberately, our honest conviction, that ANY ATTEMPT TO BRING ABOUT THE SACRED MONTH BEFORE AN UNIVERSAL ARMING SHALL HAVE TAKEN PLACE, WILL RUIN ALL.

We have said that any one of the suggestions of the Convention will save the country, if acted on, but that the people require time to understand them, and to organize themselves for the carrying of them out. It may be that some of them require also to be instructed. If the people determine as we hope they will, to delay the holiday, we shall, please God, devote some space to a careful consideration, and pointing out, of the best means of carrying out all the measures reccomended by the Convention, to precede the holiday; and we pledge ourselves that if our advice be acted on the people will proceed safely, certainly, speedily, bloodlessly, and irresistibly to the accomplishment of their purpose. Infinitely diversified as are the meshes of the law, they may be all avoided — rampant for blood as are the minions of oppression, their frowns and malice may be laughed at. The wiles of the enemy and the power of the wicked one may be equally defied.

There has never been in the history of this country so important a crisis as the present one — upon the people themselves everything depends — they are just at the very turning of the scales; their own coolness, prudence, and steadiness, or violence and impatience, will save or damn them, this time, and just now.

Every single incident which transpires around us serves to impress us yet more deeply with the truth of this statement.

The last agonies of faction, and the first struggles of the new-born spirit of freedom, are alike fearful. For some weeks past our paper has been a chronicle of occurrences exhibiting the dogged and insane recklessness of the upper and middle class factions on the one hand, and the cool, prudent and progressing determination of the people on the other hand. This is a state of things which cannot last long. Two armies in charge with their bayonets crossed do not long remain in that position. There may be some anxious watching of each other, but one of two things must soon happen — either the one or the other must give way, or the whole must be involved in one common slaughter. This is precisely the position of the people and the factions at the moment. Their strength is being tried. The two lines are drawing nearer to each other; and, notwithstanding that in the hands of factions are concentrated the chief means of exercising brute force, on which they have hitherto relied with pitiable complacency, they are now beginning to perceive something of the real danger of their position. They are accordingly exhibiting symptoms of that desperate and reckless plunging which precedes a giving way. Seeing that the people are really in earnest — they are trying to dash the weapons out of their hands. Hence the illegal commitment of WHITE and WILSON, by the Leeds, 'justices,' and the anxiety and alarm of their Manchester brethren, at being unable to trump up evidence whereon to commit HILTON and TILMAN, at Manchester, for peaceably testing the middle classes by soliciting their aid. Hence the outrageous barbarism of the police at Stockport, and all the other despicable freaks of frantic

204

cowardice which bespeak alike the fears and villany of those by whom they are perpetrated.

Let not the people, however, be disheartened — let them still keep on striving by every possible means to keep within the law — throwing the whole onus of its violation upon their enemies — concentrating their own energies — supporting their friends — finding out and letting alone their enemies and they shall succeed and that speedily. ABOVE ALL, AND BEFORE ALL THINGS, LET THE PEOPLE KEEP THE PEACE — LET THERE BE NO OUTBREAKS — NO FIRES — NO THREATS — NO INTIMIDATION. LET THEIR BUSINESS BE DONE QUIETLY — NOISELESSLY — P E A C E F U L L Y . THE DRAGONS MAY RAGE, BUT THEIR TIME IS SHORT. And we implore the monied classes — the property-men of all grades — not to shorten that short time by a general exhibition of the reckless insanity which has recently characterized their proceedings in several places. We implore them to listen, if not to our warning, at least to that of their own guardian oracle, 'The Morning Chronicle', whose Newcastle correspondent tells them that, notwithstanding the mad and fearful chafing to which their spirits have been subjected, the Northern Chartists are 'all firmness, coolness, and determination;' that in the midst of provocation 'they exhibited no inclination to turbulence or riot;' — that 'the Chartists of the present day have, what the Radicals of 1819 had not — unity and a directing energy;' — that the 'solitary Chartist of a small village is generally the best informed person in the village;' that 'there is scarcely a village in which the germ of Chartism is not;' — that 'the Northern Chartists are neither indolent nor ignorant. They are superior to the Southern confederates, both in minds and in person: They are a fine class of men, who have become convinced no matter by what means, or with what truth, that the Legislature and the classes above them have ill-used them, and are without sympathy with them, and they, if the opportunity be afforded them, will take a terrible revenge. There is a determination and unity of purpose about them that is most serious.'

We entreat the enemies of Chartism to remember that these are not our words; — they are those of one of the more rational of their own order, given as a solemn warning to them, in their own organ; and we equally entreat the people not to sacrifice the advantage of the proud position they have now attained by any ebullition of impatience, into which their enemies may strive to goad them. Let them keep their temper, and the battle is their own.

205

(a) Letter from Bolton magistrate and evidence given by the deputy constable

From H.O. 40/43

Harwood, Nr Bolton
15th July 1839

My Lord

From information I received last week that a large number of pikes was in the course of being manufactured in the town of Bolton, I have caused an enquiry to be made and today have got depositions of facts which I think it my duty to enclose to your Lordship.

I have also been informed by several respectable inhabitants that there is no attempt to conceal the making of them for two of the workshops are at the front of the street and the men are seen at work by all passers by. Till very lately I have every reason to believe there have been but few made *in this town*, But for the last few days the demand for them has increased greatly and generally — there are from ten to fifteen persons waiting to be supplied.

There have been meetings held every night for the last week and every means used to influence the lower class.

We find great difficulty in getting information of what is said at the meetings as the police are immediately detected and we have no funds to pay any reporter who could be depended upon.

If any further information comes to my knowledge worth communicating it shall be immediately forwarded to your Lordship.

I have enclosed, your Lordship, a copy of the last placard pasted against the walls.

I have the honour to be
My Lord
Your Lordship's most obedient and humble servant,

R. Lomax

to the Rt Honourable Lord John Russell, M.P.

Examinations taken upon oath before me, Robert Lomax Esquire, one of her Majesty's Justices of the Peace in and for the said County this fifteenth day of July, one thousand eight hundred and thirty nine, at the Sessions Room Bolton le Moors in the Said County.

John Burrow of Great Bolton in the County of Lancaster, Deputy Constable saith on Saturday afternoon last about two o'clock I went to visit the Smithy of John Matthews situated in Crook St, Bolton. I had heard that he was making pikes. I found the door fast. I knocked with my stick and it was immediately opened, I tried it before I knocked but I could not open it, Matthews was making a pike and another man assisting, he had the small hammer and the other the longer hammer, there were from ten to fourteen men in the Smithy, the Smithy fronts the street and there were a number of persons looking through the windows and grating, I said 'Well Matthews I've heard a good deal about this pike making but I've never seen any made and I am come to satisfy myself.' 'Yes' he said 'I've made a good deal,' and smiled, he seemed hard at work, there was nothing more said for a short time until one of the men present said 'Yes, these are to protect life and property,' Matthews said 'I made a hundred of them yesterday,' he soon finished the one he was working at and took a file out of a box near him to make another pike and there appeared to be from sixteen to twenty files in the box, some of the files had writing upon them — a mark made with chalk as if to distinguish them and each one might have his file returned to him when shaped into a pike, he might not be more than about ten minutes in finishing this pike, he laid it on the ground with two others, there was some conversation among the persons in the Smithy about the Birmingham riots and one said there would have been no disturbance if the London Police had not come. I left soon afterwards; whilst I was in the Smithy a boy about fourteen years of age came in and drew a pike from his breast and asked Matthews to alter it for him. I did not know any of the men in the Smithy except Matthews — they appeared to be weavers and spinners. From Matthews I went to the Smithy of Daniel Cowle which is in Great Moors Street, I had heard that Cowle was making pikes, his Smithy is in a cellar under his house. I met Cowle as I was going into his Smithy — at the bottom of the steps I said 'Well Dan, I've come to look at you making pikes,' he laughed and said 'are you going to give me an order for one,' I said, I must look at them first for I had been at Matthews' and

he was making them out of old files.' I went through the front
cellar into the back cellar and there was a man and a boy at the
anvil making a pike and there were two other men at the
grinding room grinding a pike, Daniel Cowle came into the back
cellar, he had a pike in his hand. He said, 'I'm making mine out
of good stuff, they will bend and come again,' he said 'I've an
order for four hundred of them but I am afraid I cannot finish
them in time.' He said, 'There are more pikes in Bolton than I
thought there were, there is many a thousand.' I said I thought
there had been two or three anvils at work and he said, there
was a good deal more making besides him in the town, Cowle is
a speaker at the Chartist meetings, I have know him for several
years and he knows me.

John Burrow

*(b) Letter to the Home Secretary and two depositions from the
magistrates at Bradford*

From the Harewood Papers

My Lord
    We beg leave to forward to your Lordship for perusal, some
Depositions we have taken today relating to the proceedings of
the Chartists in this District, also a Memorial presented to us by
the Inhabitants of Bradford praying for protection against the
designs of the Chartists. We have two Months ago as we
informed your Lordship at the time, sworn in a number of
special Constables, but we think that Body, as in fact to our
Knowledge many of them have stated, would not act in the case
of an Outbreak, inasmuch as the general belief is that a large
number of the adherents of the Chartists are under Arms and
they have nothing to oppose to them but staves, we are further
informed, indeed we know, that the peaceably disposed
Inhabitants of Bradford in consequence of the frequent and
unexpected Meetings of numerous assemblies of people who
listen to and are exited by the Violent harangues of evil
disposed and Revolutionary speakers are in the utmost alarm,
and without the protection of a Military Force they are
persuaded beyond all doubt that some violent outrage will take
place, and that neither the life nor property of the middle or
higher classes of whatever political opinion is at all safe. We are
your Lordship's most humble and Obedient Servants.

E. C. Lister — Manningham —
Matt^w Thompson — Manningham Lodge —
H. W. Hird — Low Moor House —
W. R. C. Stansfield — Esholt Hall —
Justices for the West Riding of the County of York

P.S. We beg leave to state that the Memorial presented to us is signed by parties who are known to us as respectable individuals, and we beg also to state that the Depositions sent are only instances of numbers of similar cases which might have been authenticated on Oath and transmitted —

W.R.C.S.
H.W.H.
M.T.
E.C.L.

West Riding of Yorkshire   The Examination of William Egan of Bradford Gun-Smith taken on Oath before us three of Her Majesty's Justices of the peace in and for the said Riding the 26th day of July 1839. —

Who says, on Wednesday the seventeenth instant a person whom I did not know and who appeared to be in the Capacity of a Labourer called at my Shop and asked me if I had any Guns or Bayonets by me, to which question I answered that I had not. He then asked me if I would take an Order for a quantity — I think he mentioned a hundred. I told him it was out of my line of Business entirely to meddle with Musquets and Bayonets. He then asked me if I knew any Gunmakers or Ironmongers who would take an order for them and I said I did not know any person who was likely to take an order for such articles. I have had since then almost daily applications for soldiery Guns. During the present week I have had application for ten at the least. During the last week or ten days I have been applied to to alter Musquets which have been bought to me without Stocks, the alterations required were generally to place the sight of the Musquet further from the end of the Barrel in order that the Bayonet might have better hold. I have seen a considerable number of parts of Musquets such as Locks, Barrels, Ramrods. The applications to me have become more numerous within the last fortnight than they ever were before. —

Wm Egan

Sworn before us
  Matt^w Thompson
  H. W. Hird
  W. R. C. Stansfield

West Riding   The Examination of Joseph Glover of Shipley
    of   Constable taken on oath before us, Three of Her
  Yorkshire   Majesty's Justices of the peace in and for the
              said Riding the 26th day of July 1839. —
Who says, Having been informed that Joseph North a Black-
smith residing at Shipley and carrying on his Business there, was
Manufacturing Spears for the use of Charterists. I went on
Saturday afternoon last about four o'clock, to his Workshop
and there I saw a Wooden Shaft, upwards of six feet, with a
socket at the end of it capable of admitting a Spear. I noticed
Samuel North the Son of Joseph North going out with a spear
with a Cross bar to it, and one of the Shopmen a younger Son
of Joseph North told me that he was going down to the
Mechanics Shop to get it sharpened. The same Boy then chalked
out the Shape of the Instrument and said that the Hooks on
each side the Spear were for the purpose of Cutting Bridle
Reins. Another Man in the Shop who Married one of Joseph
North's Daughters, told me that he had been at Newcastle and
had seen a great quantity of similar weapons. I did not see the
Boy come back, and I heard nothing more, except on Tuesday
last, when I had a conversation with Joseph North and he then
told me that he had only made one, and that he thought he
should make no more for he thought it was not right to do so.

                                             Joseph Glover

Sworn before us
  Matt^w Thompson
  H. W. Hird
  W. R. C. Stansfield

22 Drilling

From T.S. 11/1030/4424

(a) Prosecution case against Timothy Higgins, secretary of the Ashton-under-Lyne Radical Association

The Town of Aston underlyne is in the centre of a very densely populated manufacturing district — The population of the Town and neighbourhood amounts to from sixty thousand to seventy thousand — Ashton is the place where the well known agitator The Revd Joseph Rayner Stephens has held forth and for the last six or eight months the town and neighbourhood has been kept in a constant state of Agitation by him and others holding meetings and using violent and inflammatory language, threats, and encouraging people to procure arms and other offensive weapons to redress what is termed the people's grievances — The factory act was the first question upon which the system of Agitation commenced then the poor law bill and next the charter question — The Exhortations made by the leaders have induced the inexperienced portion of the work people to assemble together in large numbers and exhibit and discharge fire arms in the public streets to the terror and alarm of the more peaceable part of the community — The language made use of at the meetings of the Chartists will appear from the evidence has been such as to cause great alarm and excitement — For some time back a considerable number of fire arms have been sent into the town of Ashton underlyne and great numbers of pikes have been made and sold in the town and neighbourhood — Up to the month of April last large bodies of men have met together late at night and early in the morning for the purpose of training to military exercise four persons have been committed and are indicted at the present assizes for this offence — Although it was well known that arms and other offensive weapons were sold to and purchased by persons who could not want them for their own defence merely — yet the magistrates and authorities were at a loss how to proceed against persons for simply having them in their possession there being no statute warranting them in apprehending parties and it

211

being a question also whether the mere fact of having them in their possession was an offence at common law unless it could be shown that they had them for an unlawful object — but on the night of Saturday the 29th of June last it having been communicated by a person who did not wish his name to be made use of that there were a quantity of fire arms in the possession of the defendant — Robert Newton the Deputy Constable of Ashton undcrlyne proceeded to defendant's house at about two o'clock in the morning of Sunday the 30th day of June he rapped at the door and was let in by a man — Newton asked the man if there were not two large boxes come there — he replied not as he was aware of — Newton then asked a female who was sitting near the fire the same question who also denied any knowledge of there being any — He Newton then went up stairs and saw two long boxes one without a lid, the other with one fastened up — Higgins was in bed in the same room and Newton asked him what the boxes were doing there he said he did not know He then asked him where they had come from he answered from Thompsons of Birmingham — Newton said he should be obliged to take both of them into his possession and also to take him, Higgins, into custody — Higgins got up and dressed — Newton then procured a cart and put the boxes into it and took Higgins to the lockup — and on his way there Higgins spoke for the first time and said that he was an agent to Thompson of Birmingham — In the box that was opened he Newton saw muskets, and bayonets — On examining the boxes at the police office one contained 17 muskets 18 bayonets and 4 single barrelled guns — the other contained 4 double barrelled guns one single barrelled gun, three rifle pieces — 3 pistols and a bullet mould — In a corner of Higgin's bed room Newton found one horse pistol a brace of small pistols and 3 bullet moulds — In his house he also found several memorandum books and a quantity of papers with writing upon them — He also found a printed book entitled 'A New System of Defensive Instructions for the People' which see — this book purports to be wrote by 'F. Macerone' — at the commencement of it are two engravings representing soldiers in an engagement in the field of battle and the other the form of a lance and other instruments of warfare together with cartridges — In pages 4 and 5 of this book will be found a recommendation for the people to procure arms and by means of them to obtain justice their privileges etc. and the whole book then continues to show the system and practice of arms —

The other letters, papers and books all go to show that he Higgins, is the secretary of a Radical Association and that he has been all through the country within the last six or eight months attending meetings of the Chartists where very inflammatory language has been used as will appear by two sheets of paper in his hand writing produced by Newton. He is in possession of letters from Stephens McDouall and O'Brien whom it is well know are members of the National Convention and that each of them have attended and been great speakers at public meetings and have advised the people to procure arms —

Among the papers is a letter dated May 29th 1839 directed to Abel Williamson Bush Inn Ashton underlyne signed 'A true friend in the cause of Democracy' wherein it states 10 guns have been sent out of 20 which had been ordered and he asks for a case and orders when to send the others — see this letter marked 1 in supplemental brief.

Higgins was a cotton spinner by trade and resided in a house worth £8 a year two other families lived in the same house.

The defendant it will be observed was present at a meeting in Ashton underlyne on the 20th day of April last which was called by placard — headed 'The Chartists' and giving notice that on the evening of the above day there would be a procession formed for the purpose of escorting Dr McDouall (who was the representative in the Convention for Ashton) into the town — a many thousand persons attended this meeting with bands of music. Banners and flags - the procession did meet McDouall at the entrance into the Town and after parading the streets they assembled in the market place where speeches were delivered by McDouall and others — During the whole time the meeting was being held there were shouts and a constant discharge of fire arms — as they went along the streets guns were let off.

For copies of documents to be given in evidence counsel is referred to supplemental brief delivered herewith.

(b) Prosecution case against William Cox of Ashton-under-Lyne
The town and neighbourhood of Ashton underlyne has for a considerable time past been in a very disturbed state. The excitement seems to have been in a great measure caused by the violent and inflammatory addresses of several Chartist leaders at their public meetings —

In the months of November, December, January, February, March and April last there were many public meetings of the

Chartists at Ashton underlyne and at Staly bridge which is an adjacent town to Ashton underlyne.

The Rev. J. R. Stephens, Mr McDouall and several other Chartists' leaders have addressed these meetings which were generally attended by many thousand persons —

Their hearers were principally operatives of the Cotton factories and they have been openly advised to destroy their masters' property if the masters would not agree to assist them in redressing their imaginary grievances. The people were exhorted to arm themselves and were then told that their supposed wrongs must be redressed peaceably if possible, but if not peaceably that they must have recourse to their own right arms. Towards the latter end of March and in the month of April last, it was ascertained that a great number of dangerous weapons, pikes, daggers, etc. had been made and sold in the neighbourhood. The police officers had also good reasons to believe that many fire arms had been brought into the town and that the chartists had commenced training themselves to military exercises, in secluded country places and different parts of the parish early in a morning and late at night.

There was also an association called 'The Ashton under lyne radical association' formed in the town and the officers were credibly informed that its members were regularly drilled to the use of arms.

On the evening of the 20th of April (the day previous to the offence mentioned in this indictment being committed) there was a meeting of the chartists held in the Ashton under lyne market place. At this meeting it is estimated that upwards of 10,000 persons were present and the people were openly exhorted to provide themselves with fire arms. Several very inflammatory speeches were delivered and during the time of the procession as well as during the holding of the meeting there was a continual firing of pistols and other fire arms.

At about six o'clock the following morning (viz.) Sunday the 21st of April, last, witness Robert Newton who is Deputy constable of Ashton under Lyne accompanied by his brother who is an assistant constable went to a place called Well Stile in the parish of Ashton under Lyne and in a field there he found about 80 or 100 men marching backwards and forwards and going through military evolutions. The defendant and three others who were apprehended at the same time and who are indicted at the assizes were all there and in the ranks being drilled. There were persons who acted as Serjeants by drilling

214

the others, but unfortunately none of them are at present known. It will appear that witness Slater had been in the field for about an hour before the Newtons went, and that when Slater first went there were very few persons assembled. Slater who is an *Old Soldier* asked one of the men who afterwards acted as a serjeant whether they were for drilling that morning and the man replied 'yes they will be pouring in from all quarters by and by'. When the men came into the field the serjeant called out 'Fall in' and the men formed themselves into drills and commenced drilling.

From these circumstances there can scarcely be any doubt that the assembly was preconcerted and that the hour and place had been fixed upon at some previous meeting.

When the Newtons entered the field many of the persons broke out of the ranks and ran away. Upon this the Newtons walked quietly through the field and in about half an hour afterwards returned. The men were still drilling and one of them who was acting as Serjeant on seeing the Newtons fell into the ranks and marched with the others. Neither the defendant in this case nor the other man were taken into custody at the time, but informations were laid before the magistrates and warrants were granted for their apprehension. Early in the morning of the 4th of May the defendant and the others were apprehended and they were examined before the magistrates the same day and required to find sureties for their appearance at the present assizes. The required recognizances were entered into in the course of a few hours after the examination, but in the meantime a great number of persons assembled in front of the police office where defendant and the others were detained in safe custody and threatened to rescue them. The persons so assembled seemed so much disposed to commence rioting that the magistrates considered it advisable that they should have the assistance of the military. However when it became generally known that the defendants were finding bail, the people separated without any outbreak and the town resumed its usual tranquil state.

After the defendant and the other men were apprehended their houses were searched and in the house of defendant Cox was found not only a pike head, but also a bullet mould and a pint pot full of bullets. The defendant and the other three are it is believed all members of the 'Ashton under Lyne radical association' before mentioned. The secretary has since this occurrence been held to bail for his appearance at the assizes to

215

answer a charge of having about 30 stand of arms in his possession with the intent to dispose of them to persons to break the peace.

He has been convicted at the Chester Assizes which commenced on Monday last for a conspiracy.

PROOFS

To prove that betwixt five and six o'clock in the morning of Sunday the 21st day of April last he left his residence and went to a place called Well Stile near Waterhouses in the parish of Ashton under Lyne and that in the field there he saw about one hundred men. That he was in the same field close to them and could hear what they said. That they formed themselves into squads. That there were three squads and about thirty or forty in a squad. That the men went through what witness who has been a soldier calls facings. That they formed sections and marched in line across the field and wheeled to the right and marched forward and wheeled again both right and left.

(c) Brief for the prosecution in the case of William Cox

Liverpool Summer Assizes 1839

The Queen
against
William Cox otherwise called
William Braithwaite
For Training to
Military Exercise

BRIEF FOR THE PROSECUTION

Indictment charges that on the 21st day of April in the second years at the parish of Ashton under lyne in the County of Lancaster divers evil disposed persons to the number of 100 and more to the jurors unknown were met and assembled together for the purpose of being trained and drilled to the use of arms and for the purpose of practising Military Exercise movements and Evolutions without any lawful authority for so doing and that William Cox otherwise called William Braithwaite, late of Ashton underlyne, a labourer unlawfully did attend and was

216

present at the said meeting and assembly for the purpose of being trained and drilled to the use of arms and of practising Military Exercise movements and Evolutions against the form of the statute.

2nd Count Charges on the day and year aforesaid at the parish aforesaid divers Evil disposed persons (as in the first count) were met and assembled together for the purpose of being trained and that the said William Cox otherwise called William Braithwaite on the day and year aforesaid at the parish afore- said at the said last mentioned meeting and assembly was trained and drilled to the use of arms and the practise of Military Exercise movements and Evolution against the form of the statute.

3rd Count charges that the said William Cox otherwise called William Braithwaite together with divers other Evil disposed persons to the number of one hundred and more to the jurors unknown on the day and year aforesaid at the parish aforesaid unlawfully and tumultuously did assemble and gather together in a formidable and menacing manner armed with sticks staves and other offensive weapons and in Military array to disturb the peace of the Queen and being so assembled and gathered together armed as aforesaid did then and there unlawfully and tumultuously cause a great noise riot and disturbance and did then and there remain and continue armed as aforesaid making such noise riot and disturbance for the space of an hour and more to the great disturbance and terror not only of the liege subjects there being and residing but of all other the liege subjects of the Queen then passing and repassing in and along the Queen-Common Highway there in contempt of our said Lady the Queen and her laws to the Evil example and against the peace.

23 Report of Meeting to pray for Imprisoned Chartists

From the 'Northern Star', August 1840

A large meeting was held on Clerkenwell Green, on last Sunday morning for the purpose of offering up a prayer for the imprisoned Chartists. The placard calling the meeting was directed to Christians of all denominations. A short and appropriate discourse was delivered on the occasion, and was followed by an address from a Chartist brother. The prayer was then read in the most devout and solemn manner, the assembly being uncovered, with which the police, on being requested courteously, complied.

FORM OF PRAYER

Almighty God! The Parent of all living! the father alike of the Queen and the peasant! Listen at this time we beseech Thee to the voice of our united and fervent supplications. We confess before Thee with shame and confusion, that we have sinned against Thee — that we have broken Thy most holy laws, and that in the payment of rates for the support of the Established Church, which is opposed to Thee both in word and deed, we have robbed Thee of that supreme honour and regard to which Thou art entitled. But have mercy on us Oh! God! we beseech Thee. Lord! have mercy on us, Christ! have mercy on us.

And whilst, Oh Most High! we are engaged at the Throne of thy Heavenly Grace on our own behalf, we would not forget those who have placed themselves in authority over us, but whom we have never elected, and who have taken from us our 'free-will offerings', which we dedicated to support the poor, to clothe the naked, and assist the fatherless, and have appropriated them to support their own Commissioners and Agents. Lord! Have mercy on their souls, pardon their iniquities and blot out their transgressions.

King of kings! and Lord of lords! have mercy on the Queen, shew unto her the error of her ways, enlighten her mind that she may see the sinfulness of attending the playhouse on the Saturday, and taking the most Holy Sacrament, at the Lord's

218

supper on the Sunday — lead her to the examination of herself and the auful state of the country — convince her that she cannot be the mother of the country whilst so many of her children are starving for lack of food — that she receives too much money for merely living in a large house, and signing acts of Parliament, for oppressing the people, Thy servants. Oh Lord! convert her and her Royal husband. May the Lord have mercy on their souls —

Oh most merciful Father! Whose Government, except where distorted by man, is all mercy! Remember, we entreat Thee, our brethren who are at this time confined in dark and gloomy dungeons, for endeavouring by peaceful and Scriptural means to obtain possession of just rights — visit them even there — strengthen them with the consolations of the Gospel, and though they are prevented from attending the public means of grace, support their minds; and if any should perish for want of the necessaries of life, receive their spirits, and may they dwell forever more with Thyself and the patriots that have gone before them. We rejoice in the contemplation of that great attribute of Thy character, by which Thou doest behold all the actions of men, whether good or evil. Thine eyes did follow the arrest — the trial — the effort to get convicted — yes the very verdict is recorded on high in Heaven's court. Thou hast observed the minutest circumstances which have attended the persecutions of Thy servants and Thou hast and will sustain them. Deliver them out of the hands of their enemies. Hear our prayer for John Frost and his compatriots Williams and Jones, for Feargus O'Connor, for Henry Vincent, yea for the whole catalogue of patriots whose every case Thou art well acquainted with. Provide for their wives and families may the children follow the steps of their fathers, as far as they have followed Thy holy example. We thank Thee for the past, we thank Thee for the future.

And now, oh Lord! May we depart in peace. Direct the Council of the people now sitting in a distant part of the country — may the means they may resort to be consistent with the glory, and further emancipation of Thy servants. Bless our enemies — convert the lawyers, — the spies, — the soldiers, — the police, and all others that have been engaged in the unjust persecution of the people; and to Thy name, Oh, Parent of mankind, shall be the glory;

'Our Father' etc.

PART IV

Clashes with Authority

It is surprising, in view of the enormous amount of tension and suspicion on both sides, that there were not more clashes between the Chartists and the authorities in the early years of the movement. The Bull Ring riots at Birmingham, the Llanidloes clash and the Newport rising represent the three outbreaks of real violence in 1839. The account of the Llanidloes events which is reproduced here is part of a pamphlet written by Edward Hamer, a local historian of some ability, in 1867, which was partly based on eye-witness accounts of the events. Its reliability has been challenged, however, and it should perhaps not be accepted in its entirety. For a discussion of the Llanidloes events, see David Williams, 'John Frost'.

The Newport rising is illustrated here not by descriptions of the events in Newport itself, but by a letter from the local magistrate before the event, indicating how far the authorities were in the dark as to the extent of the preparations which must have been made, and the eye-witness account of a local businessman who had the misfortune to fall in with the Chartists on their march towards Newport.

This pamphlet was published anonymously in 1847, although the author was known to be a brewer named Barnabas Brough who had given evidence at the trial of Frost, Williams and Jones. The material contained in the pamphlet had mostly already been given in evidence at the trial. It does, however, provide in this form a vivid picture of the confusion of the night's march. Brough's motive in publishing was probably simply the desire to make some profit from what had been, for him, a disastrous experience financially. He claims in the pamphlet that he was driven from the neighbourhood by the refusal of the local people to have dealings with him after his having given evidence against the Chartists. His brewery was sold in July 1840. The 'Northern Star', in its review of the pamphlet (20 November 1847), said:

Bruff's treachery excited so much public odium against him that he soon found Wales too hot to be comfortable. He therefore had to leave the scene of his 'moving accidents by flood and field' and has since been dodging and scheming in different parts of the country, proclaiming his remarkable services to the government, and his deep wrongs in not having received some reward from the powers that be. We have heard, on very good authority, that Bruff has more than once petitioned to be rewarded with a situation under government in return for his treachery to Mr Frost, but hitherto in vain, the government not being able to understand the claims of a cowardly informer. The Whigs being again in power, Bruff has published his 'thrilling'(!) narrative, seemingly with the hope of attracting attention to his 'claims'. Whether the telling of his story be at all likely to prolong the exile of Mr Frost, for that Bruff cares not. 'Every man for himself' is the patriotic Bruff's motto. . . .

From Birmingham is included a unique series of reports from a police spy who succeeded in being accepted as a member of the local Chartist organisation. The notes to these reports are the comments written in the margin by Redfern, the chief of the Birmingham police to whom the reports were submitted before they were sent to the Home Secretary.

24 Extract from 'The Chartist Outbreak in Llanidloes' by Edward Hamer

Published Llanidloes, 1867

Tuesday 30th. A lovely spring morning ushered in this eventful day, one ever to be remembered, by those who witnessed its proceedings, as perhaps the most momentous in the little town's history. At an early hour, information that a police force had arrived from London, leaked out through the domestics of the hotel, and it was also stated that they had come for the purpose of arresting the Chartist leaders. This intelligence spread rapidly through the town, and caused the greatest excitement among the members of the Political Union. After conferring together, the leaders determined to call a meeting of their supporters. A Chartist, armed with a long tin horn, was sent to parade the streets, and after each flourish of this musical instrument, he announced the fact that an assembly of the members of the Union would be held on the 'Long' Bridge. The tin horn, which is still preserved as a sacred relic in the family of the 'bugler,' was styled by the Chartists the 'Horn of Liberty,' while the soldiers who visited the town after the outbreak dubbed it the 'Chartists' Bugle.' In obedience to the summons numbers flocked to the bridge, where they were addressed from the parapet by one of the leaders, whose usual high-souled courage had deserted him upon the arrival of the London police, and had converted the confident leader into a timid suppliant for a mob's protection. While still appealing to the crowd around him in the most pathetic and touching manner, that they would not allow himself and his fellows to be given up to the minions of the law, messengers from different directions were seen approaching the spot. As soon as they came within hearing, they shouted out that three of their comrades had been arrested in front of the hotel by the London police. This startling intelligence threw the meeting into disorder, every one of its members seemed to think only of releasing their friends at once, and 'To the rescue!' pealed from lip to lip; and, as if galvanised, an instantaneous disorderly rush was made towards the Trewythen Arms to set their companions at liberty. Let us leave them for a

222

moment, to explain the cause of this sudden outburst of feeling.

Strengthened by the arrival of the men sent by the Home Secretary, the magistrates assembled at the hotel, and decided upon arresting the individuals against whom the warrants were out; and, to be prepared for the worst, had sent the town crier to request the immediate presence at the Trewythen Arms of the special constables then in the town. Between forty and fifty obeyed the call, and, loitering before the inn, watching the proceedings, were the identical men whom the authorities were so anxious to apprehend: they were pointed out to the police, who at once took them into custody, and secured them inside the hotel. Upon this the tocsin of alarm was given, and the news of the arrest reached those assembled at the bridge in a very short time. This crowd, with their numbers swelled on the way, soon arrived in sight of the hotel, where they saw the police and special constables drawn up to receive them. The sight took them aback, but it was only the momentary impediment which dammed up the waters for a more impetuous rush.

Without arms of some description, their great number was no match for the police and specials, armed with their staves of office. They accordingly withdrew for a few moments to procure whatever they could lay their hands on in the form of weapons — guns, staves, pikes, hay forks, sickles, and even spades were hastily seized by the excited and turbulent mob!

Some of the women who had joined the crowd kept instigating the men to attack the hotel — one old virago vowing that she would fight till she was knee-deep in blood, sooner than the Cockneys should take their prisoners out of the town. She, with others of her sex, gathered large heaps of stones, which they subsequently used in defacing and injuring the building which contained the prisoners. When the mob had thus armed themselves, the word 'Forward!' was given, and as soon as they were within hearing of the police, they imperatively demanded the release of their friends, which demand was of course refused. What took place during the next few minutes cannot be easily ascertained; both parties afterwards accused the other of commencing the fray. The special constables, many of whose acquaintances were among the crowd, were seen to give way on the approach of the Chartists, and to seek their safety either in the hotel, or by trusting to their legs. When their request was denied them, the mob set up a terrible shout, and pressed forward towards the door of the inn; the rioters asserting that the London police began the conflict by striking one of their number, which only exasperated them the more, and caused them to shout out for 'revenge!' as well as the release of the prisoners. They further state that the Ex-Mayor, on finding that he was locked out, to ensure his own safety, suddenly appeared to sympathize with the mob, by crying out 'Chartists for ever';* and, with a stick which he had in his hand, broke the first pane of glass, thus initiating the mob in the work of destruction.

The women followed the example thus set them by throwing stones at every window of the house, while the men pressed forward and tried to burst in the front door, through which the police had retired. The thought of their prey slipping through their fingers infuriated the mob, who sent repeated showers of stones at the door and windows; the latter were soon shattered into a thousand fragments. Guns were next fired through the door, which, after resisting all their efforts for some time, was ultimately burst open. The mob quickly spread themselves over the house in search of their comrades, whom they found handcuffed in the kitchen. They were at once led off to a smith's shop, where their gyves were knocked off. Finding themselves masters of the house, the rabble proceeded to hunt out the policemen, against whom alone their animosity was now directed. The Mayor with one of the police had retired to the bedrooms, but the latter (Blenkhorn) was soon found, and dragged from under a bed; his pistol and staff were wrested from him, and the former was presented at his head. He was then most savagely abused by all who were within reach of him, till his bruised and bleeding features moved the hearts of some of the most compassionate, who managed at great risk to save his life, for only with his life would some of the ruffians be appeased. The Mayor† (a surgeon by profession) was also discovered in one of the bedrooms. He was rather frightened when brought out into the street; but a happy idea occurred to him, — he appealed to their better nature, by recalling to their memories how he had saved their mothers' lives in ushering them (the Chartists) into the world, &c. He touched the right string; their hearts were softened, and they allowed him to proceed to his home without injuring him. Two of the London

---

* The trick enabled him to pass through the crowd in safety. Having done this, he travelled with all possible speed to give the Lord Lieutenant information respecting the outbreak.

† The late David Evans, Esq. He died August 12th, 1844, aged 57, and was buried at the east end of the church.

224

policemen managed to escape into the hay-loft of a stable adjoining the hotel, where they were secreted by some labourers who took pity on them; but they were dreadfully beaten before they reached this haven of rest. At midnight they were conveyed in a chaise to Newtown. The cellar was emptied of its contents; wines, spirits and ales were conveyed into the streets, where the mob stove in the barrel ends and destroyed more than they drank. While some were thus engaged, others proceeded up the stairs, destroying everything as they went; the bedrooms were entered and the furniture smashed to pieces; the window curtains and bed hangings were torn to shreds; the bedsteads and staircase were cut with their hatchets and pikes; and they seemed to derive the most exquisite pleasure from witnessing the beautiful pier glasses being cast through the windows upon the pavement beneath. During the affray in front of the hotel, a half-pay officer of the forty-second regiment made himself conspicuous, by rushing into the thickest part of the mob with a view of arresting one of the leaders; but he was soon overpowered and knocked down. He, however, managed to escape after receiving considerable injury.

The family of the landlord were dreadfully alarmed, but they received no personal injury, although they were rudely treated by some of the ruffians who were the worse for their visit to the cellar. The hotel had formerly been the private residence of General Jones, who had distinguished himself in the American War of Independence; and the accommodation, furniture and fittings of the house were at that time superior to any in the county. The damage done was immense; the inside of the house seemed a perfect wreck. Yet, singular as it may appear, robbery did not form a part of the programme of these reckless men; they took none of the valuables from the house; even the land-lord's watch was smashed to pieces, but left in the bedroom where they found it. Destruction alone seemed to relieve the intense feeling of hatred which they experienced against the police and the house which sheltered them.

25 Letter to the Home Secretary from a Newport Magistrate about the Distribution of Arms in the Area

From H.O. 40/45

Newport, 12th March 1839

My Lord

Since I had the honour of addressing you a letter on the 9th inst. I have made minute inquiries into the subject of the guns which have been received by coach in this place and I have come to the conclusion that the information which was conveyed to me on the first inst. was calculated to give a somewhat exaggerated impression of the real facts of the case. The inquiries I have made have only enabled me to trace with certainty three distinct packages of guns and muskets, all of which appear to have arrived here from the neighbourhood of Birmingham, and one of which was accompanied by a heavy hamper. Of those packages, two were sent from here to Pontypool, two to Tredegar, both towns in this county surrounded by iron works. It is extremely probable that hawkers passing through the county finding a great demand for guns and muskets order them in the usual way of business without knowing or caring for the purpose to which they are intended to be applied. I understand that clubs have been recently established in this neighbourhood to which men contribute small periodical payments in order to obtain arms in their town, and I was informed sometime back that guns and muskets were purchased with eagerness at the neighbouring iron works. It is also within my own knowledge that active efforts are making to incite the workmen employed at the Collieries to violence and to persuade them that in any course they may pursue they will not be opposed by the soldiers who would not act against them. There has existed in this town for some months a Chartist Society — some of the members whereof make circuits periodically into the neighbouring villages and mining districts to obtain signatures to the Chartist petition and contribute to the national rent. The missionaries attend at public houses and beer shops where a party small or large as the case may be has been assembled. The missionary expounds to them the grievances under which they labour tells them that half their earnings are taken from them in taxes, that these taxes are spent in supporting the rulers in idleness and profligacy — that their employers are tyrants who acquire wealth by their labour, that the great men around them possess property to which they are not entitled that these evils are to be cured by the Chartists but that the people must sign the Chartist petition and contribute to the Chartist rent, that if their demands are not peaceably conceded they will be justified in resorting to force and that they need not fear bloodshed because the soldiers will not act and a letter is normally read to confirm the statement made with respect to the feeling of the soldiery. I cannot say to what extent these appeals may influence the conduct of the working classes in this neighbourhood — I am loath to believe that they will be hurried into actual insurrection but it is certain that sullen discontent marks their appearance that they look with aversion and dislike at their employers and that the moral influence which ought to belong to the government and without which the government itself cannot exist is altogether at an end amongst a very numerous class of the community. I do not think that anything which has yet occurred need excite apprehension of immediate violence and it may be prudent to take no step that can be construed into fear but I would urge strongly on the government the necessity for being fully prepared for an outbreak. The appeal made to the passions of the ignorant and wicked must sooner or later lead to acts of illegality and violence and it seems now openly avowed that a systematic application of physical force is the means by which the Chartists intend to act on the government and the legislature. If such a proceeding be really adopted it is obvious that it would consist of a wide spread insurrection commenced at once in parts of the Kingdom remote from each other. In this neighbourhood with an extremely large and very reckless population we are wholly unprepared for such an event having no troops of any description in any part of the county.

I have the honour to be, my Lord, your very obedient servant,

J. Phillips, Jr

26 'A Night with the Chartists' by Barnabas Brough

Pamphlet published anonymously in 1847

The incidents deeply interesting; and though strange, yet not more strange than true.

PREFACE

The following extraordinary narration of adventures may appear to ordinary readers as bordering too much on the marvellous, to be easily credited. But a reference to the diurnal press of the period, and but more especially to the 'Times' Newspaper, of November the 12th, 1839, or to the published report of the Monmouthshire State Trials, by Messrs Butterworth & Co., Fleet Street, in 1840, will fully show, that nothing but well proved facts, and veritable occurrences, are here related; in fact, such reference will prove them considerably less romantic even than the account given by the usually business-like reporter of the 'Times.'

The narrative was written at the especial request of several of the narrator's friends — then too far removed from the scene of action to be cognizant (as far as their friend was concerned) of the memorable occurrences which took place at Newport, on the night of the 3rd and the morning of the 4th of November, 1839, by the Chartist Insurrectionists. The Editor, with a desire to show the folly of such fool-hardy attempts; and to point out, to how much suffering, annoyance, and danger, innocent persons may be subjected — has obtained permission of the Author to lay before the public on its eighth anniversary, the adventures he encountered during a *night with the Chartists* in Monmouthshire, headed by Frost, Williams, and Jones.

London, November, 1847

Truth is strange, stranger than fiction.

Few of the reading public can have forgotten the insane attempt at insurrection made by the *Chartists* in Monmouthshire, at the latter part of the year 1839, when a body of misguided men, many thousands in number, led by three persons, whose names have so frequently of late been before the public, namely, *Frost, Williams,* and *Jones*, were discomfitted, and totally dispersed by a small detachment of the 45th regiment, amounting to only twenty-eight men, at the Westgate Inn, at Newport, in Monmouthshire.

The outbreak was to many a memorable one — to too many a fatal one — to myself a fearful one; and, but for an irregularity in the legal proceedings, would have been to the three leaders, a terrible and an awful one — they were all three condemned to *Death*; and, though their lives were spared, they are doomed (unless her Majesty mercifully shorten the period) to drag out the remainder of their days in the penal settlements of South Australia.

It is not my intention in this article to chronicle the incidents of that absurd conspiracy, or to trace the causes which led to its ridiculous, though melancholy, termination; but, to render the adventure about to be narrated more fully understood, it is necessary to glance at a few of the facts in connexion with its history; the more so that time has now softened down the angry feelings, and rubbed off the asperities of temper, then engendered by that most ridiculous attempt at revolution.

Mr John Frost was well known to, and much respected by, me; and, up to the time of his becoming a delegate to the Chartist Convention, I was not only on friendly terms, but in political agreement with him, both of us inclining to what was then considered the *Radical* side of *Whiggism*, now the politics of the majority. When Mr Frost became publicly a lecturer on, and a supporter of, Chartism (though our social intimacy continued), our political agreement was disrupted; so much so, that on many occasions I publicly opposed, not only what Mr Frost advocated, but also the sentiments of his friend Vincent, as well as those of Jones. Of Zephaniah Williams, I knew but little: simply that, he being a publican, and myself a brewer, I had merely a *commercial* knowledge of him.

With William Jones it was different: on my first acquaintance with him, I found that he possessed considerable mechanical ingenuity and tact, and, in consequence, occasionally employed

229

him; a farther acquaintance proved him to be a man of more than common-place talent in his rank of life; and, being a member of a philanthropic society to which he also belonged, I took some interest in his well-being: and when I found that he had joined the Chartists I did all I could (as did many others) to detach him from what I considered a dangerous party. Finding, however, that, although he received my remonstrances with respect and attention, he still persisted in connecting himself with the Chartists, and became a public lecturer in favour of that political creed: *I tried harsher means* — I assisted in causing his suspension from office in our benevolent society. That not succeeding, his friends (many of them) went further: they ceased to hold converse or communication with him, and no longer recognised him as an acquaintance.

These observations would be unnecessary, but that I shall have presently to mention an incident that, under these circumstances, redounds highly to the unfortunate man's credit. Previous to the outbreak I had been connected with our parish as guardian of the poor, and was one of the committee of inspectors of police; and stood in the relative position just stated with the three great leaders of the Chartist movement, *Frost, Williams,* and *Jones.*

The morning of Sunday, the 3rd of November, 1839, was 'ushered in with clouds,' promising a wet day. The weather does not always keep its promise in this respect — but on this occasion it did most faithfully — it turned out a regular *drenching wet day* — and what appeared worse, a wet night too; the sequel will shew, however, that the wet that night not only saved my life, but, most likely, the lives of hundreds of others also.

On the morning of this eventful day, I started from Pontypool with a neighbour, in my gig, for Newport, on my way to Cardiff, in Glamorganshire, to visit an invalid sister. On my arrival at Newport (ten miles on my journey) failing to get other conveyance on to Cardiff, and the horse's shoulder showing symptoms of being galled, I was compelled to ride him the rest of the way (twelve miles) to Cardiff. On arriving there, I was a second time wet through. (I had changed part of my clothes before, at Newport.) Again I got my clothes dried, paid my visit, and returned in the same way, in the evening, to Newport; again wet through. During the process of once more drying my dress, I was informed that the authorities of Newport had received information that the Chartists, thousands strong, were coming down that night to attack Newport, led by Frost, Williams, and Jones. On hearing this, as soon as possible, I repaired to the Westgate Inn, where I found Sir Thomas Phillips (then Mr Phillips) the Mayor, with the military and a large force of special constables. The Mayor assured me the report was to be relied on, and advised me not to proceed home.

The cry of 'The Chartists are coming,' like the cry of 'Wolf,' had so often been given before, that I turned a deaf ear to the Mayor's kind recommendation, ordered my gig, and, with my friend, started for Pontypool! Would we had not!! We proceeded slowly, in consequence of the horse's galled shoulder, for above six miles, when it was evidently becoming worse; so much so, that after considerable jibbing the horse fairly stood still, and would not proceed farther. The Cock Inn at *Cross-y-ceilog*, kept by a customer of mine, being close at hand, we determined on leaving the poor brute there, and walking the remainder of the distance (four miles) home. We saw the horse properly attended to, and set off per turnpike-road, on foot, for Pontypool, regardless of the reports that the Chartists were coming. We reckoned, however, without our host, — *they came*! We had reached the great oak at the *Race Farm*, within about three miles and a half of home, when we suddenly heard the heavy tread of a multitude of feet, and, ere we could exchange a question and answer, were surrounded by hundreds, perhaps thousands, of armed men; for the night was so pitchy dark, that the eye could not penetrate the gloom a single yard in advance. The first words I heard were from a voice which I fancied I knew (and it appears I was right in my conjecture; it was the unhappy man who first fell in front of the Westgate Inn, at Newport, on the Monday morning), uttering, with military authority, the command, '*Halt!*' He then demanded my name and business, and also my companion's; on my mentioning who I was, there was an evident sensation, whispering, and communicating around us. On this, he demanded if we were armed; and, notwithstanding he was answered in the negative, we were instantly ordered to be searched, during the performance of which ceremoney (not over gently performed) I addressed the leader, stating that I was certain I was perfectly well known to him, and to most of the assembled throng, and that, if any violence were committed on the persons of my friend or myself, he would be held responsible. The answer was, — 'Hold your tongue; obey orders, and you'll be taken care of; offer resistance, or attempt to escape, *and it will be the worse for you.*' He then ordered four pikemen to take possession of, and guard, the *prisoners*; which, to their credit be it said, they did most carefully; and, in addition to the four pikemen, two rough and determined fellows, with pistols, took me under their especial care and protection, and never left my side for hours.

I knew every turning, lane, and by-road between Pontypool and Newport. My business, for years, took me every week, sometimes twice or thrice, down to Newport, and that, too, by all the roads wherever a house in my business existed; so that the bearings of all the turnings were as familiar to me as if I had made a regular survey of the country. I, in consequence occasionally cast a furtive glance down any avenue where I knew there was a chance of a run for it; but I was always foiled. The fellows with the pistols seemed to read my intentions by the turning of my head, for it was too dark to see my face; and when I did look down a lane, I was reminded in terms the most gross and disgusting, that if I even looked aside again I should have a bullet through my head. During this time, we made several halts, and it was evident that there were communications being made between our party and some one in the rear; which I have since learned was with Jones.

And here let me do justice to that misguided man; two years after my having witnessed the awful ceremony of sentence of death being passed on him and his co-leaders, by the late Lord Chief Justice Tindal (and never was that dreadful and awful duty performed with more solemnity and truly Christian feeling than was evinced on the occasion by that great and good man), I was informed by one of Jones's friends, who was no doubt of his party, that, though then in the rear of the section of which he had the command, he was speedily informed of my capture; and that, on hearing it, he instantly forwarded instructions to the front that I was by no means to be allowed to escape, *but that no violence was to be offered to my person*. I have no doubt the first part of his order had reference to my connexion, before alluded to, with the authorities of Pontypool, fancying I might be there for information; but his care for my personal safety must have been induced by kinder and nobler feelings, — *a remembrance of my friendship in past days*. Had I been aware of this act of his, at the trial, he should most certainly have had the advantage of its being given as evidence in his favour. But to return to my narrative.

In this way we were marched (in that dark and dismal night, with the mysterious tramp, or rather the plash, of thousands of

232

feet about and behind us — the very uncertainty of the numbers making the mystery more fearful), in the direction of Newport. When we reached the *Marshes*, a series of low, flat meadows, within a few hundred yards of the turnpike-gate of that name, and within about a mile of the town itself, a halt was ordered, to wait, as it appeared, the coming up of those in the rear. Knowing that the brook which runs in a zig-zag course through the Marshes, must, from the quantity of rain that had fallen, be flooded, and being well acquainted, even in the dark, with the old road which lies immediately beyond it; having confidence in my swimming; and, above all, having been told a few minutes before that the prisoners were to be armed and placed in the front of the forces, as the insurgents entered Newport; I made up my mind to make an effort here to get away from my vigilant guards. I addressed the same silent, cold, almost wordless individual who was evidently the leader of the van, for permission to cross the hedge, assigning a reason for the request; his answer was curt, — '*Yes, to the hedge*.' I took advantage of the permission, and immediately, instead of stopping at the hedge, leaped over the fence; but, unfortunately, found myself half immersed in the water of the ditch, which I had calculated on clearing; it was nearly proving a fatal leap to me! and, as I have since been informed by the solicitor who conducted Jones's defence, would have been my last leap, but for the slipperiness of the bank. The moment I leaped, one of my guards, guessing my intention, levelled his pike, and made a lunge at me with all his might, but, providentially, from the cause stated, his foot slipped, and I escaped by a miracle from being pierced through the body by his murderous weapon. But my danger was not yet passed; on perceiving that the pike had missed me, an incarnate fiend sprung to the hedge, and, with imprecations the most horrible, pointed a rifle at my head, exclaiming that he would draw the first trigger, shed the first blood, and blow out my brains. The cold rifle barrel touched my cheek; I moved it on one side with my hand; I heard the ruffian's horrid exclamation — the click of the cocking of the hammer — of its falling on the nipple of the lock — and I thought it was all over with me!

It was rather astonishing, that though all this occupied only a second or two, I never lost my presence of mind. I said to the villian, 'for Heaven's sake don't both shoot and drown me.' Fortunately the rain had wetted his powder, his gun did not go off; and thus was I again providentially rescued from what appeared inevitable assassination. Several of the insurgents then crossed the hedge, and forced me back, at the point of their pikes, into the road; and I was again a prisoner.

After waiting some time in that heavy rain, my clothes now perfectly saturated with water, and besmeared with mud; shivering with cold, and surrounded by reckless and desperate men who had just attempted my life — we were joined by the party expected, and which I understood was accompanied by Jones; but if that was so, he studiously kept out of our sight, for neither my friend or self saw, or heard him, during the whole of that fearful night. The party were now ordered to march, and we proceeded to the turnpike-gate. On our arrival there, we, the unhappy prisoners, were thrust into a cow-shed on the opposite side of the road, and found ourselves more than ancle-deep in accumulated filth, impossible to sit, and most miserable to stand. We could hear, from the voices, that we were still guarded by the same worthies who had exercised such vigilance over us from the first: and thus we remained for nearly half an hour. The voices ceased, and one of the party who had been hovering about us during the night, and whenever he had an opportunity, attending close to my fellow prisoner — entered the hovel. (I learned afterwards that he had been trying all the night to obtain the liberation of my companion, to whom he was known.) He very kindly enquired if he could do anything for us. I instantly begged him, for God's sake, to get us out of that beastly place, and to remove us, if possible, to the gate-house, where, at least, we might get ourselves warmed. He promised to use his best endeavours; and, after a few minutes absence, returned with the desired permission. We were immediately removed, guarded as before, and soon found ourselves in the midst of the poor misguided, miserable creatures, who thought themselves capable of revolutionizing an empire. They had taken forcible possession of the turnpike gate-house; some of them had blackened faces, the soot partly washed off by the rain — some were disguised with strange dresses — some with their faces covered; but all, woefully wet, wearied, cold and comfortless. Never shall I forget the kindness, or the astonishment of poor old Mills, the gate-keeper, when he saw my condition, and was told that I was a prisoner to the ruffians who had taken possession of his dwelling. I had been long known to the old man, and had gained his good opinion by some little acts of kindness which I had rendered him. He was much excited on seeing me, so much so, that the kind old

234

fellow cried and condoled with me; got me water to wash the dirt from my face; procured me a dry pair of stockings; and, apologising for having nothing in the house to give me to drink, proffered, for the purpose of warming me (as he said), to fill me a pipe of tobacco. *I smoked it*! yes, in that company, under the awful circumstances that then environed me, I smoked a pipe! It *did warm me* — and perhaps never was a pipe smoked with greater *gusto* than was the short, blackened, and often-used pipe that I smoked on that memorable occasion. I accepted the well-darned old pair of woollen stockings, too, from the good old fellow; and a comfort they were to my wet and wearied feet. I know not if he be still alive, if he be, God prosper him in this world; if not, may he be rewarded for his kindness, in another and a better one. But to proceed. About this time, messengers were mysteriously passing and repassing, in and out of the toll-house, and it was evident something of moment had, or was about to occur. Numbers were called over and answered to; when a whispering took place, and we were ordered to be removed to an empty room above stairs. In addition to our former guard, a ruffian with a rifle — who I now recognised as the same man who had recently attempted to blow out my brains in the Marshes — was added. He took up his position at the head of the stairs of the little appartment which formed our prison. This reinforcement to our guards was certainly not the most agreeable to me, for the miscreant had just boasted that the next trigger he pulled on me should be more successful than the last, for that he had taken care to provide himself with *dry powder*, had reloaded his piece, and was now ready for me. (It may not be out of place to mention here, that whilst in the room below, so wet was the night, so saturated the men, that many of them emptied their pockets of handfuls of gunpowder in a state of semi-liquidity). How strange is human nature! Surrounded by blood-thirsty men; guarded by fellows armed with deadly weapons; particularly the ruffian who had an hour or two before attempted, and since had threatened my life; shut up in an empty room, without a chance of escape; wet through; shivering with cold; not a brick even for a pillow, or a mat for a coverlid; I stretched my wearied limbs on the bare boards and slept! yes, *slept*, gentle reader, for near an *hour*! I was awoke, shivering as in an ague, and leaving a watermark impression of my figure on the floor, by the stern voices of our guards, and by the mild one of my kind friend, who had watched over me while I slept, informing me that orders had been given to

235

march!

Of course we had nothing for it but to obey; and now came, with me, the great difficulty; for, on changing my stockings, the gate-keeper had placed my shoes near the fire to dry, and they had, in consequence, shrunk in size, and, from the excessive fatigue I had undergone, my feet had swollen considerably; so that I found it impossible, with all my efforts, to get on my shoes; the consequence was, that I had to re-commence, through dark lanes, over rough roads, wet to the skin, shivering with cold, with blistered feet, and *without* shoes, our dreary march.

It *was* a dreary march! the early part of our journey was comparative comfort to this part of our weary way. Frequently halting, for (as it appeared) instructions, I found we were not going direct to Newport, but were wending our course by *Pen-y-lan*, on the road to the *Cefn* and *Risca*. At the former place we again halted, and to our great gratification obtained some refreshment and the comfort of a warm fire, at the beer shop of kind Mrs Jones.

I had already discovered the advantage of showing — or at any rate of assuming — a confident and courageous bearing; and here, whilst my guards were discussing sundry pots of double X and rations of bread and cheese, I entered into a discussion with the fiercest of them on the *'Points of the Charter.'* This, and perhaps my having paid for a few quarts of beer, so far softened my stern sentinels, that the friend who had obtained our liberation from the cow-house was allowed, at my request, to assist me in getting on my shoes, which, after some trouble, and slashing them with my penknife, was effected. During this process my assistant whispered that Mr Frost was at the *Welsh Oak*, a short distance ahead, and that our party were waiting for his orders to join him there. I instantly saw the advantage of this information, and, slipping a piece of coin into his hand, I begged him to announce to Mr Frost, as soon as possible, the situation I was in. Again we were ordered to advance; and, at about seven o'clock in the morning, we reached the *Welsh Oak*. On our arrival there we were at once taken to the tap-room, still guarded as before. Having proved the advantage of beer amongst our guards at the *Cefn*, we again had recourse to the same innocent bribery, and ordered immediately a copious quantity to be supplied them. Here also our mysterious friend was true to his promise; he had found Mr Frost, who now entered the room with him. He looked unusually pale, haggazed, much

236

fatigued, and evidently dispirited. On entering he immediately inquired 'Where is Mr B—— ?' With unfeigned joy, I started up, presented myself to him, and answered, 'Here I am, sir.' He then asked evidently surprised at seeing me, 'What had brought me there?' I referred him for an answer (pointing to them) to the *amiable* party who had taken such especial care of us during the night, not forgetting to inform him of their kind intentions and practices towards *me* in particular. He was evidently annoyed; and, after sternly glancing round him, he turned to me, and said, with a milder look and manner than he had before assumed, 'Sir, I respect you as a friend and as a gentleman, but I *hate* your politics; you are discharged.' 'And my friend of course?' I asked. 'Who is your friend?' he demanded. I told him. 'Yes, and your friend,' was his rejoinder.

I cordially thanked him, and requested an escort through the assembled thousands, lest other parties might again detain us. This Mr Frost immediately ordered.

It was now day-break, and we were conducted through hosts of drenched, begrimed, fatigued, and many apparently frightened men, who lined the road for a considerable distance, without let, hindrance, or molestation. This party was the section immediately under Mr Frost's command, waiting for the other divisions to join them, and consisted of several thousands of men, nearly all armed, some with pikes, fixed on well-made handles or shafts, some more roughly made; crude spears, formed of rod iron sharpened at one end, and turned into a loop at the other as a handle; guns, muskets, pistols, coal mandrills (a sharp double-pointed pick-axe used in cutting coals), clubs, scythes, crow-bars; and, in fact, any and every thing that they could lay their hands on. The whole presented one of the most heterogeneous collection of instruments and munitions of war that ever were brought into the field to compete with disciplined and well-armed forces. It was folly; it was frenzy; it was sheer insanity; dowright madness!

As soon as we had passed the last phalanx of these misguided and unfortunate men, this mighty mass of all but madmen, we deemed it safest to leave the high road and fly to the mountains. We took the nearest course, regardless of bridges, boats, brakes or brambles, and made straight for the hills. A word here in favour of my *ci-devant* friend, Mr Frost: his opportune interference in my behalf most likely saved my life, and I am grateful for it. Had the party by whom we were first made prisoners pursued their original plan of entering Newport

237

at the north-eastern end of the town simultaneously with Frost's and Williams's entrance by the two great approaches from the west and north-west, there is little doubt (Jones not having appeared) that the threat of placing us with muskets on our shoulders in the front ranks would have been carried out: this Mr Frost could not have helped; he would not have been with that section; but, when the party having us in custody joined Mr Frost's division had he not so kindly interposed his authority, and so fortunately set us at liberty when he did, the same fate would have probably befallen us, and we might have been numbered with those (and innocently too) who lost their lives on that melancholy morning.

This exercise of his authority in our favour — an act which probably saved our lives — was urged by the Judge in summing up to the jury, as much in favour of Mr Frost's humanity, however it might tell against him, as proving him to have supreme command over the insurgent forces. The same learned authority also pointed out other parts of my testimony which favoured the general character of Mr Frost, as a husband, as a father, and as a friend. Yes; it was a fortunate thing for me on that occasion, that I *was* on friendly terms with Mr Frost. It was a more fortunate thing for me that Mr Frost did not forget our friendship on that perilous occasion; and, whilst memory holds her seat, I shall ever remember with gratitude his interference in my favour on that eventful morning. There are few men, who, when by their own acts they have committed themselves for life or for death, would be so considerate for the safety of others, more especially when that party and themselves are in an antagonistic position to each other, as we were in regard to Chartism. Mr Frost knew full well, that the steps which he had taken previously and on that decisive morning were a series of overt acts against the law of the land, and were in fact acts of treason. He knew also that on liberating myself and friend, he was supplying the country with evidence of that treason; yet the kindly feelings and humanity of Mr Frost towards me were paramount to all selfish feelings: he *committed* himself — but he *emancipated* me.

Soon after eight o'clock in the morning the two fugitives found themselves resting their wearied limbs at the foot of *Twym-barLwm*, a tumulus at the south-western end of a range of magnificent mountains which terminate near the little town of Risca on the Ebbw. There, with the mountain for their altar — with Heaven's canopy for their temple; they found them-

238

selves in safety offering, with grateful hearts, thanksgiving to their God for their deliverance from danger and from death!

The day opened in loveliness and splendour; it seemed as if it were a July day adjourned, to cheer the more melancholy month of November. The sun shone out most brilliantly, and his slanting rays impinging on the villages and houses, which a few hours before we had passed in darkness, in misery, and in dread, in the neighbourhood of the *High Cross*, the *Cefn*, and the *Welsh Oak*, reflected back his beams with a softened refulgence as if no crime or commotion had ever been there. Newport, too, we could partly see. We watched to see the expected fires blaze forth: we listened for the booming of the guns — but no! we neither saw nor heard either, and we hoped that the infatuated men had paused in their mad career, and had returned to their mountain homes. Alas! vain were our hopes, — at that very moment the fatal conflict was going on — at that very moment several of the misguided men were being hurried into eternity. They had, by this time, attacked the Westgate Inn, and the handful of soldiers in self-defence were compelled to return their fire and repulse their attack; and, whilst my friend and myself, so recently delivered from danger, were enjoying this glorious morning — doubly glorious to us, after that perilous and awful night, the unhappy authors of our captivity, were many of them rolling in the streets of Newport, in the last quivering agonies of a violent and sanguinary death. The romance of our adventure was now ended. After many restings on the purple heather of those lovely hills to ease our wearied bodies — and weary indeed we were — we reached home in safety. A warm bath relaxed our stiffened limbs, and a few hours sleep gave us back our strength and activity; and, though with me it has entailed a chronic rheumatism which will most likely last me for life, we suffered less than might have been expected after such severe fatigue as we endured on that fearful and never-to-be-forgotten night.

Here let me do justice to my kind friend, who was my fellow prisoner and co-sufferer on the occasion. He was a mild and unobtrusive man, and amongst the Chartists excited no suspicion of being there for sinister purposes. (Not so with me — they fancied I *had* an object in being there.) He, doubtless would have been allowed to proceed home, but for his being taken in company with me; in fact, he afterwards informed me that he had several opportunities during the night to escape. But no; he availed himself of neither, but, in the true spirit of pure

239

friendship, preferred mixing his fortunes with mine, and stuck to me until the last.

During our toiling across the mountains, he had frequently to bear nearly my whole weight on his arm, to enable me to make my way towards home. But for his aid and presence, a very different result to me might have been the winding up of that dread adventure.

I immediately, when sufficiently rested, wrote a note to, and communicated personally with, the Lord-Lieutenant of the County (Capel Hanbury Leigh, Esq.), the particulars of what had occurred to us on the foregoing night. We were, in consequence, sent for by the examining magistrates, and were bound over in recognizances to give evidence in a case of *life* and *death* against our personal friends and acquaintances. Painful as was the task, we did not shrink from it. We gave our evidence faithfully, honestly, without 'anything extenuating or setting down aught in malice;' and, though the doing so entailed commercial losses of a most ruinous nature on myself, and a great falling off in the trade of my friend, we only performed an incumbent duty — a duty which we owed to *ourselves* to our *country*, and to our *God*.

B.B.

27 Reports by a Birmingham Police Spy on Meetings of the Local Chartists

From H.O. 40/50

November 2nd

Went to the meeting at ½ past 8 in Allison Street, where I found 13 members present — two members came in afterwards, they were about commencing the business of the evening when a stranger came in, it was the same person who came on Thursday, and I was told he was there on Friday. As soon as the stranger came in the members sat down and talked about religion and began to sing.* Kircupp of Dale End was appointed to mind the door and keep watch — the stranger got in while he (Kircupp) was attending to the candles — I (Tongue) and Kircupp was walking up and down the room when he shewed me a brace of pistols which he had bought — he ordered them during the week — Kircupp said Hill would not allow any member to belong to his class that had not a brace of pistols, and if they had not got them they were to by a certain time, and a dagger; — he had one with him about 8 inches long, 3 square.

On account of the stranger being there word was passed from Hill (of Lynch Street) Parks and Smallwood (of Digbeth) to other members to meet at the top of Allison Street, corner of Bartholemew Street, in half an hour for the purpose of ascertaining whether any of the members was acquainted with the stranger, and for Hill to tell his class where to meet this morning.

The last time I saw Mr Burgess, the commissioner he asked me whether I could buy over either of the leaders.† Last night after the meeting separated (10 o'clock) I went to the 'Horse and Groom', or 'Horse and Jockey' opposite Market Street in Digbeth with Parks, after I got him pretty lushey I began to talk to him about the particulars of the meeting, and to know whether there was any meeting on the same plan as the one

* A.S.

† Not true. I found this man, contrary to my express orders at my house at nine o'clock in the morning. I examined him closely on many points of his report, as to buying over the leaders it was never even hinted.

carried on in Allison Street, in any part of the town. He said there was not, but there was one at Dudley, Bilston and Lyewaste, I asked him whether he knew them, he said he did — I asked him whether he ever attemded either of them; — he said he had attended them all, and help form the one at Bilston, I asked him whether they had many arms, and he said they had many arms at Bilston and Dudley, but he thought they had not many at Lye Waste. Lye Waste is where they make the daggers, spear heads and spears which they throw under the horses' feet. I asked him whether he thought it was safe what they were carrying on — he said if he thought there was any danger he should leave the country. I asked him if he had a tidy sum of money and everything made safe with him, whether he would leave off attending the meetings and join the opposite side, he said he would not then give me an answer but would see me again on the subject. I asked whether he knew all the parties that had arms in the town — he said yes, and all the rules that were not written in the book. It being 12 o'clock we left. I went home to my lodgings in Bellbarn Road, Bellbarn Place. Parks promised to dine with me this day.

Report of the meeting in Allison Street on Sunday evening, November 3rd 1839 — about 100 persons present

Smallwood gave out a hymn afterwards read a chapter in the Bible. Bridges then prayed, and then sung another hymn, after which gave a text from Kings, and then addressed them upon the good of a Republican Government, and advised them to do away with the present Government by any means; he told them to be prepared for the change for the time would soon come; he said there was spies attended their meetings, and cautioned them to be very particular who they spoke to Brown then addressed the meeting, stating about Mr Clarke* the Magistrate having called upon him to ask whether they did not meet for the purpose of Drilling, Training and procuring arms — he said no, they only met for the purpose of reading the papers and discussing upon them —

Smallwood got up and said they had been that afternoon to Mr *Blaxland*† of Bull street to ask him to come this evening

---

* This Mr Clarke was one of three magistrates including the mayor with whom I thought it necessary to communicate. He has acted very unwisely and done much mischief by this communication.

† A respectable tradesman.

242

(Monday) and give them a lecture, he said he could not attend until Wednesday evening having to attend the meeting of the female Chartists in Lawrence Street, this evening. Smallwood stated Mr Blaxland advised them to be prepared and organize themselves — he said there were six of the old council, mentioning *Mr Sturge's* name that were determined to carry out universal suffrage by any means — he said there would be a secret come out this week concerning a gold snuff box that was given to May. He said there would be a meeting in the Large Committee Room in the Town Hall on Saturday next at 12 to elect the Mayor and Council, he said they wanted to get Mr Muntz in as Mayor, and he (Blaxland) wished every man that called himself a Chartist to attend to oppose Muntz and all who they brought forward they did not approve of — he said he should attend the meeting on Wednesday night when he would tell them how to act. On account of spies attending the meetings they are in future going to transact their business in the classes.*

Meeting in Allison Street, November 4th 1839
    Mr Smallwood in the Chair —
The Chairman read from the 'Northern Star' about a meeting that was held in Charles Town in Ireland, after which he addressed the meeting stating they must all look to themselves as there was spies attended their meetings, he told them to be cautious what they said to prevent the Government turning it into Sedition.
    Parks then read from a paper called 'The Working Bee' — he told them they must not depend upon their neighbours, but all of them must get organised and be well read, meaning well armed.
    Brown the delegate then addressed them about F. O'Connor and told them to be prepared for the worst as the time would soon come — he then made fun of the judges and jury who attended last Warwick Assizes, he wanted the members to call a public meeting and he would pay his part towards the expenses — he said if they did not now stir themselves they would be lost and all butchered — he said they allowed the Government to put all their meetings down and put a new police in the town — he said if they had been all armed and organized at the time they could not have done it, when he said about the police being put on the town some of the members said they would

* Meetings of ten at the houses of class leaders.

soon put them off — he again told them they must all look to themselves and be prepared — he advised them to break up all secret meetings for if the magistrates got hold of them they would be either hanged or transported. When Brown came into the meeting he looked round to see if the Strangers was there, he said Mr Clarke stated there was a policeman attended the room in the pay of the Magistrates. He told them about Mr Clarke the Magistrate coming to him and asking him what meeting they held — he said there was one of the members professed to be a strong Chartist that went to Redfern every morning and told him about the meeting the evening before. Clarke asked Brown whether he had been chairman one night in the bottom room, when the speaker advised the members to get pistols, daggers and muskets. Brown said no — Clarke said he would tell him the name of the person to-day (Nov 5th) who gave the information. Brown asked whether the stranger had been there that evening, and if he came there again he hoped they would give him a smugging.

Brown said going home, if he had told Clarke they had met to get arms he expected they would all have been transported. He asked me whether I remembered the night Mr Clarke alluded to — I told him that it was Tuesday night when Smallwood told the members if they could not get arms to get a carving knife and sharpen it on both edges and give them that — he said that was the night but he dared not say so — he said that Clarke was sure to come and tell him of any information the Magistrates might receive about that meeting.

Meeting in Allison Street, Nov 5th, 1839
None but members were admitted.
At 8 p.m. I went to the Meeting, there were about 30 members present, the only business transacted was about getting the room painted by the 18th of November for a Tea Party — Smallwood, Brown, Hughes & Matty — Brown said if he could find out who it was that had been to the Magistrates, he would make him fit for a Coffin. Smallwood advised the Meeting to look out who went into Beardsworth's — An Irishman whose name I do not know advised them to go down some night to Beardsworth's and kill the lot — he also advised for the different members to go by numbers instead of names —

Meeting in Allison St, Wednesday evening, Nov. 6th, 1839
Mr Brown of Upper Gough St in the chair.

244

Mr Fussell opened the meeting by reading from the 'Sun' newspaper an account of the Riots in Wales, after he had read the paper, he said he was very glad to see the People of Wales was stirring and by this time the people of Newport had declared their independence, and that he hoped in a short time they would be prepared to proclaim themselves a Republic, he said a Man would be deputed to go to Wales and learn the particulars and that we do hold a public meeting on the day he returns, and that it should be such a meeting that had never been held in the Town. That they should petition the Queen to give them *universal suffrage* or they would *take it* by force. Many said *we will have it or die for it*.

Smallwood then addressed the meeting. He said if the Queen would not give them universal suffrage they would join the Insurrection and declare themselves a Republic—— Fussell got up and told him that if he went on in that way the Magistrates would have us up for Treason. Parks then addressed the Meeting. He said he was not so pleased to hear of the Riots as the other speakers had been but he said he could not die but once and he would sooner die fighting for his country than live a slave. *He asked how many there was in the room arm'd and prepared* when about 12 to 20 said they was. He said they were not ready. He had experienced in the past riots, he said that when the men were called upon in the last riots that held up their hands and said they were armed, he said they could not be found, and he hoped every one who said he was prepared, would be so, it was of no use for them to meet night after night if they would not take their advice. He said they had been told what to get and prepare themselves he advised the men instead of going to Public Houses to save their money to buy the requisite things, they understood what he meant. He advised them as Englishmen to provide themselves with arms and be ready.

Chapman *told me* he should be Drilling a lot on Friday night, but I cannot tell until this evening. There was from 150 to 200.

Meeting in Allison Street, Thursday evening November 7th, 1839, about 120 to 130 persons present
Mr —— in the Chair.
Smallwood read from the 'Sun' Newspaper.

Parks made a motion that the Committee should be dissolved and a new one formed of men that had spirit and would act. He said there was many men on the Committee who talked a good deal but would not act. He said he wanted to see a Committee formed of young men who was determined to do something. He wished to know what they would do in the event of Frost being condemned. He said if they let him suffer, he should consider he was the first Martyr of the great cause. He asked them whether they would go to their death for him. They said they would. He said they must be up and doing for the time was come when they would be wanted. He said he had no occasion to tell them what to get for they had been told often enough, and he should consider it an insult to tell them what to provide. They then formed a fresh Committee who meet on Sunday in Allison Street on Sunday afternoon at ½ past 2.

Lord told *me* that him, Parks — George — Chapman — Bridges and another were determined to have illumination by burning the Churches and Farm Houses on the borders of the Town. He said they should go on dark nights and set fire to them.

I have to meet them this evening at 7 at Lords Shop. 2nd Entry on the left hand going down Keel House Lane. He lives in Sun Street.

T—— account: Meeting in Lord's Shop in Lichfield Street, November 8, 1839

Lord, Parks, George, Oatridge, Chapman, Bridges and Tongue present —

Lord asked us whether we could go conscientiously to work and burn the Churches.

Parks then quoted several passages from the Bible to prove they should be justified in burning down the churches and murdering all that opposed them, they did not like. Every one offered an opinion and it was agreed it should be done.

Parks said he belonged to the Society the Dorchester Labourers did who was transported. They had an oath which he thought if made in a stronger form would do to be taken by each member. The members then stood up in a circle and joined hands. *Parks* then administered an oath to the following effect. 'I do hereby pledge myself to keep the proceedings of this Society secret from mortal man, as I hope for happiness in the world to come.'

Chapman was then chosen *Captain*, and Parks under him, the watchword was then agreed upon '*Chicken*' countersign 'Peck', if they met in the dark, and had any suspicion of being heard, they then was to touch each other under the arm, and take hold

246

of the forefinger. It was agreed they should not meet in one place twice following. They again meet in Allison Street on Sunday morning at 8, afterwards they will go about 9 to Hall Green on the Warwick Road to drill. *They will pass through Sparkbrook Gate.*

Four Churches are selected to be burnt, *two* at Edgbaston, *one* at Hollyway Head, *one* at All Saints. *Parks* says there is some of the Policemen who are Chartists and have promised him to tell of all their proceedings. He said *Fussell* was gone down to Wales to enquire into the riots in Wales. He said if things were favourable there they would be called out in a short time.

If either of the Members obtained any news, they were to go to Chapman's and he would tell them how to act.

Memm —
I have offered a room at my house for them to meet him next week — a person can be placed in the adjoining room and hear every thing.

Dec 10 1839

Mr Wilson reports he went to Lawrence Street Chapel and Mr T. P. Green took the chair. Mr Cardo adressed the meeting about Mr Frost's trial coming on, and would prove fatal, for the government [was] * sure to have a jury to prove him guilty on purpose to bring him to the gallows to execution. Therefore those that had [an] interest towards Frost, or [who] want to gain universal suffrage, ought to endeavour to rescue Frost from that horrible death of execution. London and those in that and other towns are quite ready and willing, but as Birmingham is the principal town, they are waiting to see the Birmingham men make a start, which he hopes will take place in less than three months, and then it will [be] carried on all through England. Then universal suffrage will come, and must come, and this will be a free country, and then the government will be glad to liberate the whole of the Chartists from gaol. On account of him having a cold, and very hoarse so that he can't talk very well, he would put it off till next Tuesday night, and then he will explain the thing better to them.

Mr Green then brought forward another thing. As there would be plenty of Government witnesses at Monmouth against

* [Words in square brackets are not in the original, and are inserted to make sense. Spelling has been amended.]

Frost and the others that are to be tried for high treason, the motion that from ten to fifty pounds will be paid from the 'Northern Star' office to any person that will come forward and prove that any of the witnesses that is against the welsh patriots do perjure themselves, for they shall be tried for perjury. The motion was brought forward and passed. Mr Thomas then began, after the words of Cardo, recommending the men of Birmingham to unite themselves together, and with physical force stand their ground, and the infamous government will soon give you your rights. About the spies that Mr Cardo speaks of, is employed by the government for they think of crushing the charter, but the chartists is not so easy to be crushed, and they will find it so. Mr T. P. Green he spoke of the roguish government, and that he would not petition the house of commons no more. What is the government for? Why don't they govern the working class of man, and give them their rights?

Mr Thompson he said that he had received a letter from Lord Normanby the secretary of state [in] answer to a petition that was sent to him for the liberation of Lovett and Collins at Warwick gaol, and the answer certified they must wait their time, and he said that the whole of the Secretary of State, and them at Whitehall and the Government is a bloody thumping set of rogues and thieves.

Mr Cardo stated that he hoped that the [men] of Birmingham would be cautious, for he was quite sure that there was certain persons going about to different towns to ascertain the proceedings of the Chartists. If any person should come and say to you that he was a Chartist, and came from such a town, he will ask you how you Chartists of this town is for universal suffrage, with the intention of getting out of you whether you have arms or not, but unless you know them you must not know nothing or they will entrap you. Mr W. Green then gave [a] little of his advice to the meeting, stating that if the police was to come there, he would keep his seat, and if they pulled out a pair of handcuffs and put them on, he would go quietly to the lock-up place, and [told] the [rest] of the meeting to do the same, and not speak a word, and then afterwards they could serve the police out afterwards and in spite of their teeth.

PART V

Activity after Newport

In the winter of 1839-40 the Chartists were confused and disorganised. The Newport rising spurred the authorities to intensify their efforts to find out about the activities of local Chartists, which they did by increasing police surveillance, and the use of spies where this was possible. It also seems likely that some moderate Chartists, alarmed by the events of 4 November 1839, themselves gave information to the authorities, in the hope of avoiding further bloodshed. Mail was intercepted and opened by the authorities; leaders, both local and national, were arrested. In the localities the Chartists were often without leaders, short of information, and very conscious of the need to keep their activities under cover. Very little has yet been done to draw together the confused evidence which exists of the activities of the Chartists in these months, and the documents presented here do little more than add to the confusion. There were three periods at least during the winter when uprisings were being organised. After Newport, and the arrest of the Welsh leaders, there was a strong suggestion that further outbreaks might have been planned. At this time local leaders were arrested and charged with seditious utterances — like the Bath men whose hearing before the magistrates took place only a few days after the Newport rising. The next danger period was the time of the sentences on the Welsh leaders, which were announced on 19 January 1840. The days between the verdict of 'guilty' on Frost, pronounced on 9 January, and the calling of the three men for sentence were some of the most tense in the whole period. It was at this time that there were undoubtedly considerable secret negotiations taking place in the north of England, particularly centred on Dewsbury in the West Riding of Yorkshire. As the Sheffield documents and the first of the Bradford documents show, the men of the north were expecting to be called on to rise either during or after the trial of Frost, Williams and Jones. The Sheffield 'rising' (if it can be dignified by the name) took place on the night of 11-12 of January, when there were similar events at Dewsbury. The

249

Bradford Chartists, who were originally intended to form part of the insurgent force on that night, seem to have postponed their effort until after the sentence had been passed. Robert Peddie, a Scottish Chartist, hitherto little known south of the border, came into the district and took over the leadership of the action. The story of these events has been told by A. J. Peacock in a recent publication, 'The Bradford Chartists 1838-40' (Borthwick Papers, York, 1969). This should be read for a description of the events and the identification of the individuals mentioned in the Bradford documents.

The story of the Sheffield events has not been fully written up, although Holberry, who died in prison while serving the sentence which he received for his part as its leader, was a well-known figure in Chartist history. He was a man of more than common education, who had at one time been a regular soldier. He obviously possessed qualities of leadership, although the fiasco of the attempted rising would suggest that these were not matched by organisational ability.

The men whose depositions and accounts appear in this section were all rank-and-file Chartists, or leaders only at the local level. The Bath artisans and the Sheffield mechanics are probably fairly typical of the men who made up the rank and file of the Chartist movement.

Holberry and Peddie were sentenced to two years' imprisonment, together with others who had taken part in the 'risings'. The Bath Chartists received sentences of from six to eighteen months' imprisonment.

28 Bath: Report of the Hearing before the Magistrates of the Case against the Bath Chartists Arrested for Sedition

From the 'Bath Herald', 16 November 1839

At our Guild Hall, on Saturday, *Anthony Phillips* and *Thomas Bolwell*, two members of the Bath Working Men's Association, were charged, on the evidence of two policemen, named Gould and Furness, with making use of seditious language.

The evidence against Phillips was given by Charles Gould. He stated that he was at a Meeting of the Working Men's Association on Thursday night, saw the prisoner there, and heard him speak to the people. He said, 'My friends, I suppose you have all heard the reports in the papers about how many were killed. Don't you believe it: they don't say how many of the soldiers and special constables are killed. The men had walked 30 or 40 miles, and their ammunition was so wet that they did not make use of it; but they stood their ground like men.' He afterwards said, 'They are up in the North in full earnest and I hope the West of England will be the same, and get armed and prepare for them.' He also said something about the Town Council — that they had had power a long time, and now the Chartists would see if *they* could not have power. Another thing he said was, there were the Lords and the Bishops, and the little Queen with £70,000 a year coming in for stables, or looking after stables, witness was not sure which. — Mr Sutcliffe: Are you certain he said £70,000 a year? — Mr Roberts, who attended for the prisoner, protested against the witness withdrawing his words. — Mr Sutcliffe: Justice shall be done in the case, but the proceedings are not to be interrupted by a member of the legal profession, who is here only on sufferance. — The witness resumed: ' — The prisoner then said, 'Do away with that; do away with that;' and a few more words, but not very particular. He also said that, 30 or 40 years ago, when he was 'little,' his father and mother could go to bed without locking the doors; there was no suspicion of robbery, nor anything of the sort, then; but now there were a police established, and they were the biggest rogues. He (witness) would not be certain whether it was the biggest rogues set to

251

.

catch the rogues or not. He said something, also, about the workhouse. He said, the paupers there had but one ounce of tea allowed to them to 14 pints of water, and 2 quarts of milk, which altogether made 18 pints of something, and witness could not remember what he called it; he could not catch the word. The prisoner also said he wished those who gave it were obliged to try it for one year.' Mr Sutcliffe: Did he give the people any particular advice? — Witness: He told them to get themselves armed and to prepare for it. — This closed the statements against Phillips; and the evidence given against Bolwell by Furness (the other witness) was of a similar purport. — The prisoners were both remanded till Monday for further examination.

On Monday, *George Morse Bartlett*, a young man of diminutive size and respectably dressed was brought up on a warrant charging him with having on the 7th inst, at a Meeting held in the room of the Working Men's Association, in Monmouth Street, made use of certain seditious language, for the purpose of exciting Her Majesty's subjects to a breach of the peace. Mr Roberts attended as the prisoners' attorney. — Charles Gould, a policeman being sworn, was examined by Mr Sutcliffe. He was at a Meeting of the Bath Working Men's Association on Thursday evening — saw the prisoner there, and heard him speak. He said, 'My friends if we succeed, it will be a glorious sight; and if not, it will be criminal, and we shall be punished; and if we do, we'll punish them.' He then said, 'No doubt but what some of the magistrates have sent some policemen here for a spy: never mind for that, they are merely sent to satisfy their hunger, and keep up their high establishments.' The witness added, he then said, 'If they hurt a hair of John Frost's head I hope you will prepare yourselves with arms, and go to work.' Something was also said about arming themselves by Phillips and another man. Mr Sutcliffe: How did the Meeting behave themselves when they heard this? — Witness: They cried 'Hear, hear' and clapped their hands and cheered. — By the Mayor: He could not identify any person in particular as doing so. — By Mr Wilson: The applause was both before and after what was said about Frost.

Cross-examined by the prisoner: — Are you positive I am the person who said on that occasion the words alluded to about Frost? Witness: You did. — By Mr Roberts: Witness was certain the words were uttered by the prisoner. Mr R. was about to ask him if the words were used there by any other person, when the

252

Mayor objected to such a course. Mr Roberts said, he would submit he had the right to take any course he thought proper to throw discredit on the testimony of the witness, and he could shew, on his answering his (Mr R.'s) question, the witness was unworthy of belief, the reasons for which he would shew the magistrates if they would order Gould to leave the room. This was not complied with; and after one or two questions more by Mr Roberts, Col. Bailey asked the witness if the room was full, and if Mr Roberts was present. The witness answered in the affirmative, and said, he wished he had known his character, he would [— Before finishing the remark he was stopped by the magistrates].

Alfred Furness, the other witness was called and sworn. He saw the prisoner at the meeting and heard him speak to the people. This evidence was in substance similar to that of the last witness, though in some slight respects verbally different. The witness also confirmed Gould's statements as to clapping and cheering. By Col. Bailey: Nothing was said about good news from Bristol. — By Mr Wilson: He heard nothing about intelligence from Monmouth. By Mr Roberts: Witness heard the whole of the prisoner's speech. Did you recollect hearing him say, 'It would be a glorious sight,' and the other words which immediately followed? The Mayor told the witness he was not bound to answer that question. Mr Roberts: I bow with submission, but I wished to throw all the contempt I could on the evidence, to show how unworthy it was of credit. The Mayor: You may cross-examine the witness as long as you like on his own evidence.

The prisoner was then allowed to offer his own statement in defence, but was cautioned by the magistrates that what he had to say would be taken down and, if he should be committed for trial, produced against him in evidence. — The prisoner said, he would recite as nearly as possible what he said on the occasion in question, and would prove to the bench that what the witness had said was entirely untrue. Being conscious of the purity of his intentions, he on no occasion used such language. The prisoner was going on at the same speed as when he made his speech, but was requested by Mr Falkner to speak slow enough for him to write it down. The prisoner complained of this as an arbitrary rule of the Court. — The Mayor told him the magistrates were anxious that every opportunity should be given him for his defence; but he must submit to the ordinary routine of business in having his defence taken down. — The prisoner then resumed a recitation of his speech! Which consisted of remarks on the state of the country, the poverty of the working classes, the conduct of the government and other political topics, which, after taking up some time, were considered by the magistrates not relevant to his defence in rebutting the charge. — The prisoner said, if he were allowed to go on he would soon come to that part which bore against the evidence. The words he used were to this effect: — 'If anything should take place, and you are unsuccessful, the deed will be criminal. If you are successful, according to the statement of Mr Roebuck and the opinions of the Benthamites generally, the deed would be glorious. I am not an advocate of physical revolutions. I agree with Bentham that the majority ought to rule. It is your duty who are at this meeting to win over to your side the great bulk of the people; when you have done so, the desire for reform will become more general, and the legislature must comply with your demands.'

The Mayor here interrupted the witness and told him it was of no use for him to enter into a long speech, if he could not adduce something opposed to the charge. If he did not use the words alleged he could say so without taking such a lengthened course. — The prisoner said he was ready to swear that he was not an advocate of physical force on the occasion alluded to in the evidence, nor at any other time. He never on that occasion said 'If any person hurts a hair of John Frost's head the people should take up arms and go to work.' He did not mention the name of Frost as being arrested, nor advise the people to take up arms; nor could he be so silly as to say 'Go to work.' He said to the Meeting, 'From a principle of justice, you have no right to enforce your opinions by physical means. If you are the majority, the desire for reform will become general, and the legislature will concede it. That being the case, it is a folly to force public opinion before the time. Why have we met here on the present occasion, but in order to prevent an outbreak by giving vent to popular feeling? You find that all revolutions have been occasioned by rashness and intemperance on the part of the ruling powers. We intend in future to have nothing to do with local questions, such as concern Poor Houses or Town Councils. We should adopt one prudent course of action — we should endeavour to spread our principles as widely as possible, knowing that upon the progress of information among the people depends the success of our cause.' The prisoner here said, that as he was not desirous of harassing the gentlemen of

254

the bench, and as it appeared he was restricted by arbitrary rules, he should 'relate' no more of what he said. — The Mayor told him he might go on if he thought proper, but only confine his observations to the charge against him. If there were any witnesses he wished to be called, they should be heard.

The prisoner said he was not then prepared with any. He then went on to say that he would defy anyone to assert that he ever advocated physical force. He contended for the political opinions held by Sheridan, Fox, and many other statesmen, but deprecated all revolutions by violence. This his opinion had been fully expressed and known to the Public through the channel of the Press. He deprecated popular commotions, for wherever they had occurred they had not succeeded. As to indulging a spirit of vindictiveness against any parties he was so far from doing it that he considered were he placed in the same position, under the same circumstances with those who differed from him he should act under the same feelings; and whether a man was Tory, Whig, or Radical, he must act from his convictions. He was not for putting down others by force who held different political opinions, but if men in power committed themselves was not their conduct to be condemned and publicly discussed? Must not the people canvass questions of a public nature, and seek a redress of their grievances? He was never before the magistrates previous to this occasion; he was never drunk, nor disorderly, nor did he ever advocate anything to the disadvantage of mankind. His motives and conduct were regulated by honest intentions: but if he might judge of his accusers on phrenological (!) principles they evinced those characteristics which would not entitle them to be trusted! He was of opinion with Robert Owen that the human character was formed by circumstances, and he therefore naturally expected that a Tory would act as a Tory, or a Whig act as a Whig. He did not wish to conclude that in the proceedings taken against him the bench was influenced by impure motives but he maintained that what was said by the witnesses was false, and many parts of their evidence inconsistent. He knew something of the rules and principles of his own language, and enough to make it highly improbable he should express himself in the manner represented by the witnesses. He always told the people to war against systems, and not against men. Whether they (the bench) were Whigs, Tories or Radicals, he hoped no misconstruction would be put on his words.

255

The Mayor: Do you wish the case should be adjourned to give you an opportunity of calling witnesses in your favour? The bench are willing to give you every facility you may wish to prove your innocence. — The Prisoner having expressed his wish for an adjourned hearing, the case was ordered to stand over until Wednesday, the day named by the prisoners' attorney.

The other prisoners, Phillips and Bolwell, were then called for when Mr Roberts requested an adjournment for them on the same grounds as for Bartlett. They were accordingly remanded for further examination on Wednesday. — The prisoner Bartlett asked the magistrate if he should be allowed pen, ink, and paper, in the prison? Mr Falkner told him he would be accommodated according to gaol regulations. An intimation was afterwards given him that he would probably have the indulgence asked for.

WEDNESDAY

Continued Examination of Prisoners. Charles Morse Bartlett examined on Monday, was first brought in.

Previous to any of the witnesses being called, William Hall, Serjeant at Mace, who apprehended Bartlett was sworn, and he deposed as follows: — He went to the room of the Working Men's Association on Sunday evening; people were assembled there, and the prisoner was speaking. Hall told him he had a warrant to arrest him; Bartlett told witness to be careful what he was doing, and to be satisfied that he was the right man; Hall said he was satisfied about that. Prisoner then said, 'Don't disturb the Meeting, wait a short time, and let there be no noise and I'll go with you without disturbance;' Hall remained about three quarters of an hour, and heard Bartlett speak. He exclaimed against the government for first allowing them to express their opinions at public meetings and petition them for a redress of grievances, and for now employing parties to suppress them. He said it was very likely that he himself would soon be incarcerated. He should be still ready to carry out the Charter, whether in or out of prison. He went on speaking of the different revolutions which had taken place in different countries; said that their cause was that the people had not got their rights; he begged his hearers to be firm, and complained of the authorities of Bath; said the corporation employed parties to come among them as spies. He said he knew several of the

256

Council personally and he knew that in private they were Chartists in principle; but it was very fashionable for them to deny it at the dinner table:

Mr Wilson — Did he mention the names of any of the Corporation who were Chartists?

Hall — He said he knew Admiral Gordon very well.

The first witness called for the prisoner was John Duck, cabinet maker, of No. 5, Pierrepont-Place, but his evidence applying to all three prisoners, it was proposed by the Magistrates that they all should be brought in to hear it at the same time. This Mr Roberts objected to, but his objection was overruled.

The witness being sworn, then went on to state that he was present at the meeting of the Working Men's Association, on Thursday night: heard Bartlett there.

By Mr Roberts — He did not use the expressions alleged in the depositions, that 'if a hair of John Frost's head was hurt, I hope you will be prepared with arms;' he did not use any expression against the Town Council, nor advise the people to arm themselves.

By Mr Sutcliffe — Bartlett did not say anything to the effect that, 'If we succeed it will be glorious, and if not it will be criminal, and we shall be punished, and if we do we'll punish them.'

By the Mayor — Witness continued during the whole time of the meeting; was stationed near the door; Bartlett was at the other end.

Mr Sutcliffe read from Bartlett's own statements, taken down on Monday, part of what he said at the meeting, and asked the witness if he recollected hearing him say any thing like it. He answered in the negative.

Mr Wilson — Can you recollect anything he said?

Witness — Yes; he recommended moral force; he told them there was no use in physical force, but by moral force they would get their rights; he always recommended the people to educate themselves in political knowledge.

By Mr Roberts — Witness heard Charles Bolwell speak on the same occasion. [Here a printed copy of the rules of the Working Men's Association was handed to the magistrates, together with one of the tickets given on admission to membership.]

By Mr Wilson — Witness had been a member of the Association two years; it had a treasurer and secretary, but no president; the contributions were voluntary; Phillips was treasurer; witness paid no regular subscription, but occasionally put money in the box; when he was admitted a member he had a card and copy of the rules, such as those produced; there is a secretary but he did not know who he was; his card was signed by George Bartlett (the prisoner Bartlett's brother), then secretary, but not at present; there were no other rules of the association than those on the table; the members' names were entered in a book when admitted, and in another book before, called the balloting book, but the books contained no rules. The members signed their names to support the principles of the 'People's Charter.' When he signed he was required to do so by George Bartlett, the Secretary; Phillips was then treasurer; he had to render an account of the funds every quarter; he could not say when he last audited the accounts; he never heard any of the members in the course of their speeches avert to the necessity of using physical force; the name of John Frost was mentioned by one speaker on Thursday, but all it referred to was his being arrested; no such expression was used as 'our friend John Frost.'

By Mr Roberts — No member of the association is expected to support any other principles than those expressed in the rules, and the People's Charter. Witness heard Bolwell speak that evening; said Frost was arrested and committed to Monmouth Gaol for high treason, but did not express a wish that the gaol might be razed to the ground, nor anything like the words, 'if we are unsuccessful we shall be punished, but if successful we shall punish them:' he heard Phillips speak the same evening; he talked mostly about the New Poor Law, and a resolution said to have been passed at the Bath Union; said he did not like to hear of one set of men taking arms against another set; he did not recommend the people to arm themselves, but that their principles should be carried out by moral means; that if the people trusted in God he would fight their battles for them; he laid great stress on these words; there was nothing in his speech about resorting to physical force.

Mr Wilson — As your memory appears so good as to help you to state what was not said, perhaps you can tell us who was the chairman of the meeting?

Witness — I cannot say.

By Mr Sutcliffe — He was not there at the beginning of the meeting; if he did not mistake, Bartlett was speaking when he entered, but he did not recollect who spoke next, or who next again, or how many spoke at all. — Here Mr Sutcliffe again read several sentences taken from Bartlett's own mouth on Monday, as what he actually said at the meeting; and on asking the witness if he heard them spoken, he said he did not. The room he said, was open on Sundays for service and preaching, when anyone was admitted, and at all other times except Wednesday nights when the members only met for business. During Phillips' speech great disapprobation was shown by some part of the meeting: there were strangers there who expressed disapprobation; the room was full of strangers. When he spoke against physical force part of the meeting disapproved of it.

The next witness called was Sarah Snell, a single woman, living in the Upper Bristol road. The drift of the examination, on behalf of the prisoners, as in the evidence of the former witness, was to show that they did not say what was alleged against them by Gould and Furness, and that the language used by them was the reverse. To various questions by the magistrates, she evinced the utmost reluctance and hesitation in giving an answer, and to some returned no answer at all. She neither had any recollection of any passages of Bartlett's speech as given by himself nor knew who was the chairman of the meeting.

The witnesses examined afterwards were James Huntley, plasterer, Grove-street; Mary Huntley his wife; Eliz. Selway, a young woman living in Green-street; and Wm Williams, gardener, Widcombe. Nearly all the same questions were put to them as to the two other witnesses, and similar answers returned. Each witness, however, persisted in denying all knowledge of the Chairman of the meeting, though repeatedly asked as to his person or name. — The time taken up in their examination protracted the proceedings till nearly five o'clock when the prisoners were remanded till Thursday.

THURSDAY

The examination was resumed by calling Charles Cottle, a shoemaker, of Ironhouse place as the first witness on behalf of the prisoners.

By Mr Roberts: he was at the meeting on Thursday, the 7th instant; heard the whole of Phillips' speech; it was principally on the New Poor Law. He did not recommend the people to arm. At no time had he heard him recommend the people to physical force; but quite the contrary. All he spoke that night

259

was against the Poor Law, and not to any great length.

The Mayor asked Bartlett and Bolwell if they wished to question the witness? They both answered in the negative.

By Mr Sutcliffe: Witness did not know the chairman of the meeting.

Mr Roberts here intimated to the magistrates that the chairman on that occasion was a stranger from London.

Charles Perkins, a shoemaker, of 5, St Michael's Court, was next called. He was first examined by Bartlett. Heard him speak at the meeting of the Working Men's Association, on Thursday night. He spoke about forming a constitution. He did not advise the people to arm. He did not advise them to physical force then nor on any other occasion on which he heard him; but advised them to moral force. Said nothing about taking arms if a hair of John Frost's head was injured. Did not hear him say the police were sent to the meeting to satisfy their hunger.

By Bolwell: Heard you speak the whole of your speech that night. You said nothing respecting Frost, or razing the gaol of Monmouth; but heard something about it among the people as a report. You did not advise men, and women, and children, to be armed with bludgeons.

By Mr Roberts: Witness heard the whole of Phillips' speech. He did not tell the people to get themselves armed and prepare, nor said anything about arming. He did not say there was a man going backward and forward to receive and bring news. He gave his opinion on moral and physical force, and said the charter would never be obtained by physical force. The people then would not hear him any longer and he sat down. He had heard him speak occasionally for the last 8 or 10 months. The general character of his speeches was in support of moral force, and he often spoke against those who resort to physical force. He said something that night about £70,000 granted to the Queen for building stables and only £30,000 for education.

By Mr Sutcliffe — There was a chairman elected, but he could not tell his name — there was no name mentioned. He heard nobody at the meeting recommend the people to arm — he must have heard it had it been said — others who had sworn so much had committed wilful perjury.

By Mr Wilson — Witness is a member of the Working Men's Association. He stood so as he could hear all Bartlett said.

By Col. Bailey — He did not know a man named Mealing; as a member of the Working Men's Association he sometimes subscribed, not a regular sum, but just what he liked.

260

Mr Roberts — State what are the objects of the association. The Mayor — You are not, according to your own arrangement to put questions after the magistrates.

By Mr Wilson — The nature of the discussion and speeches was various — both political and religious. There were meetings at the room on Sunday evenings, and sometimes prayer. Phillips told the people they might expect to attain their object by prayer to God.

Mr Roberts — I wish you to examine him on the objects of the association.

He was told by the magistrates the rules were sufficient to judge by.

Matilda Bath, wife of William Bath, boot and shoemaker, of Grove-Street, was next examined. Her testimony in favour of Phillips and Bolwell was similar to that of the other witnesses, as examined by Mr Roberts.

By Mr Wilson — Her husband is a member of the association, and attended the meetings sometimes.

John Davis, of 33, Walcot-street, lodging-house keeper, examined. After other statements similar to those of the other witnesses, he said, Phillips spoke respecting Wales; said there were several killed, which he abhorred, and spoke against men taking up arms against their brother men, and advised them to get the charter by moral and peaceable means. Witness heard some of Bartlett's speech, but could not make it out, he spoke so low.

By Captain Bateman — His (Phillips') speech was not more than a quarter of an hour; he said more than he could recollect; he could recollect some parts but not others.

The Mayor — You are bound in justice to the prisoners to tell all you heard.

Witness could not recollect anything more than he had stated.

Bolwell said Frost was a prisoner, but did not tell the people to arm.

By Mr Sutcliffe — Phillips was hissed by the meeting when he spoke against physical force — he then sat down. He was not aware that any other speaker recommended physical force. No speaker advised the people to arm themselves. He did not number the speakers — the prisoners were the principal. He did not know the chairman of the meeting.

By Mr Wilson — He did not count the speakers — he could not see every one who spoke. The speakers were announced by the chairman. He had not any knowledge that a man named Mealing was announced.

By Col. Bailey — He knew a man named Mealing — did not see him on the platform that night. There were 3 or 4 on the platform, but could not say whether or not he was one of them. He had been a member of the association 9 months.

By Mr Wilson — Frost's name was mentioned, but he did not recollect anything said about harming a hair of his head.

Maria Vincent the wife of Samuel Vincent of Midsummer-buildings, painter and glazier, examined by Mr Roberts, gave similar evidence as to what the prisoners did or did not say to that of the foregoing witnesses.

By Mr Wilson — The meetings were sometimes opened by prayer, she had heard Phillips pray a number of times, as he belonged to a Wesleyan Society.

After a question put to the witness by Bolwell she was examined by Mr Sutcliffe; she heard Bolwell say that he expected from what he had heard, the gaol at Monmouth would be razed to the ground by morning, but not that he wished it to be so. None of the speakers advised the people to arm. Several strangers at the meeting said 'We'll have it immediately,' meaning the charter. Two of them were put out of the room for it. Could not tell who was on the platform besides the prisoners. She had been a member of the female association 9 months. She knew a man named Mealing, but did not see him on the platform that night, she did not know if he was there.

James Britten, a stonecutter 15, Oak-street, gave the same testimony in favour of the prisoners. On the witness using the terms physical and moral force, Mr Brown asked him what he meant by them. Witness replied, by physical force he meant taking arms and fighting one against another — by moral force to do things without fighting, and by peaceable means.

By Mr Sutcliffe — Could not recollect who was chairman. Recollects hearing a horn blow and a coach pass and soon afterwards believes some came in, but did not know whom.

The witnesses' further examination by the magistrates varied little from that of the other witnesses. Being asked by Col. Bailey if the prayers used at the meetings on Sundays were read or extempore, he answered the latter and added that Wesley's hymns were used there.

Maria Gardener, wife of John Gardener, 17, Bridewell lane, brightsmith, gave testimony to the same account as the other witnesses did; after whom William Gazard, a turner of Waterloo

262

buildings was called, whose examination had only been proceeded with but a few minutes when Mr Roberts said he was willing to close the case for his client and to this also Bolwell and Bartlett consented.

The room was then cleared, and the magistrates left to consult; in which they took up about half an hour. On the reopening of the room doors, and the prisoners being again brought in, the Mayor announced to them that the magistrates, after a patient hearing were unanimously of opinion the charge against them was sufficiently made out and that they had come to the decision that each prisoner should be required to find bail for his appearance at the next sessions, to answer such indictment as might then be preferred against him, in his own personal security of £100, and two securities each in £50 and 24 hours' notice would be required.

Mr Roberts said he had already given in certain names as bail, for enquiry.

The Town Clerk and Magistrates told him that could not be considered as answering the terms, as it was not then known securities would be required, the nature and character of the offence not being ascertained or decided on as a ground for committal. The prisoners were taken away in custody till the sufficiency of their bail could be enquired into.

The following is a copy of the Warrant of their committal:–

Anthony Phillips, Charles Bolwell, George Morse Bartlett, Unlawfully on the 7th November, wickedly, maliciously, seditiously published, uttered, pronounced and declared certain scandalous, malicious, and seditious words tending to excite and influence the minds of her Majesty's subjects to the Commission of breaches of the peace.

Twelve o'Clock this (Friday) morning.
The names of the parties offering bail are — For *Phillips* — Wm Boyce, carpenter; Peter Baker, whitesmith — these two are *accepted*. — For *Bartlett* — John Milman, yeoman; Henry Wills, broker. — For *Bolwell* — Thomas Bolwell, (prisoner's father), shoemaker; John Maidment, yeoman.

263

29 Sheffield: Depositions of Two of the Chartists Arrested after the Attempted Rising

From T.S. 11/816/2688

Samuel Foxhall

I am a Native of Staffordshire 24 years of age and married — It is 6 years since I first came to Sheffield — I came to my brother — I am a file cutter by Trade and I first worked at Mr Thomas Wyng's till he died — Afterwards I worked for Messrs Pease & Ibbotson for about 2 years — since that time I went to work with Messrs Vickers & Co. as a file cutter and have continued with them ever since. Myself and wife have lived in Button Lane in Sheffield Moor with my wife's Father Francis Hough for the last 12 months I joined the Chartists about 6 weeks before the disturbance in Sheffield. I had been at their public Meetings and the time I first joined them I went to one of the public Meetings in Fig Tree Lane and when the Meeting was over they said All were to go out but the Committee. I went down and stop't some time with several others about the Door, most of them went away. Then a person came to me and said he thought there had been a spy and he followed him and he told me to go after him. I went according to his directions and then met the man again who brought me back to the Room and laid hold of me by the collar and said there was a new association formed and asked me if I would be a Member. He said there was a person inside the door to receive a Password. Then he gave the Password 'Truth' to the person inside, he said this is a new one and took me into the Room having still hold of me by the collar. I dont know who this person was never having seen him since. When I got into the Room I saw Bradwell there whom I had known before. I and several others stood round Bradwell and he went through a Ceremony the substance of it was to promise that we were to assassinate any one who should divulge the secret. I believe McKetterick (whom I afterwards became acquainted with) was there. I and the new Members were told (I think by McKetterick) where the Classes were and which was the *gainest** to each person. A person of

[* i.e. nearest.]

the name of Rose told me my class was at Clayton's in Porter Street, he told me the number of the Door and said he would take me there he said the number was 87 as I believe. While I was there Peter Foden came into the room with two new Members as he said I heard Foden given them the Ceremony. I believe that night was a Wednesday night. The next night I went to Claytons, there were 8 or 9 there. Clayton was one of them. Rose was there Danl Hands was also there. Then there was a Conversation amongst them how they should attack the Military. Clayton said he had been a Soldier. Hands said he had been a Soldier. The Class Meeting Nights at Claytons were Tuesdays and Thursdays. I think I went regularly for about 3 weeks on the Tuesdays and Thursdays at Clayton's. I have seen both old and young Booker at some of these Meetings. The talk at Clayton's used to be about what Arms we had — and the Members Names were written down in a Book and where each lived. Danl Hands was our Class leader and he wrote most of the Names and Bradwell the remainder. I remember hearing old Booker say that he had been a Soldier. Besides the Meetings at Claytons I attended Mettings in Fig Tree Lane. They were private Meetings. I think I attended 10 or a dozen times. I had seen Holberry at the public meetings before I joined so as to become acquainted with his Person. I remember his coming to our Class Meetings at Claytons about a Fortnight before the disturbance. Clayton was there, and Bradwell and Francis Rose, those were all I remember. Holberry said he had been as a Delegate to different parts, he named Chesterfield, Mansfield, Dewsbury and other places which I dont recollect. He said he had got a pound for the defence of Frost and he was to see it was laid out in something that would defend him. That they were all Chartists at Dewsbury that when they were about searching for Arms there they had pawned them to a Chartist Pawnbroker for small sums — that he had told them at Dewsbury and other places that the time for a General Rise was fixed and that they said they should sleep better that night than they had done for the last six months. I think that Holberry said the Rise was fixed for the 31st December. He said there would be 3 to lead we on. One was to be a sort of Field Marshall the other two were to be lower and the three would be distinguished so that we should know them from anyone else. That each man was to put two shirts on to keep him warm and to save every halfpenny he could to provide a Sixpenny dram as probably it would be very cold. That the Field Marshall would take possession of Sheffield in an hour and a half and that he would lead them on the next day. Soon after that time, we used to meet every night at the class at Claytons. I took my gun twice to Claytons in consequence of directions to bring what arms I had. I shewed it to the class people. I took it in my hand it was dark. I saw others in at the class shew both guns and pistols. I remember Francis Rose brought a pike head to the class and William England a pistol and afterwards a gun and he also brought an axe and a dagger. I think I saw 6 or 7 guns shown to the class and about the same number of pistols and some pikes and daggers. We were called on to pay 2d. a week which was said to be for the defence of Frost. I paid it twice and it was put down in a book. It was said to be for the defence of Frost that no one might have hold of it. Hands received the subscriptions and entered them in the book. And afterwards he produced powder and caps which he said he had bought with the money. The powder was divided and I received 2 oz and a half and it was distributed to the others in the same parcels. I received also from Hands some percussion caps. One of the Members gave me some lead and Sml Bentley lent me a bullet mould to make it into bullets. I have seen Bradwell at Claytons making ball cartridge. About 30 while I was there I think that was about a week before the disturbance. I heard young Booker at Claytons say that he had a gun at their House but it wanted a screw or two put in the lock and said he must get it done and the others said the time was short. I believe that Clayton was present at all the class meetings I have spoken to. The place where I live is about 2 or 3 minutes walk to Claytons I have merely to cross one street. I attended the private meetings in Fig Tree Lane on the Wednesday Thursday and Friday* before the disturbance. On the Wednesday, James Boardman was Chairman. Bradwell, England, Saml Bentley and Duffey were there. The chairman gave out that we were to shew up our small arms at the classes on Friday night, those arms that could be concealed. Duffey made a speech and told them that the reason he left them before was because they mixed Religion with Politics. He said he was as dear to his religion as any man. He alluded to their mixing up religion with politics in Ireland. He said he had an Irish class but he should not tell the members that night as there was not sufficient order kept at the door. That he should continue to meet as long as they met. I observed that Duffey had under his top coat about ½ a dozen daggers in

[* 8, 9, 10 January 1840.]

266

rough handles and I saw some of the Irishmen there with similar daggers. The pass word was changed that night. There were two men to keep the door, one about half way down the steps and the other inside the door. The new pass word was for him on the steps outside 'Union' and for him inside the door 'Strength'. I remember that Powell Thompson was there that night. I went to the meeting again on *Thursday night.* Saml Bentley, Bradwell, England, Duffey and some others of our class were there. I heard Duffey tell the number of his class that he had 64. Holberry was also there that night. He said he had a motion to propose that there should be 50 bills printed for a Scotch Delegate to come and lecture on the Monday night, and that a sermon would be preached on the Sunday. He said it would do them good if they heard them. I cannot say whether Foden was there that night or not but I remember one of the nights he came in and got into the pulpit and said the news had arrived about Mr Frost that he was brought in guilty, that it was in Mr Wyley's window but they were to take no notice of it, it would be a fine handle to work upon and then he left the pulpit. I attended again a private meeting on the *Friday.* Bradwell, McKetterick, old and young Booker, Duffey and England were there. Holberry was not there while I was there. Duffey was the Chairman. About 100 were there. Duffey was speaking and while he was doing so some one came in and said he believed there was a Policeman underneath a spy and Bradwell got up and said he would put a cloak on it and he made a sort of moral speech very loud. Duffey then got up and took a pistol from his bosom and held it in his hand and said lead me to the spy and I'll stop him from spying. I left about ½ past 10 o'clock before the meeting broke up. On *Saturday night* about 10 o'clock I went to the class at Claytons. I took nothing with me the first time. I went there in consequence of hearing the Night before at the Class that I was to be in attendance at that time. When I got to Clayton's I found there Clayton, Bradwell, and about a dozen others. Bradwell had a dagger in his hand and I saw others with Arms, some had Pikes on handles. I was asked whether I had brought my Gun. I said No but I hadn't far to fetch it. Duffey came in and Bradwell and he exchanged some words and Duffey said the Soldiers were out and after exchanging a few words with Bradwell Duffey went away. I then went and fetched my Gun. I remember hearing Bradwell say he would go out as a Spy, he went out, he came back about 12 o'clock, and he said an Irishman had stabbed a Watchman or a Policeman and almost throttled him and kicked him on the head. Old and young Booker had come in before them. They both had daggers. Between 12 and 1 o'clock Bradwell and Hands went out together. While they were gone, our Class moved to Old Booker's House within 3 or 4 minutes walk of Clayton's. The Party began to be afraid that if they remained at Clayton's they should be found out, that it would be better to remain and so they went to Bookers. They took their arms with them. I remained with 4 or 5 others to the last. In a Back Room a Slop Kitchen there were about ½ doz hand grenades and 2 large shells and we took them all to Bookers. I took one of the Shells. Two or three went at one time and 2 or 3 came afterwards. That must have been about 1 o'clock or after. We waited at old Bookers till between 2 and 3 o'clock when Bradwell came in and said the Orders were to Moscow the Town that each one was to set fire to his own House. A dispute arose on this. Some of them objected to it. After this dispute was over Clayton said he would go back to his own house and fetch Hands as he did not know where Booker lived. Bradwell said the Orders were that if they saw a Watchman they were to assassinate him, and if the Watchman produced a pistol they were to shoot him. That Hands was hard of hearing and Bradwell moved that Swallow should take his place as Leader. Swallow was appointed instead of Hands and then Bradwell said we were to go to the Top of Watery Lane to meet the other Bodies. Before Bradwell proposed that Hands should be displaced, Hands and Clayton had come into Bookers. Swallow was one of our Class men. He brought to Clayton's some Cats that night in an Apron. One of our Class men was a Stout Man and lame and he said as he could not run he should not go with us. Bradwell and he talked together about it and it was agreed to leave him behind. He had a Gun and a Pistol. He lent Bradwell his pistol and to Hands his Gun and Hands lent his pistol to one of the other Men. We then set off, leaving Old Booker and another or two in the House. Young Booker took two Hand Grenades and a Box of Lucifers and he had a dagger. The Party were all armed. They then went to Watery Lane. We arrived there about 3 o'clock. We only saw one there who said he belonged to McKetterick's Class. We waited there an hour I should think. Then we moved further on toward Crook's Moor Workhouse having heard a Gun or two fired in that direction. We went past the Workhouse and there met a part of Boardman's class. Peter Foden was with them. I both heard him speak and saw him. They were most of them armed. Old Booker and those that were left behind joined us near the Dams. Booker had a dagger the others had pistols. Some of Boardman's Class said that Holberry was taken at 12 o'clock and that Boardman had gone off to Barnsley. Boardman's class and ours then parted. As we were going on we heard the sound of Horses' Feet. Bradwell said they were the soldiers. Then young Booker, Bradwell, myself and 2 others parted from the rest and went together, and kept the Field roads as much as we could, and then got into the road by the botanical Gardens. I hid 40 rounds of Ball Catridges in a Field which adjoins the wall of the botanical Gardens. I covered them with some grass and a stone over it and a little lower down I flung the dagger over the wall into the same Field. Young Booker hid near that spot two Hand Grenades and another hid a Pike not a great way from the same place. Bradwell and the other person left us and I and young Booker returned to his Father's house. It was near five o'clock when we got there. Young Booker knock'd at the door and his mother got up and let us both in. He mended the Fire and we sat by it till the police came in and took us. I remember at a class meeting at Clayton's on Friday Night before this disturbance that an account of the Arms was taken. Bradwell said those who have Guns hold up your hands. Several held them up. I was one. Then he asked as to pistols in the same manner and others held up their hands. Then he asked as to Pikes and hands were held up. Bradwell took the numbers down on paper. And also the number of Ball Cartridges, Clayton having told him that he thought he had about 100, and Clayton turned to Hands and said I think there will be about 100 for thee. Bentley said he had 50 or more. The Stout lame man said he had 40, others said they had 40. Bradwell took it all down on paper and said it was for the Council.

I have heard it said many times both in the class Meetings and at the other Meetings that the object of the General Rise was to gain the Charter. I never heard the Charter explained.

The Night I gave my promise Wells acted as Door Keeper inside and received the pass word. I saw him afterwards at the private meetings several times. I have heard him reading the Newspaper aloud. I have seen Marshall both at the Secret and public Meetings in Fig Tree Lane. I have heard him say he was a class Leader and have seen him speak to others about the Class. I have heard him mention his Class.

Samuel Powell Thompson

I was apprenticed for seven years to Messrs Kidd & Law at Stockport as an Iron Turner — I once went before a Magistrate when serving them and lodged a complaint against Kidd for beating me got a Warrant from Mr Coppock the Town Clerk — My Master didn't appear and the Case was never heard — I then left my apprenticeship and came over to Sheffield — This was 3 years ago last September — About a week or a fortnight before the Christmas following Kidd and a Policeman named Earlham came to my father's in search of me — While I was in Sheffield I went to work with Booth & Co. as an Iron Turner and left them about a fortnight before — Kidd and the Policeman came — I was married at Stockport during my apprenticeship and when I quitted Stockport — I left my wife with her child to support herself as she could — I went to Stockport to fetch my goods a few days before Kidd and the policeman came over to Sheffield as above stated and returned to Sheffield the Sunday before they came — I left my wife still at Stockport — She was in a good place of work as a reeler.

When Kidd and the policeman came to my father's house they took me away to Ashley's the Waterloo Tavern and kept me there till the next morning and then took me by the coach to Stockport — There I went to work again with my Master Kidd and continued till he failed which was in the following March. My time would have been up the following July — That would have completed my seven years — On my Master's failure I came over to Sheffield leaving my wife at Stockport and went to work with the Milton Iron Company about 8 miles from Sheffield — I continued there better than 3 months and while there I fetched my wife from Stockport — I parted from the Company by reason of my putting a screw into the fire for which I was turned off by the Engineer — I then came to Sheffield and worked for Mr Revile in his Sugar House as Engine man. I continued there better than four months — I left the service on account of a quarrel between myself and the Sugar Boiler — Mr Revile gave me a written character when I left — Then I continued out of work some time — Afterwards I worked at Woods a Boiler Makers — Afterwards at Sandfords of Rotherham in the Iron way — I left him by reason of a quarrel with the foreman — Then I came to Mr Parker of the Pond Forge and worked with him till the day before I was taken up — On that day I left my service having given a month's previous notice in order to go back to Sandford — For having then left his service and I being applied to by Michael Heple the Foreman — I was to have started

270

for my work on the Monday following — I worked for Parker About 9 months — I went to work there in March and left in January — During that time I became a Chartist. The first time I attended was the day they went to the Parish Church — It was soon after Peter Foden was taken — I attended a meeting in Paradise Square where thousands were assembled previously to going to church on the Sunday Morning — they were singing a hymn — I accompanied them to church — They took possession of the pews and filled the church — I went the next night to a meeting in Fig Tree Lane — It was notorious that the Chartists held their meetings there — at first I went through curiosity — It was a full meeting the room was full — it was about 8 o'clock at night — I heard speeches made — After this I attended the evening meetings as regularly as I could — I first became acquainted with Holberry at Church it was on the third Sunday after the first that I attended the Chartists to the Church — I saw Holberry frequently at the Meetings — he was a leading speaker — I remember being at a Meeting in the Fig Tree Lane on Saturday Night the 4th January — this was the Saturday week previous to the Sunday when I was taken up — There was first a public meeting and a private one was held afterwards — At the public meetings the Newspapers were read and speeches made — Then the room was cleared and those who were made members were admitted to the private meeting. Members were admitted to the private meeting by a Sign and a Pass Word at the Private Meeting that night it was said (but by whom I do not know) that Holberry was expected home that night — I have attended the private meetings during the whole of that week and had learned there that Holberry was gone to Dewsbury and was expected home first on the Tuesday and afterwards daily — At the meeting on the Saturday night Holberry not having arrived — I and Peter Foden were at first delegated by the Committee to go in a gig to Dewsbury after him — Afterwards James Boardman was substituted for Foden — James Boardman Peter Foden, Birks, James McKetterick and James Marshall were at that meeting — Peter Foden went out to get a gig and returned saying he could not get one till 6 the next morning — Soon after the meeting broke up. I went home and at 5 in the morning Boardman and Birks came to my house — I was up waiting — they told me at first to get ready — but afterwards said that Holberry was come back — I went out with them — Birks left us and then we went to Bentley's House — and there saw a man whose name I understand to be Law and to be a Delegate who had come up with Holberrry from Dewsbury — we breakfasted with him at Bentley's and walked to the coach office with him — and I saw him take his place for London and get on the coach — about 1 o'clock on that day I went to Holberry's House in Eyre Lane, and found there two men, and afterwards 2 or 3 more came in — I knew them all by sight having seen them at the Meetings — but did not know their names, Holberry told us that he had been a Delegate to Dewsbury and they had settled when the general rise should take place — that only two men in every town should know the time besides the Delegate that brought the news — That there was a courier gone up to London from Dewsbury — I told him I had seen him off on the coach — Holberry named also that he had pledged his word at Dewsbury that no place of Worship or Provision Store should be injured — We all came away together from Holberry's to the room — This was between 2 and 3 o'clock in the afternoon — There were a few people at the room and the Meeting was a secret one — Holberrry called on the Meeting for a collection to carry him round by Nottingham and that way — he said he only set off with £1 — When he went to Dewsbury and had only 5/s. of it to keep him there — That they had made a collection there to send a Delegate off elsewhere and he had given a shilling towards it — a collection was then made and I believe 10s and some odd pence were collected — I gave sixpence — we met again on that Sunday night that was a public meeting — Holberry was there, and another collection was made for the same purpose — Bradwell made known its object. I think about 4s were collected. After the collection was made we gave Holberry the money in the Committee Room. He said he should go to Nottingham and round that District and should be back on Tuesday night if he could but he should be at home on Thursday without fail. I attended Meetings on the Monday, Tuesday and the Wednesday. I don't recollect what passed on the Monday. On the Tuesday Duffy was at the Meetings both public and secret. He made a speech about Daniel O'Connell becoming an universal suffrage advocate — On the Wednesday Duffy attended again and told the people at the secret meeting that he had got a Class of Irishmen together but he said he should not give the meeting any information as to their numbers or names until such a time as there was better order kept at the door as he did not consider it safe. He said they could hardly know who was admitted seeing the manner which the door was tyled. In order to satisfy Duffy I proposed a new pass word 'Union is strength' and that two Tylers should be placed one on the outside and the other within the outside man to receive the word 'Union' and the inside 'strength'. On Thursday night I was at the Meeting.

It was a secret meeting and a good many attended Holberry, Boardman, Duffy, Bradwell and Young Benison were there Duffy spoke first. He told the number of his Class he said they were 64. Holbery spoke, he said he had been round by Nottingham to warn them of the time when the general rise was to take place and to give information of the decision of the Convention. That the rise was to gain the Charter, that as to Mr Frost he was but an individual and the news of Frost would arrive correctly on Friday night but they must take no notice of that the Charter was their motto. That they must all be punctual at their Class on Friday night. He then brought forward a proposition that 50 Bills should be printed to announce a Sermon on Sunday night and a Lecture on Monday night by a Scotch Delegate. He said he hoped no person would ask him any questions about these Bills for time would show. Boardman spoke but I don't recollect what he said. When the Meeting broke up I and Boardman went to a Public House in Dixon Lane kept by Kirk. We found Holberry there and Law and a man whom I learnt had been a Delegate from Barnsley whose name was Ashton — We were in a back room — There was a talk about the rise and Law said he was glad they should have Wales with them at the same moment, they talked about Arms and Holberry produced a dagger from his pocket it was on a red Morocco Sheath it had an Ivory handle tipt with silver, Law asked me if I had got that dagger ready for him (that was in allusion to something that had passed between him and me when I accompanied him to the coach) I answered No but told him to come down to my House the next morning I would try and get him one I was again at the secret Meeting on Friday night Duffy was in the Chair Holberry, Bradwell, Birks, Marshall, Boardman, McKetterick were there and Foden came in afterwards late. Duffy spoke something about his Class I don't remember what he said. While he was speaking a person who was a stranger to me came in and said a policeman was underneath as a Spy — Duffy pulled out a pistol from his breast and said lead me to the Spy and I'll stop him from spying as soon as he said that Bradwell got up and said he would put a Cloak on the Meeting and then spoke in a loud voice a kind of moral lecture he spoke for three or four Minutes in that way after that they went to business again Holberry then spoke he stood on a form in the middle of the Room he had a Pistol in his hand he said that every man must be punctual at his Class at 10 o'clock on Saturday night and if he found any man out in the streets that was a Chartist after that time he would certainly blow his brains out he said that every man must put two shirts on

273

and whatever clothing they could to keep them warm he said they must get a 6d. Dram to keep out the cold and that the class meeting was for an inspection of Arms and there was a man who was a Frenchman and was in the French Revolution who would go and inspect the Arms that they must all take their arms whatever they could secretly but not pikes. The Frenchman was in the Room — Before the meeting broke up it was made known there was to be a Meeting at 7 o'clock as usual on Saturday and that there was to be an inspection of arms also there. After the secret Meeting a few stopped and discussed about the arms Holberry was one — The Frenchman spoke English during that discussion. We learnt from Holberry that the rise was to be on Sunday morning at 2 o'clock — There was also a talk about what ammunition there was — Boardman said he had a thousand rounds of Ball Cartridges — James Marshall said he had about 400 rounds — I said I had about 400 rounds, Birks said he had but a few, Holberry said he had a deal Hand Grenades and if I am not mistaken he said 12 dozen and a quantity of fire balls — Then we talked about arms — Boardman said that he could bring about 6 or 8 guns — I said we had three, Marshall stated he had either 3 or 4 — Birks said they had only 3 or 4 guns — Boardman, Marshall, Birks and myself were respectively leaders of classes and McKetterick was another leader — Then they talked about attacking the soldiers, at first it was suggested that they should fire on them as they were coming by the Infirmary, then another place was mentioned by Johnson's Waggon Warehouse in Gibralter Street, but it was left at last to the Council to determine. Then it was talked about money to buy powder and they asked Birks to get them 5s and he said that he had not it and they asked him to pawn his Sunday clothes, Birks said he would get them 5s either by pawning his clothes or in some other way. They asked me for some money and I said I would see what I could do for them. It was after 12 before the meeting broke up and then I went home and on Saturday forenoon Boardman came to our house and asked if I had money, I said I had not got any for him and he desired me to come to the room at 3 o'clock — I went and found a man of the name of Cooper there and others — Holberry came in afterwards and asked me and Cooper to go with him — Holberry left the room and we followed him and he took us to a public house in Lambert Street the Reuben's Head — he took us into a large room up stairs. We found there McKetterick, Boardman, Duffy and a few more Irishmen and a man whom I afterwards found to be a Rotherham man — Birks came in afterwards, now Holbery got up and addressed the meeting — he

274

stated the plan — First he spoke about taking the Town Hall and the Tontine.

He said every man must be at his post exactly as the clock struck 2 — He spoke about the best plan of coming to take them that they must calculate the time they would be in coming from the meeting house so they all might be there as the clock struck two. The plan was that one man of every class should come first and then two of every class but still all to keep in sight. That was to prevent alarm since they would not be alarmed at one or two as they would at a whole body, that the one and the two's were to assassinate every watchman they came across — He said that my class, James Boardman's, McKetterick's and Birks' classes and the Eckington Friends were to attack the Town Hall — Duffy's Marshall's and the Forty Row the Bridgehouse and the Rotherham People and the Attercliffe people were to take the Tontine. That the Rotherham and Attercliffe were to meet at a Beer house below the twelve o'clock public house and by the Weir head about this time Boardman interposed and said he could bring about fifty and I could bring about 50, Birks said he could bring about twenty and McKetterick said about 40. Duffy said sixty four — It was put to the vote by Boardman which classes should go to the different places and it was voted according to the arrangement laid down by Holberry as before stated — Holberry said now we have said nothing about what should be done if we are put off and he said he should say to begin to Moscow the Town and all the party seemed to approve of it — Then we discussed about getting Arms for those who had none — One of the Irishmen said we have picked upon Ward's shop the corner of Church Street — I said I should like to go after Naylors and Boardman mentioned Mr Yeardley's at West Bar — Holberry seemed to object to this and said there were Arms enough and he should object to break into any shops there was a long haggling about it, but it was put to the vote by Boardman whether they should go to the shops or not, and it was carried we should go — Boardman having suggested that instead of the whole class going eight out of each class should go and then Holberry consented. It was agreed that the Irish party should take Ward's, Boardman's Yeardley's, and mine Naylors and they were to break into the shops exactly as the clock struck two and then return to the main body with what they had got each party knowing where they had to come to as arranged. Holberry then went on to say that as soon as the party got in to the Tontine they were to shut the Gates and barricade them with

275

the coaches that were in the yard and those who got into the Town Hall one party was to occupy the Ground floor and the other party were to go on the top outside. If the soldiers brought their big guns to fire at the Town Hall or Tontine the people having guns in the Town Hall and Tontine would be ready to knock them off before they would be able to plant them and to load, and the Hand Grenades were to be divided amongst those of the classes who had no guns to throw amongst the soldiers. That the Government and all the authorities were a property Government and as soon as their property was destroyed they would become as poor as us, and when they heard it was destroyed they would leave Town and go and protect their own property and they would also give in towards giving the people the Charter. It was then discussed about throwing the cats some proposed that they should be thrown on Sing Hill on account of its being so narrow it would be sure to lame every horse that came up, Sing Hill is on the Road between the Barracks and the Tontine. Sing Hill was not approved of and an amendment was made that the cats should be laid from Woolhouses Corner to the corner of the Town Hall and from thence across the Albion, that was put to the vote and carried. Holberry then stated the plan he had adopted for firing the Barracks. He said that he and 8 more he had picked on one of whom could climb the spouting would go and throw a Fire Ball into the Straw Chamber at the Barracks as soon as the soldiers were called out and that he would set fire to the Riding School which was built of timber and they then would throw a hand grenade or two into the Barracks he said the hand grenades were to be distributed amongst the classes that from the Barracks they would go to Albert Smith's House and fire that and so on with the remainder of the Magistrates. A person then asked him if he could manage to get to Mr Parker's as that was a wide distance. Holberry said leave that to me. I will look after that business if you will look after the Town during the time that all this was going on in the room, I saw the Landlord there. He was there the greatest part of the time and only went in and out for Beer and Liquors. I knew him to be the Landlord because there was a dispute at one part of the time about paying for the Beer which he supplied and he said if they had a mind they should have it for nothing he was a stranger to me at the time but I have seen him a time or two since I don't know his name. In the course of the meetings that took place I learnt that there were various classes I was the leader of one class which met at Valentine Benison's in the Park James Boardman was the leader of another class which met at his own house in

St Phillips Road, Birks was another leader that class met at his house in Mill Lane. I have been there myself Joseph McKetterick was leader of another class that was held at Penthorpes in Spring Street John Marshall was leader of a class which met at his house the top of Coal Pit Lane. There was a class held in Forty Row I don't know who was its leader. There was another in Bridges houses and I don't know that leader and Duffey's class. I don't know where that met. We left Lambert Street about 6 o'clock when the Meeting broke up. I went to my master's, Mr Parker, to settle with him and received my wages and then went home to my father's I remained there until I went out to meet my class. I left home about 9 o'clock and took with me a sword which I had borrowed from my brother concealed in my trousers I went to the room and found no meeting there from thence I went to my former house in Forge Lane expecting to meet some of my class there but found none. I then went to Valentine Benison's in the Park where I met about a dozen of my class (young Benison was one of them) and led them to the house in Forge Lane. When we got to Forge Lane I inspected the Men and found them all armed except young Benison most with daggers and some with Pike Heads which they carried concealed while we remained at Forge Lane. William Wells came in, he was one of our class, he brought three dirks with him they were in red Morroco sheaths and had Ivory handles tipt with silver he asked me if I had got a dirk. I said no and he then gave me the 3 he asked if we had a file in the house to file out the mark on the Dirk George Morton another of my class came in and said the soldiers were out and hearing the file asked for looked on the dirks and said he would go and fetch a file he fetched one and gave it to one of my men and I gave that man the dirks and he filed out the marks. Hearing the soldiers were out I ordered the men to stop where they were till I returned and then I went out to Birks in Mill Lane who sent me to the public house in Lambert street. I found there James Boardman, Duffey and the Landlord I first went into the bar and saw the Landlord he took me upstairs into the room and then went down and fetched up Boardman and Duffey the Landlord remained in the room. I told them the soldiers were out and asked them what was to be done now. They said they knew that and the Landlord said they could not see any choice now but Moscowing the Town it was at this time about eleven o'clock Boardman gave me orders to come or send every half hour and I returned to Birks and agreed with him that my class should join his — Two of his men had a gun apiece and another had a sword. Birks was engaged in dipping torches in turpentine. I saw him dip about half a dozen. I then returned to my own class in Forge Lane and brought my class to Birks and we made when united about 20 or 24 while we remained at Birks; young Benison went home and brought back his father's pistol and some ball cartridges. A person went backwards and forwards to Lambert Street for orders and at last brought an order that we were to go to the top of Water Lane to meet the other Classes. Birks had a torch and a dagger. We went there and found nobody — We returned to Birks and then it was determined that Watery Lane must have been meant for Water Lane and then we went there up Spring Street, Allen Street and Tobacco Box Walk. We found nobody there. We were about 20 or 24 then it was turned 3 o'clock. Then we returned into Tobacco Box Walk and met with a few Irishmen seeking after Duffey. I and two of my party went with the Irishmen to Duffey's home. We found Duffey there and stayed till between 4 and 5 o'clock. There was some wrangling between him and the Irishmen. A great many Irishmen were in the house — they charged him with not coming forward as he ought and he excused himself by saying he had been to the Council and appealed to me for the truth of it. All of them were armed with daggers. I left Duffey's with young Benison another man and went to Birks' and found he was not at home. I was then making my way home to my father's when I was collared by a policeman on the bridge from whom I got away and ran down towards the Wicher then I was stopt by a body of police and brought to the Town Hall. I had then on my person two swords, two daggers and a box of Lucifer matches and a box of percussion caps. I remember to have seen Old Booker at secret meetings during the week before I was taken but I cannot tell how often or at which.

Before a member was admitted to a secret meeting he was obliged to make a promise. I made that promise and I have heard others make it. More than forty made it to me — I made my promise the second Sunday after the disturbance in Wales it was at Penthorpes house in Spring Street Peter Foden was Chairman Holberry and Bradwell were present. Foden put the question to me whether I had any objection to join a secret society — I said no then he said will you do all that lies in your power towards gaining the people's Charter even to the loss of your own life and shedding of the blood of the tyrants. I said I will. Holberry mentioned that when he was a soldier the soldiers had been putting down secret meetings where they had taken oaths, but he mentioned one place the name of which I don't remember where they could not put them down because they had taken a promise instead of an oath

278

and therefore he recommended a promise. Then Holberry and Bradwell settled a form of promise but which Bradwell wrote down and read over several times and when it was approved he gave it to Foden. Then I and several others stood round him Holberry Bradwell and Penthorpe being three of them. Foden read the form and we repeated it after him — As well as I can recollect the form was this — Each man beginning with his own name 'do most solemnly and sincerely promise that in the sight of Almighty God that I never will on any occasion make known any matters that are to be kept secret and I therefore pledge thee my troth that I will assassinate anyone that shall betray the secrets of these meetings and bear assassination if I shall betray them'. I got the promise off by heart and I saw the paper from which I read the form put into the fire and destroyed that night.

30 Bradford: Evidence Relating to the Attempted Rising in Bradford

(a) Report from James Harrison, employed by the police authorities, on the activities of the Bradford Chartists, 17 December 1839

From the Harewood Papers

On the 5th Dec. last I was going from Bradford to the Queen's Head in company with George Flinn who is one of the Chartist Delegates. I said to him what do you think about this matter, what will it come to? He said it will come to something very serious in a short time, as the time is nearly at an end, meaning Frost's trial. Nothing will be as good for us as fires — I said to him. Worsted is a thing that will not burn well — he says it won't burn as well as cotton — but I am prepared with 2 pint bottles that will fire any Mill in this county and I for one will attend that part of the work. I have the command of 250 men. He went on to the Queen's Head to a place called the School and there we met about a dozen men. I do not know the names of any who were there except Flinn. One of the Speakers said we have made up our minds and sent our determination down to Bradford. We'll have no more public meetings nor pay no more money. We have 260 or 270 men well armed and ammunition is ready at any time by the sound of a horn. We left the School about 10 and went to the Old Queen's Head where we met with a delegate from London.

In the bar there was this delegate, George Flinn, 2 men from the Queen's Head whose names I do not know and myself. The man from London looked earnestly at me and asked Flinn if he knew me — Flinn said he had known me for 3 years and that I was as good a man as any in the room — this delegate said his reason for asking that was that he was aware there were a many spies up and down the country. He said in London at this time of the year people are liable to accidents, some people by burning tobacco might set the bed on fire, or some people might leave a candle burning and then set the house on fire. Fire he said was a good Servant but a bad Master — Frost could never be tried at a better season than the present — the days are short and the nights are long. He recommended fires very much and said they were very useful as it would reduce the soldiers from different places. Geoge Flinn then answered and said it was agreed there should [be] a fire at Keighley which would take the soldiers from Bradford and after the fire took place at Keighley they would allow 2½ hours for the soldiers to arrive there from Bradford and by that time all would be quiet at Keighley and they would begin a rumpus in the neighbourhood of Bradford, meaning a large mill at Bradford should be set on fire and in this way we will keep the soldiers going from one place to another. We left the Queen's Head about half past 11 and returned to Bradford when we separated. Queen's Head is 4 miles from Bradford in the direction of Halifax.

On Sunday the 8th of Decr I was in company with John Hodgson and others. Hodgson said I am going to a meeting in Manchester and when I return I will lead my men up manfully as he expected then the row would begin as soon as he returned. Hodgson returned from Manchester on Thursday night and I saw him again on Friday 13th inst. He said he was well satisfied with the meeting at Manchester as Dr Taylor had volunteered either to stay at home amongst his own men in Carlisle district, or he would come into Yorkshire to head and assist them, or he would go into Wales. We consider him the best man we know he said that Dr Taylor had 900 men ready to rise well armed and well fit up in every respect and that he had bought 1000 shirts for his men at 2/6 each, with 2 pockets for ammunition at the breast and a belt for pistols or sword. He also said it was determined that Taylor should stay at home. I was with George Flinn on Saturday last the 14th he told me there were 3 foreigners in London who were willing to go to any part where they might be sent to. They were men who feared nothing. It was agreed that one should come to Bradford and 2 go into Wales and they had no doubt of being successful. At this time there are 10,000 men upon the mountains and have been ever since Frost was apprehended and will never return to work until they get Frost liberated. There was a Chartist meeting at Bradford on Saturday evening last which was numerously attended. I was present at it, George Flinn was Chairman, John Hodgson was one of the principal speakers and was elected at the meeting to go to London as a delegate to the national convention, to meet on Thursday the 19th. Both Hodgson and Flinn have told me that the general rising is to take place upon receiving information from London but that they expect it will be about the 27th, 4 days before Frost's trial. Hodgson also told me that in the convention a place would be settled to meet the Judges and to shoot them in their carriages on their way to Frost's trial but that that was to be finally settled by the convention in London.

James Harrison

Sworn before us at Bradford Yorkshire
this seventeenth of December in
the year of our Lord 1839 being three
of her Majesty's Justices of the Peace
for the West Riding or Yorkshire
    J. G. Paley
    Matt^w Thompson
    H. W. Hird

(b) Evidence given by Harrison at the trial of Robert Peddie for sedition, February 1840

From T.S. 11/814/2678

The further Examination of James Harrison of Bradford in the said Riding Labourer taken on Oath in the presence and hearing of the Prisoner Robert Peddie the twenty first Day of February 1840.

Who says 'On Saturday the 25th of January last the Charter and its final object was mentioned at Hargreaves Beer Shop at a Chartist Meeting by the Prisoner George Flinn and Isaac Holloway, John Turner, William Brook and Marsden and others — Peddie said that if they brought up half the quantity of men they said they had he could beat the soldiers and establish the Charter — he could insure the people that they could have the Charter in two or three days — that it could not be obtained without physical force and that they would use physical force — after taking Bradford they would go and take Dewsbury and after taking Dewsbury they would take all the places on their way to London — after they got to London they would upset the Government, and do all this in three or four days — Peddie said that when they came from Low Moor down to Bradford they would have the piece-hall as a depot for ammunition and the news room as a depot for the men the pillage of different places bread clothes and provisions were to be taken to the newsroom and when they left Bradford to be taken in the baggage waggons — Peddie said we'll have the miners agate with their picks and make port holes thro' the walls we can soon do it — Peddie and the others said that they wanted annual parliaments universal suffrage — no qualification — vote by ballot, that there should be an equal division of property thro' the Country — take all and sweep all before them — especially the money — that they would upset the Government by physical force when they got to London as nothing else would do — that when they had upset the Government they would establish the Charter — that he Peddie would have the management of every thing — that there was to be a national convention — to give every poor man his own rights and that they could do nothing without it — these subjects were agitated both on the Saturday night and Sunday night the 26th of January — on the Sunday at Turner's and they all agreed to what Peddie said — Peddie and Marsden, George Flinn, Isaac Holloway and myself William Brook, Thomas Drake and John Turner were all at his Turners house — Peddie was to be the head Leader and all were Leaders who were there on the Sunday night and agreed that he should be head Leader there were about twelve or fourteen people at Turners — On the Saturday night a little after seven I went with Marsden as far as the Junction Inn on the Leeds New Road in Bradford on his way to Leeds to set fire to the magazine at Leeds and then bring the Leeds Chartists to Bradford — he said he should bring a hundred men from Leeds — all this was stated in the Room at Turners so that every body could hear it — Marsden went forward to Leeds and I have not seen him since — on Peddie stating what his object was they said they were all ready to join him — they approved of his plans — I had heard physical force and the Charter talked about very often by all the parties — I have named at different times and places — and all agreed to join Peddie in his plans —

James Harrison

Sworn before us
H. W. Hird
B. Hague

(c) Evidence given against Peddie by John Ashton, a Bradford Chartist who turned Queen's Evidence

From T.S. 11/814/2678

The voluntary confession and deposition of John Ashton late of Bradford Wool Comber taken this 6th of February 1840 at York Castle.

On Sunday the 26th January at eight o'clock in the evening I received a message through my wife that a person had been to desire I would go up to John Smith's orange cellar Nelson's Court. I went after eight o'clock when I got into the house there were 8 or 9 people there drinking ale, they handed me some. We remained until one in the morning — I sometimes went out and came in again — In the room there were myself Peddie, G. Flinn — Woolcomber Nelson Court, Holloway, Tailor lodging at Holcombs a Shopkeeper in Nelson Court, Paul and James Holdsworth both Woolcombers living with their Mother in-law of the name of Smith, in Nelson Court. When I went in I enquired who Peddie (the stranger) was and what they had met for I asked of G. Flinn this, He said there was going to be an insurrectionary movement, and that Peddie was to be a leader the movement was to take place in Bradford, that they were to take possession of the Town next morning he said if I would join I might but that no person joining after the victory would be allowed to partake of the products of the night, he would take care they did not, Flinn told me that Peddie had told him that, there were two companies of Soldiers at Halifax whom he knew were coming and who would join their party Flinn said that Peddie told him that he was partly acquainted with nearly all those soldiers and knew that they were on their side. Flinn Peddie and Holloway were armed with pistols I do not know whether they were loaded — I saw Flinn and Holloway with about 40 ball cartridges each in a bag in front and I heard Peddie say he was prepared, the others were armed with pikes — about a quarter before two on Monday morning Peddie made a speech and at the end said 'England expected every man to do his duty' he and Flinn led the way out — We followed all armed, to the Bowling Green there was a watchman sat there on Butcher's block Holloway went up to him and took him prisoner, and told him, he must go along with us we took him to a shed in the green market. Peddie set me as sentinel and gave me strict charges not to let him escape. When I had been

there a quarter of an hour Peddie had placed three sentinels at
the three openings leading to the market place. Shortly after he
and Flinn brought another watchman prisoner from the sign of
the Nelson, and after they had been together Flinn came and
took their rattles from them, Peddie had placed Paul
Holdsworth as sentinel over the second watchman. About a
quarter of an hour after this Briggs came and took me into
custody — I delivered up my pike when Mr Briggs took hold of
me, the rest of my companions immediately ran away and left
me. The prisoners who are in custody here are strangers to me
and are of another class they were not in John Smith's house
where we met. When Peddie was in John Smith's house he was
dressed in a drab great coat, with a pistol belt round his waist,
he took his pistol out of this belt when we got out of the house
and carried the pistol in his hand — Flinn gave me my pike in
Smith's house — I have not seen Peddie in York Castle since I
came here — I make this confession in the hope of benefitting
myself as I was led into it without knowing what they were
going to do I have a wife and three children who are destitute
and I will give this evidence in any court if I am allowed to be a
witness.

John Ashton

York Castle
10th February 1840

The Pike now produced to me by Mr Shepherd was given to me
early on the Monday morning by George Flinn at John Smith's
house the blade was put in by Holloway and Flinn who heated
the head red hot before it was put into the shaft. When it was
done Peddie examined it to see that all was right. I was under
Peddie's orders and went out with an intention of taking the
possession of the Bazaar in the Green Market where we were to
remain till five o'clock when we expected reinforcements from
Leeds and Dewsbury — and were to take possession of the
Town I was four or five hours with Peddie at this house and am
sure the Prisoner is the man.
    Cross examined by prisoner —
The words insurrectionary movement were the words of Flinn
— the light I took it in was a rebellion or an outbreak — About a
quarter past eight on the Sunday evening on my return home
my wife told me that somebody had sent for me as I was

285

wanted at John Smith's — I went immediately to Smith's and found you there — John Smith was sat on one side the fire and you on the other — no conversation took place between you and me I was not introduced to you I remained about an hour before I went out — Flinn had a rough fustian jacket on — At the time he went out he put on a rough top coat something like a watchman's coat a light coloured rough one — When I came in at a quarter past eight you had a belt on and a pistol in it — I swear this positively the belt might be six inches broad — Flinn had no arms on him just then but he fetched them before he went out — When I went out I was absent about ten minutes or a quarter of an hour — I am certain I was back by half past nine — I saw nearly the same persons when I came back Flinn was there and you were there. I went out before twelve o'clock — to the best of my recollection Harrison was not there. I did not see him — if he had been there I think I should have seen him — I received no orders to destroy property — I received no orders from Flinn or yourself to use our arms against anybody — I had no conversation with you during the night — When Flinn and I had the talk about the insurrectionary movement you were four or five yards off — Flinn told me he had his instructions from Peddie I received no instructions from Peddie — We were above half an hour in the market place — if I had received instructions it was not my intention to have used my weapon against any one — the conversation between me and Flinn was in a low tone, the door was not locked and the people kept going in and out — You had set forth such eloquence about the Military coming from Halifax and people they could spare from Dewsbury and Leeds this was told me by Flinn and not by you these words I did not hear you say it was Flinn that told me — I did not hear you say any thing like this in the course of the evening.

John Ashton

Further cross-examined by prisoner.

    I saw no muskets in Smith's but I saw you have a pistol. I saw no muskets in the market-place. If there had been muskets at Smith's I must have seen them — if there had been muskets in my own party in the market place I must have seen them but you had a dagger on you — a spear put into a short handle I was in the market place the whole time the Chartists were there until I was taken into custody.

John Ashton

286

PART VI

Reorganisation

After the events of Newport, the arrest, trial and deportation of the Welsh leaders, and the wave of arrests which took place of Chartist leaders throughout the country, there was a lull in activity, although the continued sale of the various Chartist journals showed a remaining fairly high level of interest. A number of the older men in the movement withdrew from activity at this time, either directly, or after their release from prison. But the summer of 1840 saw a new Convention meeting at Manchester, and it was here that the rules and organisation of the National Charter Association were drawn up. The N.C.A., with its elected leadership, formed the pattern of Chartist organisation from that time onwards, and appears to have been successful in establishing a legal framework for the first nationally organised party of the working class to exist in the world. In issuing the rules and proposals for the new organisation, the delegates also issued an address which ended:

It is not for the delegates to speak further upon their labours. But they are desirous of effecting union among the working classes, by which they may become powerful. Let, then, a strenuous effort be made. Let the people immediately meet in every city, town and hamlet, to make themselves acquainted with the nature of the proposed National Charter Association, and at no distant period. Let there not be a working man, a working woman, or child, who is not a member of this great and glorious Association — properly arranged in classes, and other divisions, as is pointed out, as is for proper government deemed necessary. The delegates may be applied to at all times for information.

And now, let Englishmen, Scotchmen, Welshmen and Irishmen arouse themselves to struggle, legally, for their rights and liberties! Let our motto be 'Universal suffrage and no surrender' — to obtain which let us effect a national union, which tyranny and injustice cannot resist. 'England expects every man to do his duty.'

31 Aims and Rules of the National Charter Association

From the 'Northern Star', 1 August 1840

A PLAN FOR ORGANISING THE CHARTISTS OF GREAT BRITAIN

Agreed upon at a meeting of delegates appointed by the people and held at the Griffin Inn, Great Ancoats-Street, Manchester, on Monday, July 20th, 1840.

DESIGNATION OF THE ASSOCIATION

1. That the Chartists of Great Britain be incorporated into one Society to be called 'The National Charter Association of Great Britain'.

OBJECTS

2. The object of this Association is to obtain a 'Radical Reform' of the House of Commons, in other words, a full and faithful Representation of the entire people of the United Kingdom.

PRINCIPLES

3. The principles requisite to secure such a Representation of the people are:— The right of voting for Members of Parliament by every male of twenty-one years of age and of sound mind; Annual Elections; Vote by Ballot; no property qualifications for Members of Parliament; Payment of members; and a division of the kingdom into Electoral Districts; giving to each district a proportionate number of Representatives according to the number of electors.

MEANS

4. To accomplish the foregoing object none but peaceable and constitutional means shall be employed, such as public meetings to discuss grievances arising from the present system; to show the utility of the proposed change, and to petition Parliament to adopt the same.

CONDITIONS OF MEMBERSHIP

5. All persons will become members of the Association on condition of signing a declaration, signifying their agreement with its objects, principles and constitution, when they will be presented with cards of membership which shall be renewed quarterly, and for which they shall each pay the sum of twopence.

REGISTRATION OF MEMBERS

6. A book shall be kept by the Executive Council (hereinafter described) in which shall be entered the names, employment and residence of the members of this Association throughout the kingdom.

CLASSES

7. Wherever possible, the members shall be formed into classes of ten persons; which classes shall meet weekly or at any other stated periods, as most convenient; and one out of, and by, each class shall be nominated as leader (and appointed by the Executive as hereinafter ordered) who shall collect from each member the sum of one penny per week, to the funds of the Association.

WARD DIVISIONS

8. Each town, wherever practicable, shall be divided into wards and divisions according to the plan of the Municipal Reform Act. Once in every month a meeting of the members of

the said ward shall be held, when addresses shall be delivered, and Society's business transacted. The leaders within the said wards shall attend the said monthly meetings, and give such a report of the state of their classes as they may deem best, provided always that such report be given in temperate and lawful language.

ELECTION OF WARD COLLECTOR

9. At the first meeting of each ward or division, a collector shall be nominated (afterwards to be appointed by the Executive as hereinafter ordered) to whom shall be paid the monies collected from the classes by the leaders; and the said collector shall pay the said money to the Treasurer (assistant) of the town or borough, at the weekly meeting of the council.

LOCAL OFFICERS

10. Each principal town, with its suburban villages, shall have a council of nine persons, including an assistant treasurer and secretary.

DUTIES OF LOCAL TREASURER

11. The aforesaid local treasurer shall receive the money from the ward collectors, and all the monies subscribed for the Association in the said township and suburbs; he shall keep an exact account and transmit the proportion (one moiety) due once a month to the General Treasurer.

DUTIES OF LOCAL SECRETARY

12. The aforesaid secretary shall keep a minute book of all the transactions of the Town Council, and a record of all meetings connected with the Society in his jurisdiction, and shall, with the sanction and under the direction of the said Council, transmit for publication such portions of the said minutes or records as may be deemed necessary.

DUTIES OF LOCAL COUNCIL

13. The Town Council shall meet for the transaction of business once every week, and shall have the power of appropriating to the purposes of the society in their own locality a sum not exceeding one half of the subscriptions and other monies received in the said locality. They shall also see that the recommendations and instructions of the Executive Council are carried into effect, and they shall have full power to adopt such means as may seem to them meet, provided such means are in conformity with the fundamental rules of the Association and do not contravene the decisions of the Executive Council.

COUNTY AND RIDING GOVERNMENT

14. In each County or Riding there shall be a council, the number to be according to the circumstances and population of the said County or Riding, with a sub-treasurer or secretary.

GENERAL GOVERNMENT

15. The general government of this Association shall be entrusted to a General Executive Council, composed of seven persons including a Treasurer and Secretary.

DUTIES OF GENERAL TREASURER

16. The General Treasurer of this Association shall be responsible for all monies entrusted to him, in such penal sum as may be determined upon by the Executive Council; he shall keep an exact account of all monies received and expended by the Association, and shall once every month, publish a statement of the same in the 'Northern Star', 'Scottish Patriot', and in such other of the the Chartist newspapers as may be selected by the Executive Council, and once every three months a full balance sheet, which shall be first examined by auditors appointed for the purpose by the Executive Council.

NOMINATION AND ELECTION OF THE
EXECUTIVE COUNCIL

17. The nomination of candidates for the Executive Committee shall take place in the Counties and Ridings, each County or Riding being allowed to nominate one candidate on the first day of December each year — the names of the persons so nominated shall be returned immediately by the secretary, called sub-secretary of the County or Riding to the General Secretary — (this year to the Secretary of the Provisional Committee who have full powers to carry this plan into effect in the best possible manner) — and a list of the whole to be transmitted by him, per post, to all the local (assistant) Secretaries, who shall take the elections of their localities on the first day of January following, and immediately forward the result of such election to the General Secretary, who shall lay the same before the Executive for examination, and by their order publish within one week of receiving the whole of such returns in the 'Northern Star', 'Scottish Patriot', and in any other Democratic Journal, a list of the majorities, and declare who are the persons duly elected. The Executive Council shall be elected for twelve months, when a new Council shall be chosen in the manner and at the period aforesaid, outgoing members being eligible for re-election.

POWER AND DUTIES OF THE EXECUTIVE

19. The Executive Council shall be empowered to adopt any measure for the advancement of the objects of this Association as may be consistent with its fundamental laws, for which purpose they shall have the disposal of one half, at least, of the monies collected throughout the Society and lodged with the general Treasurer. They shall appoint all the members of the County or Riding and Local Councils, and all officers throughout the Association, in the appointment of whom, however, they shall be confined to those who may be nominated by the members resident in each place.

TIME OF NOMINATION AND APPOINTMENT OF
SUBORDINATE COUNCIL AND OFFICERS

20. To prevent any interruption of the election of the Executive Council, the nomination of County or Riding Councils

shall annually take place on the 1st day of February of each year, and the appointment on the 1st day of March following.*

REMUNERATION OF OFFICERS

21. The General Secretary shall be paid for his services the sum of £2 per week, and each member of the Executive Council the sum of £1. 10s per week during the period of their sittings.

COMPENSATION

22. The members of the Executive shall be entitled to compensation for the loss consequent upon their acceptance of office, either by being employed as missionaries during any recess that may happen while they continue in their official capacity, or in such other way as may be most convenient for the Association; the question of compensation to be determined by the County or Riding councils. When members of the Executive shall be employed as missionaries, their salaries shall be the same as when employed in the Council. Coach-hire, and one half of any other incidental expenses shall be paid to them in addition, by the parties who may request their services, or in the event of being employed by the Executive to open new districts, the same proportion of expenses shall be allowed out of the general fund.

SOME MEANS FOR THE ATTAINMENT
OF THE GREAT END

1. The People shall, wherever convenient and practicable, put in operation Mr O'Brien's plan of bringing forward Chartist candidates at every election that may hereafter take place, and especially select, where possible, those as Candidates who are legally qualified to sit in Parliament.

2. The Members of this Association shall also attend all public Political Meetings, and there, either by moving amendments, or by other means, enforce a discussion of our rights and claims, so that none may remain in ignorance of what we want, nor have an opportunity of propagating or perpetuating political ignorance or delusion.

3. It is urgently recommended that strict sobriety be observed by all members and officers of this Association.

4. The diffusion of Political Knowledge.

* This clause, it will be seen at once, must be carried into effect for the present year as *soon* as can be by the Provisional Committee.

Suggested Further Reading

What follows is an attempt at a working bibliography for students, confined to the years covered by the documents. A fuller bibliography of the whole movement can be found in G. D. H. Cole, 'Chartist Portraits', the 1965 edition of which has a bibliographical foreword by Asa Briggs which brings it up to that date. F. C. Mather's admirable Historical Association pamphlet 'Chartism', also published in 1965, contains a comprehensive review of writing about Chartism, and a fuller bibliography of recent material can be gathered from a file of the 'Bulletin of the Society for the Study of Labour History', which lists all relevant publications, including many articles which have appeared outside the usual historical journals. The 'Bulletin' also contains occasional review articles on Chartism, as well as listing unpublished theses and work in progress. It should certainly be consulted by any one intending to begin serious work on Chartism. The most recent bibliographical article is by W. H. Maehl, in the 'Journal of Modern History' of September 1969, which covers publications up to that date.

Some further bibliographical references will be found in the notes to the Introduction.

Since the study of Chartism takes in so many aspects of the social history of the middle years of the nineteenth century, most general histories, biographies, memoirs, etc. which cover those years make some reference to it or throw some light on its background. In the same way almost every newspaper and periodical published in the relevant years contains some reference to it. It would be impossible, and not very useful, to list all such sources. I have therefore only listed here books and journals which throw considerable light on the subject, or which contain important information which cannot be obtained elsewhere.

The publications of the Chartists themselves, locally and nationally, were considerable in number and variety in the early years. A check list of all Chartist publications is in preparation, but since my own list is very far from complete, and inevitably contains many items which are extremely rare, I have not tried to make even a partial list of pamphlets and broadsides, but have listed only the journals of the period, many of which can be seen at the British Museum newspaper library at Colindale, and some of which are now available on microfilm and can be seen at provincial or university libraries.

MANUSCRIPT SOURCES

Home Office Papers (Public Record Office)
Series 40/ Mainly correspondence relating to disturbances. The series is divided into bundles by counties, dates and subjects.
Series 41/ Entry books corresponding to series 40.
Other relevant bundles include 41/26 (London), 48/33 and 49/8 (Law Officers), 61/22 (Metropolitan Police), and 79/4-5 (Entry books private and secret, which contain warrants for opening mails in the post).

Treasury Solicitor's Papers (Public Record Office)
Various bundles relating to Crown prosecutions, including
T.S. 11/499: Papers re Frost, Williams and Jones and others, indictments and abstract of evidence.
T.S. 11/1030, 4424 A, B, C, D, E, F: various provincial Chartist trials, mainly for drilling, but including (F), that of J. R. Stephens.
T.S. 11/814, 2678: Queen *v*. Peddie; T.S. 11/816, 2688: Queen *v*. Holberry and others.

Place Collection (British Museum)
Add. MSS 27,819:Historical narrative of the formation of the London Working Men's Association, proceedings of the society etc.
27,820: Continuation of above; proceedings of the Birmingham Political Association.
27,821: Continuation 1839.
34,245: Letter-books of the National Convention of the Industrious Classes.
37,773: L.W.M.A. minute book, 1836-9.
Place Newspaper Collection, especially Set 56, Vol. 1, newspaper cuttings relating to the early period of the Chartist movement.

Lovett Collection (Birmingham Public Library)
Two volumes of cuttings, leaflets, MSS correspondence, etc., nearly all relating to the Convention.

Harewood Papers (Leeds Reference Library)
Correspondence of Lord Harewood, who was Lord Lieutenant of the West Riding of Yorkshire during this period.

Linton Collection
20 volumes of cuttings, presented by Linton to the British Museum in 1895, covering the years 1836-86.
MSS and correspondence in the Feltronelli Institute, Milan.

Frost material
A full list of the MSS and other material relating to Frost and the Welsh Chartists is in David Williams, 'John Frost' (1939).

REPRINTED DOCUMENTARY MATERIAL

G. D. H. Cole and W. H. Filson, 'British Working Class Movements' (sections xii, xiii, xiv).
Francis Place, ed. D. J. Rowe, 'London Radicalism 1830-1843, a Selection from the Papers of Francis Place'
(London Record Society, 1970).
John Collins and William Lovett (introduction by Asa Briggs), 'Chartism, a New Organisation of the People'
(published 1840, reprinted Leicester U.P. 1970).

NEWSPAPERS AND JOURNALS

Chartist and Owenite journals published in English in the years 1837-40
'Ayrshire Examiner', July 1838-Nov 1839.
'Bronterre's National Reformer', 1837.
*'Birmingham Journal', 1837-40.
'The Charter', Oct 1838-March 1840.
'The Chartist', Nov 1838-July 1839.
'The Chartist Circular' (Glasgow), 1839-42.
'The Champion', 1836-40.
'The Dundee Chronicle', 1835-6, 1840-2.

* Papers which, although not Chartist publications, contain much more than the usual amount of Chartist news in the years indicated.

'Edinburgh Monthly Democrat and Total Abstainers' Advocate',
  July-Oct 1838.
'English Chartist Circular'.
'The London Democrat', April-June 1839.
'The London Dispatch and Peoples' Political and Social
  Reformer', 1836-9.
'The London Mercury', 1836-7.
*'The Manchester and Salford Advertiser', 1837-40.
'The Midland Counties Illuminator', 1839-41.
'The New Moral World', 1837-9.
'The Northern Liberator', 1837-40.
'The Northern Star', 1837-52.
'The Operative', Oct 1838-June 1839.
*'The Scots Times', 1839-40.
'The Scottish Patriot', 1839-41.
'The Social Pioneer', 1839.
'The Southern Star', 1840-1.
'The Star of the East', 1838.
'The True Scotsman', 1838-42.
'The Working Bee', 1839.
'The Western Vindicator', 1839-42.

SECONDARY WORKS

(a) General studies

R. G. Gammage,	'History of the Chartist Movement' (first published 1854, 2nd ed., with plates, index, etc., 1894).
Mark Hovell,	'The Chartist Movement' (1918).
Julius West,	'History of the Chartist Movement' (1920).
H. U. Faulkner,	'Chartism and the Churches' (1916).
F. E. Rosenblatt,	'The Social-Economic Aspects of the Chartist Movement' (1916).
Asa Briggs,	'Chartism re-considered', in M. Roberts (ed.), 'Historical Studies 11: Papers Read before the Third Conference of Irish Historians' (1959).
J. T. Ward (ed.),	'Popular Movements, c. 1830-1850' (1970).

* Papers which, although not Chartist publications, contain much more than the usual amount of Chartist news in the years indicated.

(b) Regional studies

Asa Briggs (ed.),   'Chartist Studies' (1959).
Leslie C. Wright,   'Scottish Chartism' (1953).
Alexander Wilson,   'The Chartist Movement in Scotland' (1970).

Bradford
A. J. Peacock,   'Bradford Chartism 1838-40' (York, 1969).

Birmingham
Trygve Tholfson,   'The Origins of the Birmingham Caucus', in 'Historical Journal', ii 2 (1959).

Trygve Tholfson,   'The Chartist Crisis in Birmingham', in 'International Review of Social History', iii 3 (1958).

Conrad Gill,   'History of Birmingham', i, ch. xii.
G. Edwards,   'Personal Reminiscences of Birmingham and Birmingham Men' (1877).

Bristol
John Cannon,   'The Chartists in Bristol' (Bristol, 1967).

Coventry
Peter Searby,   'Coventry Politics in the Age of the Chartists' (Coventry, 1965).

Dundee
Anon.   'Memoranda of the Chartist Agitation in Dundee' (Dundee, 1889).

Halifax
G. R. Dalby,   'The Chartist Movement in Halifax and District', in 'Transactions of the Halifax Antiquarian Society' (1956).

Leicester
A. Temple Patterson,   'Radical Leicester' (1954).
Robert Barnes,   'The Midland Counties Illuminator, a Chartist Journal', in 'Transactions of the Leicestershire Archeological and Historical Society', xxv (1959).

London
I. J. Prothero,   'Chartism in London', in 'Past and Present', no. 44 (Aug 1969).

D. J. Rowe,   'The Failure of London Chartism', in 'Historical Journal' xi 3 (1968).

D. J. Rowe,   'The London Working Men's Association and the People's Charter', in 'Past and Present', no. 36 (April 1967).

D. J. Rowe,   'Chartism and the Spitalfields Silk Weavers', in 'Economic History Review' (Dec 1967).

Newcastle

W. H. Maehl,   'Chartist Disturbances in North-eastern England in 1839', in 'International Review of Social History', viii (1963).

Norwich

J. K. Edwards,   'Chartism in Norwich', in 'Yorkshire Bulletin of Economic and Social Research' (Nov 1967).

Nottingham

R. A. Church,   'Economic and Social Change in a Midland Town — Victorian Nottingham' ch. vi (1966).

Peter Wyncoll,   'Nottingham Chartism' (Nottingham, 1966).

Wales

Edward Hamer,   'A Brief Account of the Chartist Outbreak in Llanidloes' (Llanidloes, 1867). See also bibliography in David Williams, 'John Frost'.

Spen Valley (Yorks.)

Frank Peel,   'The Rising of the Luddites, Chartists and Plug Drawers' (1880, reprinted 1970).

(c) Biographies and biographical studies

G. D. H. Cole,   'Chartist Portraits' (1940).

William Lovett,   'The Life and Struggles of William Lovett in his Pursuit of Bread, Knowledge and Freedom' (1876).

L. Barbara Hammond, 'William Lovett 1800-1877' (1922).

G. J. Holyoake,   'Life of Joseph Rayner Stephens' (1881).

J. T. Ward,	'Revolutionary Tory: The Life of J. R. Stephens of Ashton-u-Lyne', in 'Transactions of the Lancs and Cheshire Antiquarian Society', lxviii (1958).
A. R. Schoyen,	'The Chartist Challenge' (1958).
David Williams,	'John Frost' (1939).
Benjamin Wilson,	'The Struggles of an Old Chartist' (Halifax, 1887).
Donald Read and Eric Glasgow,	'Feargus O'Connor, Irishman and Chartist' (1961).
Thomas Ainge Devyr,	'The Odd Book of the Nineteenth Century' (New York, 1880).
Lord Broughton (J. C. Hobhouse),	'Recollections of a Long Life' (1911).
W. J. Linton,	'A Memoir of James Watson' (1879).
William Dorley,	'Henry Vincent, A Biographical Sketch' (1979).
Ambrose G. Barker,	'Henry Hetherington' (n.d. c 1922).
F. W. Fetter (ed.),	'Selected Economic Writings of Thomas Attwood' (1964).
M. R. Lahee,	'The Life and Times of Alderman Thomas Livesey' (Rochdale, 1871).
Matthew Fletcher,	'Letters to the Inhabitants of Bury' (Bury, 1852).
Alexander Somerville,	'Cobdenic Policy, the Internal Enemy of England' (1854).
Graham Walls,	'The Life of Francis Place' (1898).
R. E. Leader,	'The Life and Letters of J. A. Roebuck' (1897).
C. S. Sprigge,	'The Life and Times of Thomas Wakley' (1897).
T. S. Duncombe,	'The Life and Letters of Thomas Slingsby Duncombe' (1865).
W. J. Linton,	'Memories' (1895).
William Napier,	'The Life and Opinions of General Sir Charles Napier' ii (1857).
H. A. Bruce, M.P. (ed.),	'Life of General Sir William Napier, K.C.B.' (1864).
Henry Solly,	'These Eighty Years' (1891).

Brian Harrison and Patricia Hollis,	'Chartism, Liberalism and Robert Lowery', in 'English Historical Review', lxxxii.
W. H. Maehl,	'Augustus Hardin Beaumont, Anglo-American Radical', in 'International Review of Social History', xiv (2) (1969).

(d) Other studies which include relevant material

F. C. Mather,	'Public Order in the Age of the Chartists' (1959).
L. Radzinowicz,	'A History of English Criminal Law', iv (1968).
E. Midwinter,	'Law and Order in Early Victorian Lancashire' (York, 1968).
Donald Read,	'The English Provinces', section iii.
J. L. and Barbara Hammond,	'The Age of the Chartists' (1930).
Donald Read,	'Press and People 1790-1850' (1961).
Jacques Godechot (ed.),	'La Presse Ouvrière 1819-1850' (Paris, 1966).
Peter Brock,	'Polish Democrats and English Radicals 1832-1862', in Journal of Modern History', xxv (1953).
Rachel O'Higgins,	'The Irish influence in the Chartist Movement', in 'Past and Present' (Nov 1961).
D. J. Rowe,	'Chartism and the Regions', in 'Economic History Review' (1969).
Y. V. Kovalev (ed.),	'An Anthology of Chartist Literature' (Moscow, 1956).

TRIALS

Gurney,	'Trial of John Frost for High Treason' (1840).
W. C. Townsend,	'Report of the Trial of John Frost': 'Modern State Trials', vol. 1 (1850).

| John MacDonnell (ed.), | 'Reports of State Trials', n.s. iii: '1831-1840' (1891), for trials of Henry Vincent and others for conspiracy and unlawful assembly; Howell and others for riotously demolishing a house; John Collins for publishing a seditious libel; William Lovett for publishing a seditious libel; J. R. Stephens for seditious words, riot and unlawful assembly. |
| John MacDonnell (ed.), | 'Reports of State Trials', n.s. iv: '1839-43' (1891), for trial of John Frost. |

'The Trial of William Lovett, Journeyman Cabinet Maker, for a seditious Libel' (Hetherington, 1839).

PARLIAMENTARY PAPERS

Parliamentary Debates (Hansard), 2nd and 3rd series.

Index of persons, places, and periodicals

304